THE GATHERING STORM

How to avoid the next crisis -
from the minds that predicted the crunch

THE GATHERING STORM

How to avoid the next crisis -
from the minds that predicted the crunch

-

An Altana Charitable Trust Project

Created by Lee Robinson
Edited by Patrick L Young

Derivatives Vision Publishing

"Clear thinking and expert analysis are both all too rare, but "The Gathering Storm" has both in abundance, thanks to a remarkable array of contributors."

Bill Emmott
Columnist, Author, former Editor of The Economist

"The Gathering Storm is a collection of essays... each chapter focuses on a slightly different area, the recurring theme is that the actions of governments and central bankers are no longer helping, but if anything are prolonging the financial crisis and adding to its eventual costs. You don't have to concur with that thesis to agree with the conclusion that Western economies in particular face some tough choices, and yet their populations are largely unaware of how tough these are likely to be."

Anthony Hilton
Evening Standard

"if you want some stimulating articles, The Gathering Storm is worth a read."

Buttonwood Blog
The Economist

"The Gathering Storm," a quirky compendium of distinctly dark views and analysis on the next financial crisis from some prominent... hedge fund managers, analysts and pundits."

FT Alphaville

"The trouble with weather forecasting is that it's right too often for us to ignore it and wrong too often for us to rely on it."

Patrick L Young

THE GATHERING STORM

"We find that respectable commentary and academic opinion are increasingly divorced from reality.

A new orthodoxy has been created, centred around an incredibly complacent and self-satisfied view of the world.

The consequences of this delusion are becoming painfully visible in global financial markets - but equally so, in the politics of some of the leading Western nations."

Eric Kraus

Also by Patrick L Young:

Capital Market Revolution
New Capital Market Revolution
The Promiscuous Investor
Single Stock Futures - A Traders Guide
An Intangible Commodity (Editor)
The Exchange Manifesto

Lee Robinson is co-founder and portfolio manager of the hedge fund Trafalgar Asset Managers Ltd.

Prior to founding Trafalgar in 2001, Lee built and managed Tudor Capital's Global Event Driven business. Previously, Lee worked in credit and derivatives at Deutsche Bank from 1996-1998; interest rate derivatives at Bankers Trust 1992-1996; and equities and derivatives at Paribas 1991-1992, where he traded equity, interest rate and credit derivatives. Lee has a BA and MA in mathematics from Cambridge University.

Patrick L Young is a leading expert on financial markets and their infrastructure. He is the Principal of Kolonna Asset Management, a boutique family office / asset management firm headquartered in Riga, Latvia.

The author / editor of several books, Patrick has more than 20 years experience in all aspects of markets world-wide. A seasoned advisor to investors in exchanges and financial market infrastructure, Young is also an active investor in Eastern Europe.

He has appeared on BBC, Bloomberg, CNBC, CNN and other television stations world-wide as well as contributing Op Eds to major financial newspapers including the Financial Times and the Wall Street Journal. He is a regular speaker at conferences and, like Lee, lives in Monaco.

Published by Derivatives Vision
c/o Projekt Vistula s.p. z.o.o.
Piastowska 7A/1
Torun
87-100

First published October 2010
(500 copies)

Reprinted world-wide

ISBN 978-83-62627-00-4

For all discussion as to rights please email in the first instance:
Patrick@DerivativesVision.com

About The Gathering Storm

Amidst concerns about the world economy, the transparency and under-standing of finance and, indeed, with a desire to try to help the world at a time of economic difficulty, the concept of *"The Gathering Storm"* was created by Lee Robinson, a leading equity and credit hedge fund manager based in Monaco.

In a rather hectic process, Lee approached a series of contributors who agreed to give their time for free to produce a chapter for the book. Each contributor receives a proportion of the book profits to be donated to a nominated charity of their choice (listed at the end of their chapter).

Thus, a unique perspective on world economics and markets has been created by a truly remarkable group of individuals who have all managed to discern the gathering storm which is about to hit financial markets in the wake of the recent *"credit crunch"* and subsequent market ructions.

Patrick L Young, an experienced financial professional as well as an author and editor, was drafted in to bring the project fruition.

Like so many things related to financial markets, events moved rapidly and volatility was not uncommon in the attempt to render a low latency straight through processing model of the authors' thoughts in a convenient user-interface... For those not used to financial gibberish: this entire project has been completed in a fairly remarkably brief period throughout what was a rather hectic summer!

The end result is a book we hope you will find stimulating and educational as well as entertaining in parts. Perhaps, most importantly of all, by purchasing this book, we thank you for assisting a broad range of charities throughout the world which have been nominated by the contributors themselves.

All proceeds from this book will be distributed to charity.

DEDICATION

To Laura
&
To Wyatt

Lee Robinson
Patrick L Young
Monaco, September 2010

THE GATHERING STORM

"Man must cease attributing his problems to his environment and learn again to exercise his will - his personal responsibility."

Albert Schweitzer

Acknowledgements

The genesis of this tome has not been quite as frenzied as the demise of Lehman Brothers but, well, you get the gist...

Lee created the concept, emailed a group of top level names in financial markets, and suddenly found himself holding the basis of an interesting book. However, he was slightly unclear as to how pertinent STP (*"Straight Through Publishing?"*) technology could be deployed to realise his vision of a book that would be available in good time for Christmas 2010 with the aim of elucidating readers while also raising money for charity.

Thanks to the good offices of Raymond M. Cheseldine III, otherwise known as the *"irrepressible Kip"*, Patrick L Young was introduced to the project and appointed Editor with a brief to produce the book itself. Suddenly wrapped in a vast array of articles, diagrams and related papers, and musing on just how many competing formats remain in computer processing, Patrick took up the challenge, arranged the articles into a manuscript, headed for production and, ultimately, publication! To that end, Patrick would like to note that any errors, omissions and other faux pas are his.

Naturally, this required assistance and, to that end, we have many people to thank for their generous input to this tome:

For a start, there are the contributors - a range of esteemed names in financial markets who have all selflessly devoted time and effort to produce the core contents of this book:

James Ferguson
Albert Edwards
Thomas Thygesen
Lee Quaintance & Paul Brodsky
Stephen Lewis
Dylan Grice
Howard Marks
Marc Lasry
David Rosenberg

Peter Tasker
Tom Burnett & Linda Varoli
Andrew M Lees
Prieur du Plessis
John Mauldin

We also wish to thank all our contributors' employers for allowing them to work with this project and similarly their colleagues who have assisted them in the preparation of their chapters.

Amongst the myriad of helpful and highly efficient assistants, colleagues and PA's we have dealt with, we particularly thank Julie Baumann, Kara Evans, Dana Goldstein, Caroline Heald, Amy Ivanoff and Jennifer Pratt. Within Trafalgar, we particularly thank Lauren Banner, Victoria Silcock and Elizabeth Van Der Lande. You probably have little idea just how invaluable your timely interventions were to helping this project be produced in record quick time.

Our colleagues have been a huge help. From Lee's side, Caroline Castel, Nerissa Ventanilla and Patrick notes the remarkable input of Magda Bak, Lynne Spaight and Caryn Fortune. Our thanks to Dawn Dudek whose cover designs really bring the book to life. We particularly owe a debt of gratitude to Lee Hadnum for his considerable input into this project. John Parry and Simon Rostron have diligently provided their PR services in the best interest of the project.

At home, Lee's wife Lucinda provided support and feedback while, throughout summer, Beata and Laura managed to put up with the fact that Patrick could not always accompany them to the beach when the sun was shining. Flora remained relaxed throughout while Patrick suspects his Mum Lucy Jone, is prouder of her son's publishing escapades than his more purely financial business activities.

Feedback relating to the book will be welcome and can be sent either via the web site www.altanabooks.com or to: patrick@derivativesvision.com.

Lee Robinson & Patrick L Young, Monaco, September 2010

THE GATHERING STORM

Contents

THE GATHERING STORM

"U.S. dollars have value only to the extent that they are strictly limited in supply. But the U.S. government has a technology, called the printing press (or, today, its electronic equivalent), that allows it to produce as many U.S. dollars as it wishes at essentially no cost."

Ben Bernanke

Introduction
by Lee Robinson

The Queen of England asked after the credit crunch *"Why did nobody notice it?"* The answer was that some people did notice it, some voiced their concerns, some of those ignored the warnings and some acted. At Trafalgar Asset Managers we noticed it and, thanks to many of the authors in this book, acted and hence became part of a small group of successful investors in that period. This book will help me, and hopefully you, think through the coming crises.

The old trading floor joke used to be that an economist has predicted 14 of the last 2 crashes - making the subtle point that if you say something often enough you will eventually be right. In truth, most economists never predict a recession as there is simply too much personal risk to the individual who makes such a call and is wrong. Many of the authors collected here were brave and shouted their concerns loudly. I thank them and urge you to follow their work as we work through the gathering storm.

What many of us have struggled to understand is why the central bankers, with so many contacts at their disposal, seem to be late to act; and in this extended period, between the beginning of the crisis and the actions by the government and its bankers, often makes it harder to repair. Alan Greenspan's often repeated line that it is better to clean up bubbles after they burst, will not console the millions who lost life savings and are now out of work.

What could have been noticed? Let's look at a simple chart like the one below watched by top economists. This is the change in the *ECRI weekly leading indicator of United States growth. As you can see the US economy was slowing at a dramatic rate in the summer of 2007 as credit conditions tightened.

This period was just a few months after the market for mortgage securities had started to unravel, which in itself, was a huge red flag. The credit

* *The Economic Cycle Research Institue (http://www.businesscycle.com/r)*

3

market froze in Aug 2007 within another 3-4 months it took another leg lower to -10%, historically a near certain harbinger of a recession. Northern Rock was soon to be nationalised, Bear Stearns had to be saved by JP Morgan at close to zero value, yet the European central bankers raised interest rates! I still wonder what indicators they were watching.

Many investors buy and then hope to find a good exit point to sell. Professional investors work out where they would sell and then decide where they should buy. The best professional investors work out where they will sell and try and calculate potential pathways that lead back from the exit point to work out the best level and the timing for entry.

Once the US housing market began to unravel in early 2007 the pathway was clearly toward large credit losses by banks and individuals. The pathway from credit losses is higher refinancing costs and wider credit spreads. Wider credit spreads lead to short term refinancing problems that lead to bankruptcies. These pathways always lead to a recession.

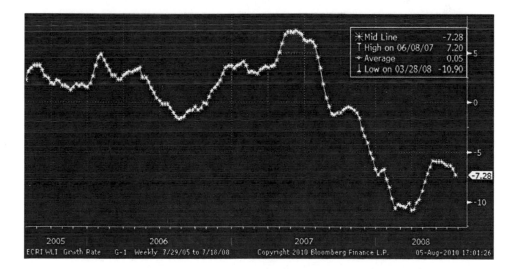

The big problem now is that transferring the private sector debt to the country's balance sheet is a pathway to either default or a large reduction in the value of the currency.

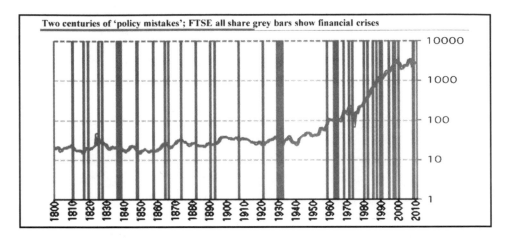

Source: Charles Kindleberger, SG Cross Asset Research

Who will bail out the central banks?

I ask the question - Has the increase in credit, and hence leverage in the system caused by repeated bail outs by central banks, actually made crises more likely to occur?

Crises are arguably becoming more regular due to global imbalances and central bank policies:

- 1997 Asian Crisis
- 1998 Russian collapse followed by hedge fund LTCM failing
- 2000 Dot com burst
- 2001 Sep 11
- 2002-03 Recession (e.g. Enron, Worldcom bankruptcies)
- 2007 Sub Prime disaster and bank failures such as Northern Rock
- 2008 Bear Stearns/Lehman, General Motors, Commodity price crash Iceland/Ireland
- 2010 Hungarian and Greek Sovereign crises

Compared to the other decades in the last 50 years we really seem to either be very unlucky or is it that in those other decades we lived within our means and not on credit? If it is due to excess credit then should we not be prepared for further crises along the way?

So I created this book for three reasons:

First of all, to help many charities and the good causes they support. All the profits from this book go to the Altana Charitable Trust which will distribute an equal share to each contributor's choice of charity or non-profit organisation.

From a purely personal point I chose the charity the Batten Disease Family Association (BDFA: www.bdfa-uk.org.uk). This is a small charity run primarily by parents and is focussed and excellent at providing relevant information for families, getting families involved, and funding research. Aged 9, my Goddaughter was diagnosed with Juvenile Batten Disease, a debilitating and rare motor neurone disease that has sent her blind which will eventually put her in a wheelchair limit her life expectancy. You have to be mentally very tough to trade a performance based fund every day for many years as I have but this pales compared to having to cope with losing your sight and knowing your other abilities are deteriorating. She has handled the loss better than almost any adult could. She has my admiration and at the very least I will try to help the charity raise monies to help counter the effects and support other families in the same predicament and offer real hope for a cure in the future.

Secondly, to introduce these wise men to help you through the coming crises with some of their more helpful thoughts and ideas. I hope you will read and refer back to many of the chapters again and again. Many of you have access to these men and I urge you to listen and learn from them. The great thing about my work is that I learn something new every day. I thank all the authors for their selfless contribution.

The final reason was to try and improve the image of our industry. The financial industry and its participants have a bad reputation yet many participants sit on the boards of charities, donate time and money to worthy causes.

Hedge funds did not create the crisis nor arguably did the banks yet political spin is used to cover up the great failings of government and its regulators. Not one politician or regulator has been deemed culpable. Not one has said *"sorry, we need to do better"*. The people, however, always understand in the end. The Queen of England has asked the question; I suspect she will never get an honest answer.

I hope you enjoy the book. Feel free to post feedback to:
www.altanabooks.com

In addition to the authors I would like to thank Patrick Young for his expert advice. Without him the whole project most likely would still just be floating around in my head. I particularly appreciate the assistance of the two main trustees, Sean Laird, probably the only man to make double - digit returns buying volatility when volatility was already at 10-year highs in Oct 2008, and Neville Newman, my long suffering accountant of many years who set up the trust at no cost. I am grateful for the endorsements. Your words are kind and will help us raise valuable contributions to the many charities mentioned.

Lee Robinson
Monaco, September, 2010

"What Went Wrong?"
James Ferguson

"You'd think it would be quite hard to arrange such a confluence of events but actually the path the developed world had set itself upon in the aftermath of the dotcom crash and particularly post the 9/11 attacks on the Twin Towers, made a banking crisis of this sort, at least with the benefit of hindsight, virtually inevitable. Three major policy mistakes by the authorities can be held responsible for the majority of the subsequent carnage."

THE GATHERING STORM

About the Author

James Ferguson is Chief Strategist at Arbuthnot Securities in London. He previously held the same position at Pali International. James has also worked at Tokyo Mitsubishi International, Dresdner Kleinwort Wasserstein, Swiss Bank Corp/SBC Warburg, Robert Fleming & Co. and Nomura Securities.

James was based in Tokyo for 3 years between 1995 and 1997 where he witnessed the Japanese banking crisis at first hand. He now lives in London and is beginning to feel a little paranoid about his proximity to banking collapses...

What went wrong?
Build-up to a global banking crisis.

"Those who don't know history are destined to repeat it."
Edmund Burke

Some twelve months after the October 1929 stock market crash, The Great Depression, which saw real GDP drop by a third, was originally triggered by rising farming defaults that set off runs on over 4,000 mostly small local banks. Yet the Great Depression is not known by history as the farm debt crisis. In the same way, history will not record what we are currently going through as the US subprime crisis.

The current crisis was also preceded by a market collapse, this time in residential mortgage backed securities. But, again, the real problems ran both much deeper and much wider. In both cases overleveraged borrowers with weak or impaired cash flows were the first to default but however spectacular the market implosions, the chronic damage to the wider economy will be just as it was in the 1930s, the true legacy of the preceding credit bubble.

If we are to avoid suffering the same fate in the future, it is vital we understand as fully as possible what went wrong. Failure to do so will not only risk a recurrence but may mean we choose the wrong policy options and future regulatory prescriptions as we try to navigate our way out of the current crisis. Instead of looking at the manifestation of the global bank crisis it is more important to look at what sparked the global credit bubble that preceded it; why the regulator let banks run their capital bases down so far and why the central bankers first mistook a solvency crisis for merely a market seizure-related liquidity crisis.

Some banking crises are caused by the State allocation of credit, some by financial deregulation and some by innovation and deregulation. But one thing remains an unfailing constant: credit growth goes through the roof. Let's take Britain as an example. UK banks' lending to UK residents at the start of the new millennium was around £1 trillion (i.e. approximately

15

100% of annual GDP at the time). By the peak in October 2008, lending to UK residents had more than doubled to £2.4 trillion; 163% of GDP.

Foreign business grew at an even faster rate. Lending to non-residents totalled just over £100 billion at the start of 2000 but by early 2008 it peaked out above £450 billion (31% of GDP). This more than fourfold increase illustrates the over-weaning ambition at the top of the UK banks to expand at all costs. Briefly, RBS, a bank headquartered in Scotland, population 5 million, became the largest bank in the world with $3.74 trillion in assets, equivalent to 166% of UK GDP. The top six UK banks' assets (loans as well as securities, derivatives, gilts, etc) at the peak of the credit bubble had reached more than £7.5 trillion ($11.2 trillion); a level in excess of five times the level of UK GDP. And this whole edifice rested on a mere £120 billion of the pure, loss absorbing, definition of capital known as *"tangible common equity"* (TCE).

What this meant was that average losses of a mere 1.6% across the board would have been sufficient to wipe the banks' capital out altogether. Though rare, bank crises typically inflict 10% losses on risk assets like outstanding loans, though it can be more. Japanese banks have endured a more than 20% loan loss rate during a crisis that has lasted for over a decade. The largest six UK banks had about £3.9 trillion of risk assets at the peak, so typical bank crisis losses of 10% on these can be expected to generate as much as a £390 billion hole in the banks' capital base. The only problem is that with just £120 billion of loss-absorbing types of capital to start with, UK banks were on track for being wiped out three times over. Aided by new capital of £124 billion raised, loss realisation progress to date exceeds £200 billion. Nevertheless, the UK is perhaps now only at the mid-point in the loss realisation process. To go any faster than the rate at which new trading profits can be generated would erode capital - perhaps enough to trigger new solvency scares.

Indeed, the first lesson from the history of bank crises is that resolution is a process, usually lasting 5-6 years, not an event. The event stage is the initial market liquidity seizure either preceding or closely following the realisation that the banking sector is partially or wholly insolvent, through balance sheet problems that had been accumulating for several years prior. This time was no different, though the authorities and even the banks' own managements were often slow to appreciate that, though the crisis was manifesting itself as a liquidity crisis, the underlying cause, right from the start, was a bank solvency crisis.

A banking crisis, by definition, is when the bank sector's capital is wiped out (sometimes many times over) and taxpayer funds are required to prevent wholesale failures; sometimes involving full-scale nationalisation, as with Northern Rock. Therefore, it stands to reason that the precursor to a crisis is an erosion of the capital to asset ratio. The assets are the risks the banks take to generate profits whereas the capital is the fund they retain to absorb losses in the event of defaults. Either the capital layer becoming too thin or the assets that capital is supporting growing too fast should be obvious red flags. If both are happening at once, then ensuing crisis is ensured.

From an income statement point-of-view, banking is always profitable. Banks borrow money at one rate and lend it on at another, higher, rate. Simple; though usually banks borrow short-term to lend at a longer term, which means there is a risk that, come rollover time, the short-term cost of funding has risen above the return that the banks expect to earn on their longer-dated assets. This, essentially, is the nature of a liquidity crisis and can be relatively easily solved by selling the institution to a better capitalised rival or, in the event of systemic liquidity freeze, the central bank can provide sufficient cheap liquidity as an alternative to more expensive market funding.

Intractable, solvency type problems, on the other hand, arise on the balance sheet when some of the banks' borrowers fail to honour their debts.

In order to minimise this risk, banks often take a charge on the loan in the form of collateral. This means that in a downturn, the banks' assets aren't really the loans that it has outstanding, so much as the value of the collateral backing those loans. Even defaults, in a normal environment where collateral values are still rising, present few problems. Once the loan is foreclosed and collateral is sold, banks rarely face a significant loss, even net of administration costs. Thus, as long as the recovery rate is high, even a high level of defaults on its own doesn't necessarily present a problem.

The balance sheet risks of a full-blown solvency crisis only become truly dangerous in a perfect storm scenario, where problems are systemic, collateral values are falling, recession crimps cash flows, triggering defaults and the banks find they had built up insufficient capital to absorb losses from collateral sales. You'd think it would be quite hard to arrange such a confluence of events but actually the path the developed world had set itself upon in the aftermath of the dotcom crash and particularly post the 9/11 attacks on the Twin Towers, made a banking crisis of this sort, at least with the benefit of hindsight, virtually inevitable. Three major policy mistakes by the authorities can be held responsible for the majority of the subsequent carnage. First, central banks held rates too low for too long, boosting the demand for credit. Second, the regulator allowed too broad a definition of capital, exaggerating the numerator of the capital-to-asset ratio. Third, the new risk-weighting rules also allowed banks to under estimate assets, the ratio denominator. Between the three of them, the result was a massive, low margin and dangerously under-capitalised credit bubble.

Interest rates were too low for too long

The first problem was that interest rates were too low going into the new millennium and they stayed too low, encouraging excessive credit demand, for far too long. Alan Greenspan, as Chairman of the US Federal Reserve, miscalculated the severity of several earlier threats to the economy starting with the Y2K non-event. Not only was the dotcom crash fairly well contained within the technology sectors but the economic impact of 9/11 (as opposed to the political, cultural and sociological effects, which were immense) was fairly muted. There wasn't even technically a recession in 2001, in that the two negative quarters weren't back-to-back. Fed Chairman, Alan Greenspan, however, not only orchestrated a steady decline in the Fed funds interest rate to a record low of 1%, he kept rates at that level until mid-way through 2004, some four years after the dotcom crash began and three years after the 9/11 attacks.

Since 1987, the real Fed funds rate (that is the overnight policy interest rate less the prevailing rate of inflation) had ranged between 2-4%, though in the 1991-1992 recession it had been briefly lowered to a real rate of around zero. After the Dotcom crash and the 9/11 attacks, however, policy radically became chronically stimulative. For three years, from 2002 to late 2005, the Fed kept the real Fed funds rate at negative 1-2%. This was even though, throughout 2004 and 2005, real GDP had recovered and was growing in the 3-4% range. Such real rates were not only far too accommodative for the state of the US economy, they forced other developed countries to keep their rates artificially low too, so as not to be too far out of kilter with the US.

In the UK, for example, between 1994 and 2002, UK base rates had stayed at a narrow 2.5-4% premium to Retail Price Index (RPI). During this time, credit growth was steady and normal and real GDP grew in a healthy 2-5% range. However, during the credit bubble, 2002-2007, base rates were only 0.5-2% above RPI; a level of real rates that fuelled the demand for credit and hence facilitated the expansion of banks' loan assets. UK bank lending growth surged at a consistent double-digit rate from 2001 right the way through early 2008. However, it takes more than low rates stimulating the demand side to create a credit bubble. The supply of credit had to be expanded even faster than demand or the result would have merely been the widening of banks' net interest margins. Instead, these steadily narrowed, halving in the UK between the late 1990s and the peak in lending in late 2008.

Capital defined too loosely

The other two policy errors related not to the demand for credit but its

19

supply and both concerned the regulatory environment that the banks were allowed to operate in. The first was the definition of capital, the numerator in the capital-to-asset ratio. The second was the definition of assets, the denominator. By expanding the definition of capital and facilitating the exclusion of much of the asset base, the quality of the capital adequacy ratio was eroded from both sides of the dividing line. Whilst the banks appeared to be well-capitalised according to the published capital-to-asset ratio, what was actually happening was that by old-fashioned unadulterated measures, capital ratios were deteriorating to dangerously low levels. That meant that when recession hit, it wouldn't take much of a fall in the value of assets before the banks' capital was in danger of being wiped out and taxpayers would have to be called upon to pick up the tab.

In order to make sure, at least in theory, that banks don't privatise their gains on the up-cycle and socialise their losses on the down, the idea is that the industry regulator forces them to accumulate a certain amount of capital, sufficient to absorb any losses they may make through the cycle. Definitions of what constitutes *"capital"* can vary and banks employ ranks of highly intelligent, motivated lobbyists who are fully incentivised to persuade the regulator to inflate the calculated value of the capital they hold, in order to facilitate a further expansion of their assets. More assets means more profits on the income statement but, come the downturn, it means more losses on the balance sheet too.

However, whilst banks were growing assets, lending was free and easy and real estate values kept rising, meaning losses in the event of default were either low or non-existent. But lower and lower policy rates were combined with banks narrowing margins to compete for business, so that borrowers who had trouble covering interest payments were rarely forced into default but were able to refinance instead at ever lower rates, keeping actual default rates very low. Naturally, low and declining default rates made the risk of default appear to be shrinking too, so risk spreads narrowed yet further, reinforcing the positive feedback loop. What should have been clear, at least to the regulator, was that this positive feedback loop, whilst keeping both default rates and the loss in the event of default very low on the way up, would work in reverse on the way down. Banks should be forced to build up more capital, not less, when times are good and lending is growing.

Besides, the whole point of banks' regulatory capital is to absorb losses when they occur. Any definition of capital that is not able to absorb losses should, therefore, be explicitly excluded. However, that increasingly was not the case. Loss absorbing capital is called Tangible Common Equity (TCE) by accountants and is defined as the bank's share capital, the additional paid-in capital and the retained earnings (after tax and dividend payments) after the explicit deduction of intangibles such as brands and goodwill. No deferred tax assets that can only be used against future profits. No debts, obviously (or so you'd think). No impairment loss provisions (a loss you're sure you're going to have to take, but haven't taken yet, is not available to support other assets) and no gains on equity holdings. As the Japanese banks discovered, these tend to evaporate at exactly the time you most need them. Yet *"innovative"* Tier 1 and Tier 2 capital definitions can include any or all of these latter items, even though none can absorb losses and so, in the case of recession-induced losses, are worthless.

Let us say, for illustrative purposes, a hypothetical bank (we'll call it Hypothetical Bank) has $5 of TCE-defined capital and $100 of total assets; that's a 5% leverage ratio. If a recessionary downturn comes along, the bank has sufficient capital to withstand an eventual loss of 5%, after recoveries, on average across its assets. Most banks hold a variety of assets across the risk spectrum. Some assets might see losses well above 5% but the majority of their assets would experience much lower loss ratios.

As we saw above, the regulator had already allowed the banks to include non-loss absorbing items in *"capital"* for Tier 1 and Tier 2 regulatory purposes. Barclays Bank, for example, reported Tier 1 capital of £26.7 billion as at the end of 2007, yet by the stricter TCE definition, capital amounted to just £15 billion, almost half as much. German giant Deutsche Bank similarly reported €20.8 billion in TCE at the end of December 2008 but counted 50% more, or €31 billion, under the *"Tier 1 Capital"* definition.

If Hypothetical Bank similarly inflated its measure of capital from $5 to $9 by including items that count towards Tier 1 for regulatory purposes, then the capital to asset ratio appears to rise from 5% to 9%. Assets can now be inflated by 80% to $180 to bring the capital ratio back to 5%, even though no new loss-absorbing capital has actually been added. To extend the Deutsche Bank example, TCE capital was €20.3billion at the end of December 2003 and had remained virtually unchanged at €20.8 billion by December 2008. However, over that same five-year period, total loans rose 83% from €148 billion to €271 billion, whilst total assets, including securities and derivatives, almost trebled from €804 billion to €2,202 billion.

Banks like the US giant, JPMorgan Chase, often argued in the past that the US leverage ratio capital requirement was unfair to banks, like themselves, which had better quality clients, and consequently, less risky assets. In fact, very large banks, those with the better clients, most diversification and (theoretically) least risky assets, were allowed to run a leverage ratio of just 3%, whilst all other banks required at least 4%. So, in reality, this argument was at least partially hollow. Making it even more hollow, a vast swathe of assets were and still are effectively excluded altogether from the US banks' capital ratios under American Generally Accepted Accounting Principles (known as US GAAP).

No accounting for derivatives

Whereas Europeans follow the International Financial Reporting Standards (IFRS), which include all derivatives at gross fair value, in the US, the Financial Accounting Standards Board (FASB) rules allow American banks to effectively assume that almost all derivatives are hedged and so net their holdings to almost zero. US banks are therefore incentivised to hold huge amounts of derivatives because they hardly need to hold any capital against these positions.

As an example of how this works in practise, JPMorgan Chase's annual report shows the bank held $79 trillion of notional exposure to derivatives at the end of 2009. When you consider that JPMorgan held about $2.1 trillion worth of all other types of asset as at 31st December 2009, it becomes clearer why Warren Buffett has called banks' derivative holdings potential *"weapons of mass destruction"*. Like Iraq's WMDs, however, these derivatives can't be found; and the reason is predominantly accounting sleight of hand which works like this.

The $79 trillion measures the underlying value of the securities and contracts that the derivatives give JPMorgan exposure to. By the time this has been translated into the gross fair value (approximately akin to the market value of the derivatives themselves) the value of JPMorgan's derivatives shrinks to $1.57 trillion of receivables and $1.52 trillion of payables. This is now where US GAAP comes in. Unlike in Europe, where JPMorgan's derivative assets would be reported in the annual accounts as $1.57 trillion, in America banks can net off legally enforceable payments. In the case of JP Morgan the netted off value of their receivables against their payables amounts to $1.49 trillion, so the carrying value of net derivative assets in the accounts falls to just $80 billion; only 5% of the fair value and about one-thousandth of the gross notional value.

The role of AIG

But netting off legally enforceable payments assumes these payments will always be honoured, or in the parlance of the market, that there's no counterparty risk. Enter AIG. Banks naturally become incentivised to increase assets that require little or no capital, which makes it very dangerous whenever the regulator changes the rules or when a basic assumption supporting the rules proves unsound. One increasingly popular type of derivative during the credit bubble was the Credit Default Swap (CDS). CDSs are, effectively, insurance policies against the underlying bonds defaulting. AIG was the largest general insurer in the US and so saw CDS as a natural area of expertise. However, AIG made at least two fundamental errors of judgement.

Firstly, CDS, unlike insurance for anything else, can be bought in unlimited amounts and even by people who don't own the bond that is being insured. As any insurance man worth his salt will tell you, that distorts incentives somewhat. If I insure my house against fire, I am still incentivised to be careful about burning candles but at least I'm covered if the worst was to happen. If, however, I was permitted to insure my house for twice what it's worth and I hit financial troubles, I might start to harbour dark thoughts. If, instead, I can insure my neighbour's house for ten times its market value, I'm now incentivised to squirt petrol in through his letterbox.

The second big mistake that AIG made was that the company was unfamiliar with financial markets and misinterpreted the risks surrounding default data. 5-year borrowing costs had been on a pretty much steady downtrend since as far back as 1984. The speed with which the US Fed had been cutting rates since the mid-1990s after the financial scares of LTCM, the Asian Crisis, the Russian default, the, dotcom crash and 9/11, came to be known as the Greenspan Put. Under Greenspan, the Fed was no longer waiting for the economy itself to turn down, as previous central bankers had. At the first sign of trouble in the financial markets, rates were being cut. This realisation, that they'd get bailed out either by a stronger market or by lower rates, made borrowers and lenders alike increasingly reckless.

Added to the downtrend in underlying rates and the moral hazard that came from knowing rates would be cut as soon as there was a wobble, the banks, as we have seen above, were gaming the new regulatory environment. By expanding the range of items that could be included in the regulatory definition of capital, banks were able to expand loans and other risky assets, without essentially adding anymore actual, proper, loss-absorbing capital. Since this happened equally to all banks at once, they were all trying to expand their assets at once. Naturally, when everyone is trying to compete on price, lending spreads narrow. Net interest margins for the UK's six major banks were 3.25% in 1989. By June 2009, they had steadily contracted to less than 1.5%. In this way, falling underlying rates were accompanied by narrowing loan spreads. Any business model that proved too weak to service its debts at the old rate, rather than defaulting, could just re-finance at a lower, less arduous rate. The default rate plummeted to new lows, which insurers like AIG interpreted as a sign that risks of default were very low. In fact, the opposite was the case; all that was needed was a recession to prove it.

The big mistake the banks made, on the other hand, was that sellers of CDS, and AIG in particular, were holding all their insurance policies. This meant, of course, that if the counterparty failed, the hedge would become worthless and explains why, at the first signs of trouble, the banks enforced their margin calls so vigorously - though it was these very actions that pushed AIG into default, long before most of the bonds AIG had effectively insured, had failed. Complacency was rife. Just as the regulator was implicitly dismissing counterparty risk as irrelevant, AIG, too, was writing insurance policies with the assumption that very few would ever require paying out. What AIG missed was that in financial markets, expectations matter. Actual defaults don't have to occur for those holding the policies to demand additional margin collateral off the seller and for the issuers of CDS obligations to explode.

The Wholesale Funding Gap

One additional feature commonly marks the build-up to a crisis; so commonly in fact its emergence should have been another clear red flag to the authorities that disaster was afoot. Banks that have become incentivised to leverage themselves up at an excessive pace, whatever the root cause; be it deregulation, financial innovation or merely overly successful lobbying of the regulator; soon find they meet liquidity constraints. Whatever the required capital holdings to protect against insolvency, banks also have to fund their lending and normally this is done by recycling deposit liabilities. One very clear indication that the capital constraint may have been relaxed too far, for whatever reason, will be that banks extend loans at a faster rate than they can grow deposits.

Obviously, as lending grew faster than deposits did, the banks needed to source funds to lend out from somewhere other than deposits. Using the disingenuous concept of risk diversification, Western banks started to rely increasingly on non-deposit funding sources. Norway, Finland and Sweden all did this in the run up to the Nordic Banking Crises of the early 1990s. Japanese banks did it ahead of their bank crisis in the late-1990s. And UK banks did it aggressively from early 2002 through to late 2008. The difference between the level of loans and the level of deposits is called the wholesale funding gap and the UK banks' wholesale funding gap reached more than 50% of GDP at its peak in 2008.

As lessons for spotting future crises go, this one is a must because banks always make the same (erroneous) case that diversified sources of funding are less risky than the single source of bank deposits. This is not true. Banking, as we saw above, is always profitable at the income statement level. It's just after adjusting for default and securities impairments that losses can result. The main reason why it is profitable is that banks borrow short-term and lend at (higher) long-term rates. This exposes banks to two core vulnerabilities. The first is that if defaults exceed retained capital, banks are also unable to honour their near-term obligations. The second risk is the liquidity risk, where if creditors or depositors want their money back in the short-term, banks have no way of liquidating their longer-term loan assets in time.

However, depositors, especially retail depositors, rarely demand their money back all at once, no matter what the state of the economy. Indeed, in recessions, the savings ratio usually goes up. The one exception to this rule is, of course, a bank run, which is why the authorities do their damnedest to curtail bank runs at the first sign of trouble. All other types of bank funders, whether bond holders, wholesale depositors or other banks in the interbank market, have no such behavioural constraints and, indeed, are all likely to act both in concert and in a contra-cyclical manner. At the first sign of trouble in the summer of 2007, when the wholesale interbank market started seizing up and bank funding rollover costs skyrocketed for Northern Rock, the UK's first bank run in living memory was triggered.

Each banking crisis shares many of the same features with its forebears but each also brings its unique characteristics too. The introduction of securitised private sector loans, like the US subprime Residential Mortgage Backed Securities (RMBS) means that the banking sector's true wholesale funding gap should be seen as the difference, not just between deposits and loans, but securities too. The US banks, for example, in the run up to the crisis, did not seem at first glance to be running a wholesale funding gap, as loans never really grew above the level of deposits. Add in their ballooning private sector securities holdings, however, and a $1.2 trillion funding gap was revealed.

Risk-weighting assets

The role the ratings agencies and the monoline bond insurers played was the final icing on the cake and played particularly to what was perhaps most egregious lapse in regulatory oversight; that of the risk-weighting of assets, the denominator in the all-important capital-to-asset solvency ratio. The main reason why apparently high capital ratios were, in fact, just a mirage also had to do with banks' lobbying of the regulator; this time for fairer treatment of risky assets. US banks are the only ones that currently have to adhere to minimum leverage ratios. Those with very low-risk assets, such as government debt and top quality corporate borrowers, felt aggrieved that they had to hold the same proportion of capital as risky sub-prime mortgage lenders, where losses in a downturn might be proportionally much worse, and they lobbied hard for risk-adjusting different banks' quality of assets. Risky assets should require more capital because they are more likely to generate losses, after all. Unfortunately, whilst in principle a good idea, the methodology employed contributed significantly to the eventual crisis. The problem was that risk-weighting assets works to shrink the denominator in the capital adequacy ratio. It stands, therefore, that the required minimum hurdle ratio needed to be set far higher than with unadulterated ratios, yet, mysteriously, at least to any significant degree, it was not.

Once again, let us use the example of our imaginary Hypothetical Bank from above, which now has $9 of regulatory capital (though only $5 of TCE) and its original $100 of total assets. Let's assume those assets are split equally between government bonds and mortgage loans. Government bonds are zero risk-weighted, which means that they simply don't exist from a regulatory capital point of view. Therefore, our bank now officially has just $50 of assets resting on $9 of regulatory capital. Yet mortgage loans themselves tend to be 50% risk-weighted, so, actually, the Tier 1 capital to risk-weighted assets (RWA) ratio - the one that matters to the regulator - is now $9/$25, or 36%. Hypothetical Bank is now in a position to go on a lending frenzy. Even a trebling of total assets without the addition of any new loss-absorbing capital wouldn't take the regulator's risk-weighted capital ratio below a robust-sounding 12%.

As an illustration of what a poor job the official BIS ratio does in measuring actual capital adequacy, one needs only to look at recently failed banks. Lehman Brothers' last reported capital adequacy ratio at the end of May 2008 stood at 16.1%. This is twice the US minimum required ratio and yet just three-and-a-half months later, the bank was gone. The UK's Northern Rock, in December 2006, and just eight months before disaster struck, sported a capital adequacy ratio of 17.5%; whilst Iceland's Kaupthing officially had an 11.2% ratio in June 2008, just ahead of its delisting.

Even if Northern Rock hadn't failed due to a sudden liquidity crunch (total lending grew 25% in the final twelve months to an unsupportable 3.2 times the size of its deposits) it seems impossible to believe the residential mortgage lender would have been able to absorb the subsequent losses on its loan book and still remain solvent. In December 2006, whilst in the midst of its 25% surge in mortgage lending, the bank reported £87 billion of customer loans and over £100 billion of total assets, yet only had to count risk-weighted assets (RWA) of £17 billion for the purposes of calculating its regulatory capital requirement. On top of that, rather than using the lower figure of £1.7 billion of loss-absorbing TCE capital, the regulator allowed Northern Rock to use a regulatory capital figure of £3 billion. The regulatory capital to risk-weighted asset ratio was therefore reported as 17.5%, whereas, in reality, loss-absorbing capital was less than 2% of total advances to customers.

Risk measurement begets more risk

There was another, less predictable problem with risk-weighting assets: it distorted banks' incentives and made their behaviour more risky. Once banks were told they didn't have to carry any capital against AAA-rated AFS (Available-For-Sale) securities (originally meant to be government bonds) on their Treasury accounts, there was a huge incentive to package illiquid loans into securities and then get ratings agencies or monoline insurers to reclassify slices of such assets as AAA. Then the lower rated securities could be sold off. Once zero-risk weighted in this way, there was no longer an obligation to hold capital against such loans. Instead, the value would be marked-to-market which, in a rising market, even meant booking a profit and was dangerously pro-cyclical. By late summer 2007, over 80% of US banks' supposedly government-issued, liquid AFS securities were, in fact, wholly illiquid, private sector loans masquerading as largely risk-free AFS.

Similarly, whereas it was deemed that a 50% risk-weighting was sufficient to cover the maximum likely loss in default for a residential mortgage based on the historical record, the incentive with a fixed 50% risk-weighting immediately changed from risk aversion to risk enhancement. Once the amount of capital required against a mortgage was risk insensitive, then the rational course of action was to increase the riskiness of new loans. In the UK this led to mortgage rates previously reserved for owner occupiers being offered to higher risk buy-to-let landlords and with maximum loan-to-value (LTV) caps rising from 90% to 125%. In the US, lenders embraced jumbo borrowers, adjustable rates, payment holidays, low introductory *"teaser"* rates, piggy back loans, low and no-doc loans, Alt-A and, of course, subprime borrowers. There was even an acronym for the most infamous borrowers of all - the NINJAs (no income, no job or assets). The way RWA worked encouraged banks to push out along the risk curve, thereby making the historically based risk-weighting metrics irrelevant.

RWA ratios are set too low

Indeed, there's a logic fault at the very heart of the whole RWA concept. The old-fashioned leverage ratio was founded on the concept that the capital cushion should be sufficient to absorb the losses emanating from a mixed bag of assets, many of which were over-collateralised. In a normal recession scenario, average loss rates on risk assets might reach 4-5%. However, in a banking crisis when Non-Performing Loans (NPLs) typically reach 25%, that loss rate rises to more like 10% on average. If 75% of assets are *"risky"* to some degree, then a banking crisis could be expected to generate losses equivalent to 7-8% of total assets. With the added ability to supplement capital from trading profits throughout the down cycle, a minimum leverage ratio of 4% (though preferably 6%+) of overall assets, as is the case in the US, should be expected to prove adequate for any, but full-on, bank crisis conditions.

Risk-weighting assets is a different concept altogether. The idea is to work out, in advance, for each type of asset (cash, government bond, private sector security, collateralised loan and uncollateralised loan) what the maximum loss is likely to be in the event of default. Government bonds (at least in a free-floating currency regime) won't usually default, so they are risk-weighted at zero; whereas a residential mortgage in default is assumed to lose no more than half its value, so such assets are 50% *"risk-weighted"*. Taken to its logical conclusion, the capital to risk-weighted asset ratio should, therefore, be very high (perhaps even 100%) yet the BIS and US minimum requirement is 8%. Capital should equal the likely loss in the event of default, so why such a low ratio was acceptable has never been adequately explained.

There was suspect mathematics behind the role that the ratings agencies and the monoline insurers played as well. The ratings agencies became convinced, not least because of the conflict of interest arising due to the fact that the investment bank issuers of private sector loan-backed securities paid their fees, that combining a large selection of BBB-rated risks together could somehow produce a slice (also known as a tranche), some of which somehow carried zero risk and could be rated AAA. Since the risk of default is a probability calculation, the validity of such a conclusion is moot. What was certainly the case was that ratings are not, in theory, intended to be pro-cyclical (i.e. the measure of likelihood of default is not supposed to go up as the environment deteriorates) but actually proved to be more volatile in reality than anyone feared, with some CDO ratings being downgraded 9-10 notches at a go.

The fact of the matter is that banks benefited if illiquid loan assets, that required capital to be held against them in case of default, could somehow be transformed into zero-risk weighted securities assets, requiring no such capital. The ratings agencies obliged, for a fee. For those portions that even the ratings agencies couldn't ascribe zero-risk weightings to, the banks turned to specialist monoline insurance companies, which could insure BBB rated securities against default for a nominal fee thereby turning them into zero-risk weighted AAA equivalent debt, for regulatory purposes. The fact that these monoline insurers had even thinner capital cushions than the banks, and in some cases would prove unable to honour their insurance commitments, also seemed to slip by the notice of the regulator at the time.

The Liquidity Crisis

One remaining question about the build-up to and the arrival of the crisis therefore remains: why did a fundamentally bank capital adequacy and solvency credit bubble, when it blew up, at first largely manifest itself as a subprime security and bank liquidity crisis? The first part of the question is easily answered. Banks across the developed world were largely following the same regulatory rules, although with some local variations. As such, banks were all extending their balance sheets at pretty much the same time and for the same reasons; hence the steady downward pressure on net interest margins visible across the board from the late 1990s onwards. Problems were always going to appear first in three ways. The first economy to go into the downturn was always going to be the first to show fault lines in the loan book. Secondly, securities were always going to discount defaults ahead of loans. Thirdly, the most recent vintages of the weakest creditors in the above two categories were always going crack first. The mistake was in thinking that the problems would remain ring-fenced within US subprime mortgage securities alone.

The second part of the question, why a liquidity crisis first, is also easy enough to explain but confounded policy-makers for at least the first year of the crisis and will ultimately leave a legacy of higher final bailout costs in its wake, as a consequence. Because the banks had either forgotten, or never much cared in the first place, who the net lenders in the wholesale interbank market were, it came as a complete surprise when these lenders took fright.

Whilst the West was running deficits, Asia and the oil-producing countries were running surpluses. In Japan, for example, bank lending is 30% less than deposits. Excess deposits were lent into the overnight and short-term wholesale funding market as interbank loans. Interbank loans are deemed so low-risk that they're often included with cash on the balance sheet, so when the banks that were net lenders to the interbank market realised that banks like Northern Rock (where loans were three times the size of their deposits) were their counterparties, they fled en masse. The resulting liquidity freeze was described by net debtor banks as both unprecedented and unexpected, yet it was neither. Unfortunately, because central banks initially bought into this conclusion, they stepped in to provide almost unlimited liquidity to replace that withdrawn from the interbank market. This mistook the symptom for the cause.

Liquidity dried up because the providers perceived the borrowers to be at risk of insolvency. Because central bankers misread this, they solved an immediate, but largely secondary, problem - shortage of liquid short-term funding - at the expense of recognising and dealing with the underlying disease: a shortage of bank capital. Not only are central banks still providing this liquidity almost three years on, but history suggests they have inadvertently added to the final bailout costs by doing so. Whereas banks could have started balance sheet repair, however painful, from a lower base and as early as late summer of 2007, instead risky bank assets continued to be accumulated for a further fifteen months. In both the US and the UK, bank loan assets didn't peak until October 2008 and balance sheet repair didn't begin until November 2008. Given that bank crisis resolution usually takes up to six years, this delay might mean the developed world private sector remains credit constrained until as late as 2014.

Conclusion

In order to generate the perfect storm scenario, there needed, as always, to be a credit bubble first. The fact that this time it was fuelled by unintentional regulatory lassitude had a secondary and equally dangerous consequence. Bank capital cushions, at least as measured in terms of capability to absorb losses, which is frankly the only way that matters in a crisis, did not keep pace with the explosion in banks' risk assets. While capital was being double counted, risk-weighted assets came in as a small fraction of total assets, as well as distorting banks' incentives to manage risk. The result was both an artificial boosting of the numerator and shrinking of the denominator of the capital adequacy ratio, leading to fatally dangerous over-leverage. The fact that a significant proportion of these risks found their way off balance sheet, especially so soon after the Enron affair, is yet another black mark against the regulatory authorities who can fairly be accused of being almost negligently oblivious to the systemic vulnerabilities their own actions were generating.

Actual bank crises aren't the cause of systemic failure. Instead, they reveal the imbalances that had been building for some time. As a consequence, the academic literature of past crises strongly suggests that if the monetary authorities respond to the original crisis with the provision of extremely liberal liquidity, then the ultimate bailout costs are higher. In other words, stepping in and providing liquidity early encourages the banks to keep lending and it's these late stage loans that prove the most costly. It is a great shame, therefore, that most banks' senior management and nearly all central bank authorities misdiagnosed the earliest seizures in the financial system as purely a liquidity crisis, rather than as merely the symptom of a much more profound underlying disease: a full-blown solvency crisis.

Even now, a full three years after widening LIBOR spreads and the failure of a pair of Bear Stearns hedge funds first alerted markets to impending disaster in the late summer of 2007, it is by no means clear that law-makers have fully understood what transpired. To make sure we don't allow such events to recur, it is essential that we fully understand what went wrong. Excessive credit growth and burgeoning wholesale funding gaps (the difference between deposits and private sector securities plus loans) should be textbook red flags. Government bond holdings are generally deemed Available For Sale (AFS assets) but banks securitised private sector loan assets and designated these almost wholly illiquid securities as AFS. Getting ratings agencies to ascribe them with AAA ratings made such assets appear to qualify as fully liquid, very low risk, government-issued securities which, sadly, they most clearly weren't.

The authorities allowed the banks to obfuscate the quality, range and liquidity of their assets, whilst facilitating the exaggeration of capital calculations. Whilst the banks were clearly successfully (too successfully) lobbying a regulator who wasn't frankly up to the standards we should be able to expect, who spoke for the shareholders? Who spoke for the taxpayers who ultimately bail out the banks each time there's a systemic failure? In the absence of a second opinion, daylight has always proven the best disinfectant. Regulators should be impelled to explain why they support banks' capital and risk-weighting decisions and be encouraged to offer alternative capital ratios under differing assumptions.

In short, conservative capital measures and extravagant asset aggregations should be the order of the day from a regulatory perspective. Then it would be up to the banks to try and convince us that things were better than they looked; rather than the current system, where the regulator has been allowing the banks to present a view of capital adequacy that the rest of us only found out was dangerously rose-tinted after it was far too late. History will show that banks are still sitting on massive legacy loan losses that they will only be able to crystallise gradually at the same rate they can generate trading profits, or faster, if they can tap markets or the long-suffering taxpayer for further capital. Either way, bank loan growth will remain negative for the duration of the banks' balance sheet repair and the history of past crises suggests this process is rarely complete in less than 5-6 years. From the peak in bank assets in both the UK and the US of October 2008, that sets an exit date from the credit crunch sometime in 2014.

James Ferguson has chosen to donate to Child's i Foundation:

This charity seeks to wipe out the endemic problem of of child abandonment in Uganda by setting up our 'Child Abandonment Project'. Developed with leading experts in social care in the UK and Uganda, this unique model has three parts: a support programme to help mothers at risk of abandoning their babies; a transitional home to provide short-term life-saving care; and a family placement programme to ensure every child grows up in a loving family.

The Child's i Foundation website is:
http://www.childsifoundation.org/

CHAPTER TWO

-

"This awful catastrophe is not the end but the beginning.
History does not end so.
It is the way its chapters open."

St Augustine

A Hedge Fund Manager Hits Back
John Veals

"Does any of this matter? It shouldn't, but all I'm saying is that I come from an ordinary background and am just an ordinary bloke, in most respects; but not all. I look and I listen and I form my own opinions and stick to them. Sounds simple, doesn't it? It isn't. Being a dyed-in-the-wool contrarian, immune to the zeitgeist, treating other people's emotions as nothing more than data points - for that you need a certain kind of mind, one that can shut down any twinges of empathy. Because if you do empathise, if you do see other people's point of view, then you're probably going to think like other people and act like other people. And in the investment world that means you're going to get the same results as other people; which is a recipe for mediocrity. Come to think of it, the mentality you need to be a good investor is pretty much the opposite of what you need to be a good novelist."

About the Author

John Veals is the villainous hedge fund manager in Sebastian Faulks' best-selling credit-crunch novel *"A Day in December"*. He is a man with no friends, no culture, and no interest in anything other than making money. His nefarious machinations lead to the failure of a major British bank, enabling him to make huge profits from his short positions. Other characters in the novel include Gabriel Northwood, a virtuous lawyer, and Roger Malpasse, a retired banker of the old school.

A Hedge Fund Manager Hits Back

My name is John Veals. You may not have heard of me, but I used to run High Level Capital - an outfit which shot the lights out in the credit crisis. I'm going to use the space I've been allotted here to give you my take on what happened and why.

I expect you're wondering about my reaction when I saw what Sebastian Faulks wrote about me in that book. First, anger and disappointment. Second, disappointment and anger. Third, more anger and more disappointment. Fourth - well, you get the picture.

If he'd only listened to me, the book could have been so much better. He could have written The Great Gatsby of our age. The movie would have been a smash too, with Jude Law or Clive Owen playing yours truly.

Whatever. It's not my nature to dwell on what might have been. Jobbing backwards never gets you anywhere, does it? But what I've been pondering is why he got me so wrong and why he got the financial crisis wrong too. Because it's not just our Sebastian. Nobody really gets it.

As it happens I've always been a big fan of Seb. Birdsong, Charlotte Gray, Human Traces, The Fatal Englishman - quite a track record, isn't it? After that streak his literary Sharpe ratio must have been off the charts. I also rate Engleby, which is a story about a weirdo at Cambridge in the seventies. It took me back some, did that book. After all, that was my era, more or less.

You see, naughty Seb has distorted quite a few facts about me. The real John Veals is somewhat older than the "John Veals" in the book; somewhat better-looking too, if I do say so myself. And he didn't study law at a grey-brick university and quit halfway through. Nor does he have an undertaker for a dad and an *'alkie'** for a wife.

*'alcoholic'

Not to worry - I understand the requirements of financial fiction. It's not that different from fictional finance, which is something I came across a lot in my career as a hedge fund manager. Yeah, cooking up a story must be something like cooking up a CDO squared or some other exotic derivative. It's not whether it reflects the fundamentals that counts. It's whether you can get people to think it reflects the fundamentals.

Have you read Seb's James Bond book? Not much alpha there, in my view. You might say a minor drawdown, even. Maybe he's just too nice a guy to get his brain around Bond and Fleming. Not nice, those two. Bastards - and proud of it. Just like me. And as for all the hoopla at the book launch - speedboats down the Thames, helicopter escorts, blonde bimbo in red jumpsuit - that was loadsacredit Britain at its pre-crisis naffest. Stunts like that may be okay for Dan Brown, but surely not for a grand man of literature.

It was that kind of nonsense that made me so bearish about the way things were heading. Monumental excess, delusion, every kind of bullshit and drivel - it was like a tide that was getting higher and higher, month by month, year by year. And you know what happens to things that are unsustainable? They stop. That's why I was shorting all the overpriced rubbish I could lay my hands on.

See, it wasn't just investment bankers who were dancing to the music. Footballers, TV chefs, brain-dead celebrities, freeloading politicians, conceptual artists flogging traffic bollards, drunken berks on stag nights in Prague, middle-class plonkers installing heated swimming pools in their gardens, shop-girls hiring stretch limos for a Saturday night on the town; the smart-arse at the office who accumulated a couple of dozen buy-to-let apartments; your own dear wife who was so ecstatic at the rise in house prices that she took to doing her Christmas shopping in Manhattan. In other words, almost every bloody person in the entire bloody country - all hooked on funny money, all living the big lie. Famous writers were no exception - instead of bonuses they had advances. They could have refused the dosh or donated it to charity, but if they did nobody told me·

When it all went tits up, I made a stonking profit - how stonking I leave to your imagination - and now I've retired to Lucerne where I manage my own money without having to justify what I'm doing to whingeing clients and out-to-lunch regulators. I have a new wife, a beautiful baby daughter, and a lakeside villa designed by a well-known architect. Sickening, you say? That's your problem, mate, not mine. Best of all, everything panned out just as I expected. I was proved right on the biggest trade of my life. And that's better than sex, better than money, better than any drug that's ever been invented.

Now it's just me, though. I got rid of the others when I shut down High Level. Most of them I kept around for appearances. All the big decisions were mine and mine alone. Not one of them was capable of coming up with the ideas, let alone putting them into action. Do I miss living in London? You must be joking. I pass my days in peace and quiet, taking long walks in the mountains, even learning to ski, which is no picnic with my dodgy knees. I also have time to catch up on my reading, for the first time in years.

May I bring up a slightly delicate subject? In the book, Seb has made me Jewish. Though he takes pains to show I don't give a toss about religion or culture and don't mind showering racial abuse on other Jewish people. Deracinated, that's what he makes me. The latest in a long line, stretching back to Shylock, Fagin, and Trollope's Melmotte. If you must know, the real J.V's mum is Liverpool Irish and his Dad was a car-worker from Birmingham.

Does any of this matter? It shouldn't, but all I'm saying is that I come from an ordinary background and am just an ordinary bloke, in most respects; but not all. I look and I listen and I form my own opinions and stick to them. Sounds simple, doesn't it? It isn't. Being a dyed-in-the-wool contrarian, immune to the zeitgeist, treating other people's emotions as nothing more than data points - for that you need a certain kind of mind, one that can shut down any twinges of empathy. Because if you do empathise, if you do see other people's point of view, then you're probably going to think like other people and act like other people. And in the investment world that means you're going to get the same results as other people; which is a recipe for mediocrity. Come to think of it, the mentality you need to be a good investor is pretty much the opposite of what you need to be a good novelist.

So, yeah, let's admit it. I am a bit anti-social, borderline Asperger's, as my ex-wife used to say. Market mood-swings don't affect me a jot, nor all the gossip and the blather of so-called expert commentators - muppets the lot of them. That's my strength. I doubt everything and everybody. I follow the chain of events to its logical conclusion.

Does that make me evil? Not at all. It's the detachment that makes me useful. Socially useful, to use a phrase that makes my skin crawl. An ex-management consultant came up with that one, and what could be more socially useless than a bloody management consultant.

The *"John Veals"* in the book is supposed to be a nasty piece of work. Remember how good old Roger Malpasse tore me a new one in that dinner party scene? I didn't answer him at the time. He was drunk, and anyway Seb wouldn't allow me to stand my ground. Which is a pity. I wanted to give the tosser both barrels. As for Gabriel bloody Northwood - he shouldn't even have been there. He should have been red-carded by the end of chapter three for the offence of being a sanctimonious twat. To my mind there's nothing virtuous about a closed-minded, back-to-the-fifties, anti-commercial, anti-foreign mentality. And there's nothing bad about prosperity, as such, or technology, as such. They give you more freedom which, of course, includes the freedom to be stupid.

As for scape-goating the financial industry, I don't agree with that either. It's like blaming the pub for your hangover. That's not to deny that some of the barmen were idiots and some of them gave you the wrong change. But they didn't force the drink down your throat, did they? You were gulping it down as fast as you could. As were the barmen themselves, of course.

You don't agree? You think the UK should downsize financial services, get back to making things, instead of just moving money around? In the words of John McEnroe, you CANNOT be serious. Have you forgotten the nineteen-seventies? Manufacturing didn't work out so well then, did it? And now the Chinese, the Vietnamese, the East Europeans, the Turks - in fact, three quarters of the population of the entire planet are in the manufacturing game. You think we should compete with that lot? Are you having a giraffe? The UK downsizing financial services would be like the Saudis downsizing oil or the Eskimos downsizing fishing.

Ah, the bonuses. Obscene, you say? Look, you're mixing up two completely different things here. Those wallies who ran their banks into the ground while picking up knighthoods and sitting on government committees and sponsoring sports clubs and all that crap - regular pillars of the community, right? Well, it might surprise you to learn that I totally agree with you. The money they trousered wasn't earned. They should give it back, and more. The same goes for the regulators, the rating agencies, the accountants, the politicians who stitched up rotten deals that impoverished hundreds of thousands of pensioners, just to save their own miserable hides. They should all be on trial for financial crimes against humanity. But nobody wants to go there, right?

That's got nothing to do with me, though. I earned my money fair and square. The only people with a right to complain are the people who paid me, my investors - and they were satisfied with what happened, very satisfied indeed. It's nobody else's business, is it? And there are thousands and thousands of others like me too - though they don't operate on the same grand scale. Do a good job of work and you get paid what was agreed. What's wrong with that? Isn't it what you tell your kids when they clean the car?

In the middle of the crisis the regulators suddenly banned shorting. We had archbishops in funny hats ranting and raving about how evil speculators were targeting perfectly sound banks and wrecking the lives of ordinary working people. That was a nice Monty Python-type touch. If you want a proper witch-hunt, why not bring in the crew who originated the concept?

I had a good chuckle about that. Not because I don't give a stuff about ordinary working people - I do actually, though I don't make a fuss about it - but because of the total misunderstanding of what was going on. I didn't force these mortgage lenders and real estate companies into bank-ruptcy. They did it all by themselves. I was the little boy in the kids' story pointing out that the emperor had no clothes.

You see, none of this happened because of me. It would have happened anyway, whether I was there or not. It was baked in the cake, a long time ago. Historical inevitability is one way to put it. Most trades are questions of probability. There's always some doubt in your mind, some margin of error. Sometimes you lie awake at night wondering if you've missed something important. Not this time. I had total conviction, right from the start. Didn't another John, John Keats, say something about truth being beauty and beauty truth? Well, my trade was the truest trade I've ever done - it went straight to the heart of the matter. And in my eyes, that makes it a thing of beauty.

If you want to do some real good in this world, as opposed to just giving yourself a self-righteous glow, you should show these ordinary working people how to protect themselves against bubbles. You should make new easy-to-understand financial instruments available to everybody. Instead of banning shorting, you should teach everybody how to do it. Courses in financial self-defence. Yeah, I'd be up for that. Though I don't suppose anyone would ever ask old J.V.

Here's what really gets my goat. You have a bubble, and everyone thinks the world is lovely. Not me, though - I see it for what it is. The bubble bursts, and the economy goes down the bog. Now everyone blames me for being right. They say I'm the cause of their misery. Malpasse even ac-cuses me of siphoning off other people's money, like some sort of Madoff-style fraudster.

Sorry, Roger, old pal - you've got it arse over tit, as usual. If there were more people like me, if there had been more shorting of the banks and the property market from day one, the bubble would never have grown to the scale it did. But everyone loved that bubble, didn't they? The politi-cians preening themselves on their brilliant economic management, the regulators so proud of their light touch regulation. And let's not forget those fine people, the general public. You can't have a proper bubble without their full and enthusiastic participation. Getting richer and richer by the simple expedient of going to sleep every night in your own bed - of course they loved it, bless their little cotton socks.

Okay - let's cut to the chase, shall we. The biggest distortion in Seb's novel, the one that really got me fuming, concerns my methods. The fictional J.V. trades on insider information, spreads false rumours, manipulates and blusters and threatens people. That's how he gets his results. Comforting, isn't it? Flattering to the readers, I would say. It tells them that the only difference between them and me, the only reason they got stuffed in the credit crunch while I hit the jackpot, is that they are good honest blokes while I am a conniving crook. Sorry, folks. That's not the way it was. The difference between them and me, the only difference that counts, is that they were living in la-la land and loving it. I wasn't. They believed in fairies and I didn't.

The real John Veals doesn't break the rules. For one thing, he doesn't need to. For another, it would take away the thrill, the existential vindication, of being right about the deep structure of the world we inhabit. Let me pause there for a moment. I'd better apologise for the abrupt change in register. In the book Seb forced me to talk like a man in a fish-and-chip shop queue, but keeping up the facade has become too much of a strain. From now on, I propose to use my normal diction. You may be surprised to learn that I'm at least as articulate and well-read as Seb's pet characters, Northwood and Malpasse. This isn't mentioned in the novel, but I was actually at university with Malpasse. He got a third in Land Economy and spent all his time swilling real ale at the JCR bar. Amusing enough in his own way, but hardly un homme serieux.

Anyway, as I was saying, my methods are perfectly above board. Obviously I go through the relevant corporate and macro-economic data with a fine-tooth comb. I also try to apply a context to contemporary events by studying the patterns of the past. Economic and social history is a much under-utilised resource in the investment business. Human nature drives markets, indeed all social phenomena, and human nature doesn't change.

The arrogance of the present leads us to believe that the men of the past were foolish and backward, that we have outgrown their obvious errors and mis-judgements. The men of the future will probably think the same of us.

The first book of what we now call behavioural finance was written by Dickens' friend, Charles Mackay - the classic Extraordinary Popular Delu-sions and the Madness of Crowds. Mackay's key insight, rarely appreciated today, is that financial bubbles are merely a subset of the greater category of manias - what he calls moral epidemics. These he saw as deeply rooted in human nature. As he put it, *"men, it has been well said, think in herds; it will be seen that they go mad in herds, while they only recover their senses slowly, and one by one."*

My copy of the book runs to over seven hundred pages, but only the first one hundred concern financial matters. The rest deals with other examples of delusive thinking - alchemy, fortune-telling, the crusades, the witch trials, belief in prophecy and fortune-telling, belief in the imminent end of the world, and so on. According to Mackay, his entire work is *"a chapter only in the great and awful book of human folly."*

It's not hard to find parallels for many of the phenomena he described in today's world. The peddlers of quack medicine deplored by Mackay now have their products on the shelves of stores in every shopping precinct. The mythologizing of outlaws like Dick Turpin and Jack Sheppard would find an echo in the films of Tarantino and Guy Ritchie. Instead of fortune-tellers and diviners we now have economists and futurologists. Little harm done, it might seem, but the same human failings can have dire con-sequences. In Mackay's words:

We find that whole communities suddenly fix their minds upon one object, and go mad in its pursuit; that millions of people become simultaneously impressed with one delusion, and run after it, till their attention is caught by some new folly more capti-vating than the first. We see one nation suddenly seized, from its highest to its lowest members, with a fierce desire of military glory; another as suddenly becoming crazed upon a religious scruple; and neither of them recovering its senses until it has shed tears of blood and sowed a harvest of groans and tears, to be reaped by its posterity.

What I took from Mackay's book is the proposition that financial market behaviour is just one aspect of the psychological state of society as a whole. It follows that excess and delusion in society is likely to be mirrored by excess and delusion in the markets. Furthermore, such phenomena are dynamic and cyclical. Calibrating exactly where we are in the cycle is crucial to my investment approach.

Today's conventional wisdom is that the global financial crisis was caused by fundamental flaws in the global financial architecture. Therefore, runs the thinking, if we make appropriate alterations to the architecture - splitting up banks, reducing bankers' compensation, increasing the number of regulators and regulations - we can ensure there will be no repeat. Mackay would consider this a fundamentally ahistorical and mistaken view, and I would agree with him.

Financial bubbles and busts have occurred throughout history, in very different circumstances and under very different economic systems. The most extreme case in recent times was the Japanese real estate and stock market bubble of the late nineteen-eighties. In its climactic phase, the Imperial Palace grounds in central Tokyo had a greater theoretical value than the entire state of California.

The interesting point, from a present-day perspective, is how different the Japanese system was from the Western systems that spawned our own recent credit bubble. Almost the opposite, in many respects.

Japanese banks had wafer-thin profit margins, and the compensation of senior executives was very modest. There were no stock options and bonuses. The financial system was strictly compartmentalised; securities companies were not permitted to conduct banking business and vice versa. Rather than a small number of *"too big to fail"* institutions, the Japanese system was made up of thousands of financial intermediaries, including hundreds of regional banks which were listed on the Tokyo Stock Exchange. Perched at the top of this structure was the all-powerful Ministry of Finance, which coaxed and bullied senior executives into carrying out its wishes for the sake of the national interest.

Let me put it another way. The financial system that gave birth to the greatest financial mania of the second half of the twentieth century contained many of the features that reformers are proposing as remedies for the defects of our own Western systems. That is an irony that Mackay would have relished. I fancy he might have considered the flood of new regulations, proposals, and taxes to be another example of delusionary thinking.

It is never the system that creates the bubble, but the people within it. The Japanese bankers, bureaucrats and corporate leaders were not venal. They believed they were acting for the good of Japan. Why did they let the bubble inflate to such a preposterous extent? Because they had no understanding of the risks. To a man, they had bought the narrative of Japan's inevitable rise to global supremacy. They fervently and sincerely believed what they wanted to believe, and there was no Japanese John Veals on the other side of the trade.

To quote Mackay one last time, *"sober nations have all at once become desperate gamblers, and risked almost their existence upon the turn of a piece of paper."* He probably had Holland in mind, but he wouldn't have been surprised about what happened to Japan three hundred and fifty years later.

You'll never stop people reading horoscopes or using herbal remedies by making them study science. Likewise you'll never put an end to financial bubbles by reforming the financial system. The tendency to mass delusion is hard-wired into the human brain, part of the same deep instinct for imitation that enables us to acquire language and feed ourselves with the right foods. The impulse to blame others for our own failings - the bankers, the politicians, capitalism itself - may be similarly hard-wired too. It makes the world more bearable, but also prevents us from learning from our mistakes.

There is only one way to alert society to the worst excesses of mass delusion - not just in finance, but in other areas that are potentially more destructive. That is to encourage the activities of aggressive contrarians like me, John Veals. For I'm not just a character in a book. I am a feedback mechanism, a critique of the prevailing orthodoxy. I am the man in the

New Yorker cartoon, sitting in the cinema laughing his head off while everyone around him is weeping. I am the hero of Ionesco's *"Rhinoceros"*, the one man in town who does not turn into a rhino. I am Camus' definition of a rebel: *"the man who says 'no'"*. I am the outrageous stand-up comedian, the heretic, the mad scientist. A healthy society needs as many people like John Veals as it can get.

So there you have it. That's my riposte. Take it or leave it - it doesn't matter to me either way. I'll be back, of course. When you create your next bubble, I'll be there, following the logic of the situation to its inevitable denouement. And no doubt you'll blame me then too. You always have done and always will.

For the time being I'll stay here in Switzerland, enjoying the food and scenery, playing with the baby and listening to my wife practice her music. Maybe at some point I'll set pen to paper in a more organised way. After all somebody has to set the record straight.

John Veals*
Switzerland, Summer 2010

* As recounted to Peter Tasker

Mr Veals has magnanimously opted to give
his charitable donation to:

An anonymous half-way house for alcoholic authors located in a former
Anglican rectory in the home counties.

THE GATHERING STORM

CHAPTER THREE

-

"To be optimistic is to be an idiot. That seems to be the mood of the times. The end is nigh, we are endlessly told, so we'd better get used to it."

Rob Lyons

THE GATHERING STORM

Remember the Ice Age?
by Albert Edwards

"At the end of both the Japanese late 1980's bubble and the US late 1990's bubble, expectations for long-term EPS growth rose higher and higher due to New Paradigm nonsense, mathematically justifying extremely high PEs. Indeed, at one point in his cheer-leading for the New Paradigm, Alan Greenspan cited the IBES long-term expectations series as evidence why high equity valuations were justified. After all, surely all those hundreds of individual analysts were unlikely to be wrong. But due to collective delusion on a grand scale, they all were!"

About the Author

Albert Edwards is the Global Strategist at Societe Generale. He previously worked for Dresdner Kleinwort Bank of America Investment Management and the Bank of England. In the world where sell-side investment bank analysts have a strong bias towards optimism, he is well-known for having been extremely bearish on the macro-economic and equity market outlook for many years. One indication of this is that he has been recommending clients underweight global equities for 14 years and seek the safer haven of government bonds. He still believes we are in the grip of a structural equity bear market.

Remember the Ice Age?

It's coming back. And it could destroy your portfolios.

Looking back over the last few years' economic debacle, one key factor that blindsided most equity investors and asset allocators alike was not realising that equities had entered a structural bear market for valuations. The Ice Age thesis I first postulated towards the end of the 1990s, would wreck the solvency of most defined benefit pension schemes with their bull-market heavy overexposure to equities. The article below, written in February 2008, was a restatement to investors of the Ice Age thesis calling for, what seemed at the time, outlandishly large decline in equities of 50-60% as the credit bubble burst.

What now? I continue to believe the equity bear market is incomplete. Long-term valuation measures such as the cyclically adjusted PEs (e.g.: the Shiller or Graham and Dodds PE) or Tobin's Q ratio, never left equity valuations looking rock-bottom cheap at the nadir of the 2008 bear market. As in Japan during the 1990s, the secular bear market takes many cycles to play itself out. It is not reasonable to expect this process to end with equities looking only moderately cheap as they did in early 2008, following the biggest valuation bubble in history. Valuation bust will inevitably follow the valuation boom that peaked in 2000. I believe the market will look for an "excuse" to complete this process and that will come as the withdrawal of fiscal and monetary stimulus sends the global economy into a renewed downturn. Investors should be prepared to see the major indices bottom far below their 2008 lows.

* * *

There is a widespread belief that in any imminent recession, equity multiples will expand as bond yields decline, cushioning the extent of any price decline. But what if multiples contract because we are in a secular bear market for valuations? The Ice Age has not gone away. It has enjoyed a cyclical snooze and is ready to come back refreshed and re-invigorated. Hide.

We formulated our Ice Age thesis a decade ago. It conjectured how financial market valuations would change in a world of very low inflation. After one last equity hurrah, we expected equities to embark on a multi-year de-rating in absolute terms and relative to bonds, which themselves would re-rate sharply. Equity yields would decouple from bond yields and traditional valuation criteria would pull investors into incredibly cheap equities, only for them to slump further.

Despite much angst in the markets, we still remain relaxed about inflation despite unprecedented cost push pressures, in very large part because we see a pronounced cyclical downturn unfolding. We consider the global economy to be more vulnerable to the likelihood of deep recession than for 25 years. Inflation jitters could soon vanish with deflation fears very firmly placed back on the agenda.

After a 17-year bull market we have invested for the Ice Age, having a bias against equities and towards government bonds for the last decade. That has made us a hate figure for many. Yet, despite global equities just cresting the end of a long bull run and our turning cautious too early in 1997, government bonds have outperformed equities over a 10-year period *(see chart below)*. Indeed they have outperformed on a 20-year view as well.

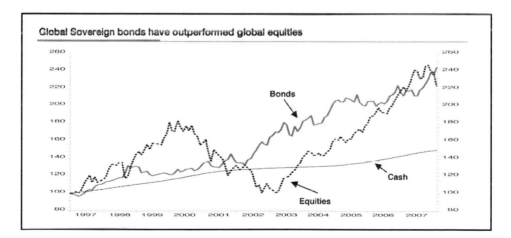

We remind investors of our Ice Age thesis in this note. If, as we believe, we remain in a secular bear market for equity valuations, a torrid time lies ahead.

While equity investors believe that the most damaging event for their portfolios would be a deep recession, they remain comforted that any equity bear market will be moderate. After all, aren't PEs the lowest they have been for 20 years *(see chart below)*?

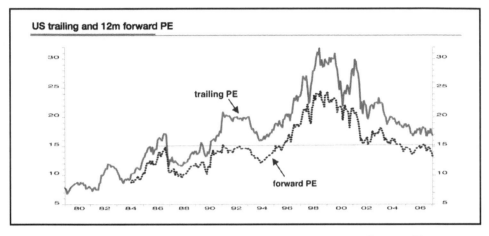

Source: Datastream

Hopes of a moderate bear market are underpinned by the belief that in recessions, falling bond yields typically allow PEs to expand as the present value of future earnings rises. That is the natural course of events, isn't it? Well, it was, until the last cycle *(see chart on following page)*. The 2001-2003 bear market shocked investors by its severity, in large part because multiples contracted in tandem with declining profits and bond yields.

Investors now seem comfortable that the unusual pro-cyclical behaviour of PE multiples during the late 1990s bubble and its aftermath is now behind us - a one-off as bubble equity valuations deflated. And having observed that booming profits have driven PE multiples even lower in recent years, most investors believe equities are currently cheap enough. Hence the usual counter-cyclical behaviour of profits and PEs can resume. *But what if they are wrong?*

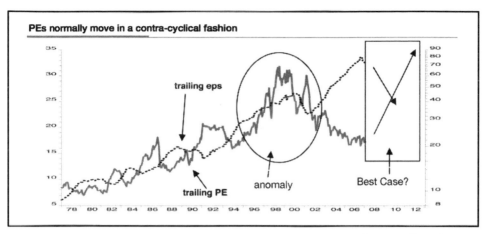

PEs normally move in a contra-cyclical fashion

Source: DataStream

To assess whether the normal counter-cyclical behaviour of PEs has resumed, one must step well, well back and take the long view. The tendency for short-termism in this industry is well-known, with increasing pressures to outperform on shorter and shorter time scales. Naming the individual trees in the wood may all be very well and comforting, but if we don't know which wood we are actually in, then incorrect strategic decisions can be made.

Stepping back and trying to see the strategic wood from the cyclical trees is instructive. For during 1950-2000 we believe there have only been three major structural phases of the equity market *(see chart below)*. We are all familiar with the spectacular equity bull market since 1982-2000, but who now remembers the dismal years of 1965-1982 where the Dow went precisely nowhere for 17 years in nominal terms - and collapsed in real terms?

The Ice Age

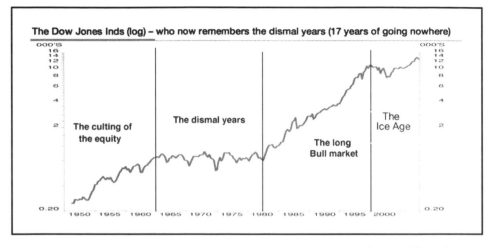

The Dow Jones Inds (log) – who now remembers the dismal years (17 years of going nowhere)

The culting of the equity

The dismal years

The long Bull market

The Ice Age

Source: DataStream

History books can remind us of the 1950-1965 period. Equities fared well, re-rating from extremely depressed levels, despite rising bond yields, as the nightmarish investment memories of the 1930s were forgotten. As the *"cult of the equity"* grew, equities established themselves as the dominant long-term investment asset class in institutional portfolios.

So while we run around getting excited about short-term cyclical and technical developments, correctly identifying the secular investment environment we are in is absolutely crucial, i.e. the default asset allocation decision that might work in one 17-year period might have been the totally wrong strategy for the following 17-year period.

It was around a decade ago that we developed our Ice Age thesis. We conjectured that after one last equity hurrah, the investment landscape would be radically transformed by very low (maybe even excessively low) inflation backdrop. We believed that the long equity bull market investors had enjoyed since 1982 would come to a shuddering halt, but the bull market in government bonds would continue. This was the Ice Age.

The reasoning was simple. The long bull market in equities had been driven predominately by a collapse in inflation from its early 1980s peak. This was a complete mirror image of the dismal 17-year period before 1965-1982 *(see chart below).*

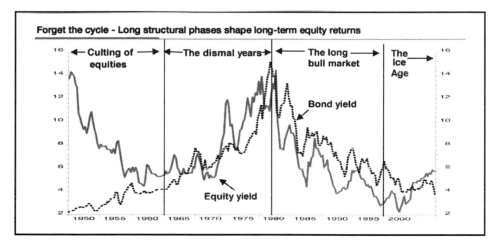

Source: DataStream

During the 1982-2000 bull market, lower inflation had led to lower bond yields which, in turn, had driven equity multiples substantially higher (falling equity yields). PE expansion had accounted for well over a half of the capital gain of equities over this period. In contrast, the previous 17 years had seen multiple contraction entirely offset earnings growth.

The first step to the Ice Age thesis was, we conjectured, that with inflation already so low this engine as a driver for further multiple expansion was over. Equities prices would now only rise in line with profits - at best - producing much-reduced returns. This relatively non-controversial idea was also expounded by some other strategists.

It was the second stage of our Ice Age thesis that marked our view out as separate from the most of the investment community. We believed that in a world of very low inflation, the Ice Age would produce a secular trend towards rising equity yields whilst bond yields (and interest rates) would carry on declining. Equity valuations would enter a secular bear market which would be a mirror image of the 1950-1965 period *(see chart on fol-*

lowing page). Among other unwelcome outcomes, the Ice Age would destroy the solvency of many equity-heavy, defined benefit pension schemes. They-would become caught in a vicious pincer movement of falling asset values (due to their excess equity exposure) and rising liabilities (due to the declining bond yield). As you can imagine, this was a hard story to tell at the end of the 1990s and not one which made me popular - especially with the equity sales force!

For what we were conjecturing was a return to the sorts of bond/equity valuations seen in the 1950s and early 1960s *(see chart on previous page).* We believed that the outlook for equity and bond yields would become a mirror image of the 1950-1965 period. The Ice Age would bring about the *"De-culting of the equity"* and we would return to a period where the equity market as a whole would yield more than the bond market - not a few stocks that seem to excite people currently. The reverse yield gap would return to being just the plain vanilla yield gap.

Before we explore the drivers of the secular bear market in equity valuations let's see what has happened and why events in many ways closely resemble Japan's experience of a secular equity bear market over the last 17 years.

What has happened since the late 1990s bubble burst? The normal positive correlation between bonds and equity yields has indeed broken down *(see chart on following page).* Cheap equities just seem to get cheaper and cheaper, relative to supposedly expensive bond markets. The bulls hope this is a one-off adjustment that has ended. But the Ice Age thesis calls for a lot more of the same to come.

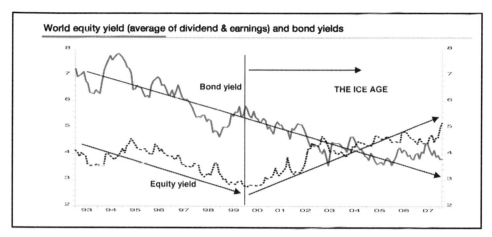

Source: DataStream

Of course we have seen this all before - in Japan when their bubble burst in 1990 *(see chart below)*. So one does not need to dig into the history of the 1950s to see how this might unfold.

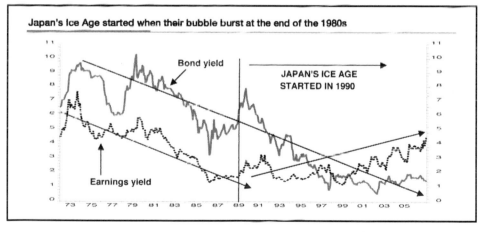

Source: DataStream

The comparison with Japan is uncanny. It has less to do with the economic comparisons (although those are perhaps more similar than many suppose) and more to do with how an equity market adjusts to a world of very low inflation (or deflation) combined with the anatomy of an equity bubble bursting. At the end of the 1990s Japan, like the US a decade later, was regarded as a model for a *"New Paradigm"* of strong and stable economic growth with a backdrop of low inflation. Equity multiples expanded in Japan to what seemed ridiculous, but at the time had all sorts of plausible explanations. The simple fact was that strong and stable growth was built upon an asset bubble that eventually burst.

Successive cycles saw Japanese equity valuations grind lower and lower, both in absolute terms and relative to bonds. The US valuation experience is not so different to Japan a decade before *(see chart below)*. PEs were a lot higher in Japan's bubble than the US but the cash flow yield was pretty similar. The tried and tested valuation metrics that had worked extremely well in Japan began to break down as seemingly "cheap" equities just carried on de-rating against what appeared to be very expensive bonds. This went on and on and on. Even now the de-rating is not over with the 12m forward TOPIX PE just falling below the S&P.

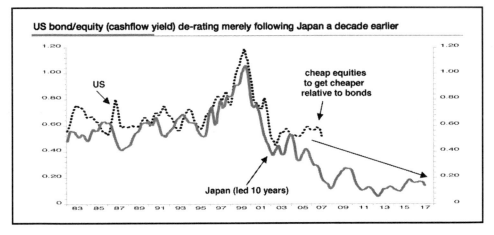

Source: DataStream

Hence, we have for the last decade cautioned that we would enter a period in the western markets where valuation metrics would flag up equities as incredibly cheap *(see chart left below)*. But the siren strategists' voices enticing investors to increase equity exposure would surely wreck portfolios. Like Odysseus' sailors, stuff your ears with wax or if you do want to listen to the bull market song, tie yourself to the mast and go nowhere near balanced portfolios. Indeed, the voices are even more alluring than normal. Our own tactical asset allocation tools developed by James during the last bear market shows that the investors regard equities as far cheaper than at the market bottom in 2003 *(see right hand chart below).*

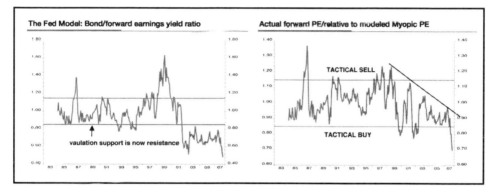

Source: DataStream, SG Research

Now I'm not too good with all this equity valuation nonsense (I normally leave that stuff to James), but in some ways it seems pretty simple to me. Using a discount model, a 12-month forward PE is determined by expectations for near-term earnings and long-term (trend) EPS growth, discounted by a bond yield and a cyclical risk premium (which can vary). The Myopic PE models the PE on just the bond yield and analysts' long-term earnings expectations. We then compare the actual 12m forward PE to what the model is saying *(right hand chart above).*

Declining long-term earnings expectations are the core as to why, in the Ice Age, forward PEs decline despite falling bond yields. Mathematically, the reverse should occur but only if everything else is kept equal. The problem is we are now in a period where long-term earnings expectations are in secular decline and also the equity (cyclical) risk premium is rising.

For this is where the bulls have got it so wrong. Yes, in a world of low inflation and low bond yields, PEs should be high, ceteris paribus. But in a low inflation, low nominal GDP growth world, long-term earnings expectations should also be low. At the end of both the Japanese late 1980s bubble and the US late 1990s bubble, expectations for long-term EPS growth rose higher and higher due to New Paradigm nonsense, mathematically justifying extremely high PEs *(see chart below)*. Indeed at one point in his cheerleading for the New Paradigm, Alan Greenspan cited the IBES long-term expectations series as evidence why high equity valuations were justified. After all, surely all those hundreds of individual analysts were unlikely to be wrong. But due to collective delusion on a grand scale, they all were!

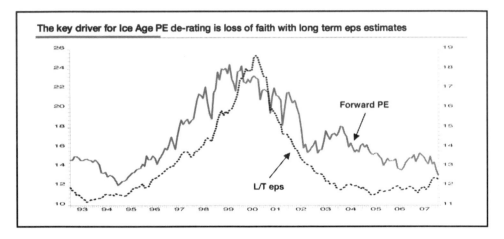

Source: DataStream

The modelled myopic PE is currently suggesting that equities are regarded by the market as unusually cheap because sharply lower bond yields have combined with a recent ticking up of long-term EPS expectations. Something similar happened in the bear market of 2001-2003 as declines in long-term EPS expectations lagged the market on the way down. Together with Bull/Bear and other technical indicators the Myopic PE was helpful in timing the explosive bear market rallies that occurred.

This time around long-term expectations have been ticking up in former cyclical sectors that have been re-designated as *"growth"* sectors due to the China/Emerging Market inspired super-cycle for industrial cyclicals and commodities. But, to be sure, it is notable that despite one of the most explosive four years of profits growth in history, long-term EPS expectations have remained pretty becalmed.

Japanese history of the last 17 years suggests that that a secular bear market has a tendency to accelerate in each successive cyclical downturn, especially if we are coming off bubble valuations *(see chart below).*

The timing of these equity slumps was crucially synchronised with cyclical downturns at a time when valuation models repeatedly told investors that equities were cheap. Equity and bond yields had become decoupled and buying into Japanese equities too early in the downturn repeatedly crushed investors. (That does not preclude the possibility of huge 40%, cyclical inspired rallies - Japan regularly enjoyed these - but they were interludes in the context of a long drawn out secular bear).

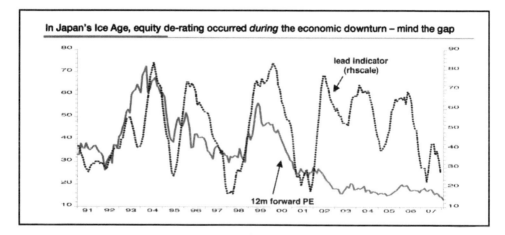

Source: DataStream

One lesson from the Japanese secular bear market is that it is perfectly normal for investors to clutch onto new *"growth"* straws in each successive cyclical rally. Back in the late 1990s, for example, the bubble in Japanese technology valuations made the Nasdaq bubble look like a small insignificant pimple. Similarly, newly formulated hopes for *"growth"* protection from industrial cyclicals and commodities will be shown to be pipe dreams and, in the unfolding downturn, analysts will take an axe again to their estimates of trend earnings.

Another similarity with Japan a decade ago is that a secular equity bear market seems to be combining with the bursting and unwind of an economic bubble (defined as unsustainably high rates of private sector debt leveraged against unsustainable asset and credit bubbles).

As successive economic upswings crumble in investors hands, the realisation that strong stable growth is actually an illusion brings huge disappointment (like recent talk of The Great Moderation). Investors then demand a higher cyclical risk premium to compensate for the increased volatility that results as the asset and credit bubble bursts and, in extremis, deflation takes a hold. But, even within the supposed Great Moderation of recent years, there is already ample evidence to suggest that in a world of very low inflation the profits cycle has already become much more volatile *(see chart below)*!

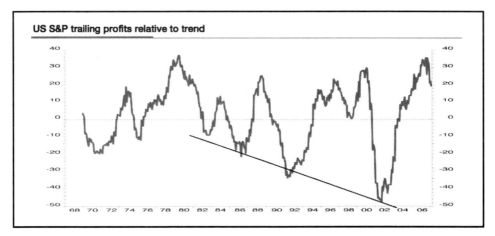

Source: DataStream

As we move deeper into this secular bear market for equity valuations, the Ice Age reality of low nominal bond yields will continue to be underpinned by unusually low real yields. In recent weeks real yields have crashed back towards 1%. But, once again, looking back into the 1960s we can see that all that has happened is that the old valuation metrics have re-established themselves *(see chart below)*. Certainty is re-rated relative to cyclicality.

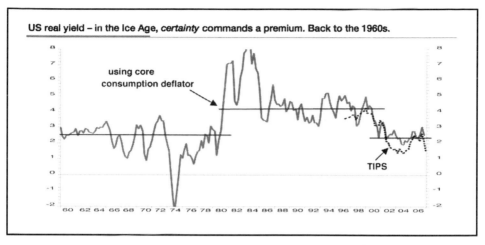

US real yield – in the Ice Age, *certainty* commands a premium. Back to the 1960s.

using core
consumption deflator

TIPS

Source: DataStream

The crux of the arguments above is that investors should be wary that equity valuations are not cheap for we may be in a secular bear market for equity valuations. A seemingly low US 12-month forward PE of 13 x (albeit with inexplicably high analysts EPS estimates) may continue to de-rate in any upcoming cyclical downturn. In a deep recession the mathematics are scary. In the last downturn, forward operating S&P profits fell 20% (peak to trough) but the S&P declined about 50% from its peak. Suppose we get the sort of economic downturn the global economy has not seen for 30 years. If profits slump 40% and the forward PE continues to contract towards single digits, then a 60% decline in the equity market would come as a bit of a shock to those who think that multiple expansion will cushion any profits recession.

One separate piece of evidence that the secular bear market in equity valuations is not over is found by comparing equity prices to cyclically adjusted earnings. On this comparison US equity valuations remain over 20x cyclically adjusted earnings and, putting aside the Nasdaq bubble years, the market remains very expensive *(see chart on following page)*. Indeed James Montier uses the Graham and Dodds PE (it uses a 10-year moving average of reported earnings instead of trend earnings) to show that apart from the Nasdaq bubble years, equities are as expensive as they have ever been - and just as expensive as just before the 1929 crash!

(One argument, that the de-bubbling process has a lot further to go because we are in a secular bear market, was subject to an excellent review by John Authers at the FT, *When are the Bulls actually Bears?* (http://www.ft.com/cms/s/0/bc33194a-ce0f-11dc-9e4e-000077b07658.html) which I would thoroughly recommend reading).

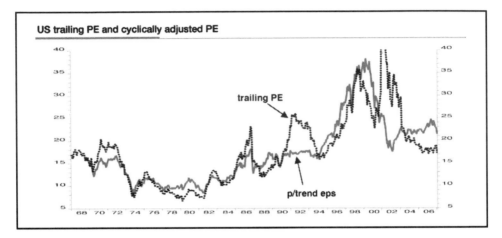

Source: DataStream

Investors in European equities might be reassured by the fact that the cyclically adjusted PE in Europe is some 5x EPS below that of the US and much more in keeping with the experience of the mid-1980s to mid-1990s *(see chart below)*. They are probably right, but we remain about one-third above levels that saw a valuation floor back in 2003. Not so comforting, hey?

Source: DataStream

The valuation gap between the US and Europe began to open up in 1994, exactly at the time that US long-term earnings began their bubble assent *(see chart on page 71)*. This valuation gap is confirmed by work Andrew Lapthorne has done using implied perpetuity growth rates. This gap should close as it is unwarranted. Since the 1994 New Paradigm re-rating began, relative to the rest of the world, the US equity market has produced consistently poorer earnings outturn *(see chart below)*. Investors have been paying more for less.

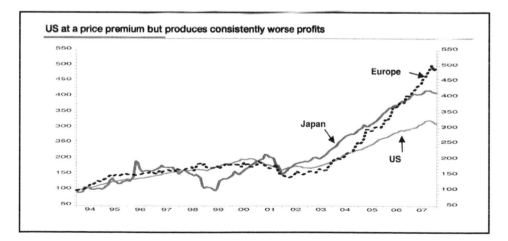

Source: DaluStream

But at least back in the late 1990s, investors could cite estimates of trend GDP growth in the US being far higher than elsewhere. Higher trend GDP growth should have resulted in higher profits growth. But in recent years US trend GDP growth has slipped *(see chart below)*.

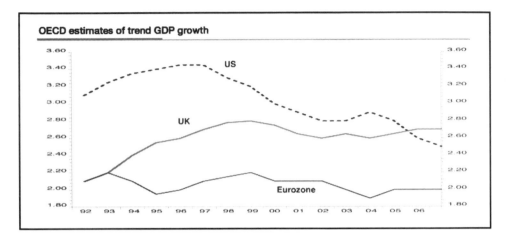

Source: OECD

So we have an expensive equity market, possibly in the grip of a secular bear market. At the same time we have a global economy at high risk of deep recession, with investors retaining the belief that commodities and emerging markets can decouple. An Ice Age equity de-rating prompting a 50%+ bear market is the one thing that investors have not factored into their economic projections for consumer confidence and the saving ratio. The housing slump is bad enough. But they should think about it because it might yet happen.

Albert Edwards has chosen to support:
The Friends of The Citizens Foundation
(TCF, UK charity number 1087864)

There is much in the media at present about Pakistan. The rise in extremism in that country should be of concern to us all. Ignorance and illiteracy can often be fertile ground for extremism. Some 47% of males above 15 years are illiterate and this rises to 72% for women. The Citizens Foundation builds and runs schools offering high-quality primary and secondary education to both boys and girls in the most undeveloped areas of Pakistan. TCF have a clear no-discrimination policy and their schools are open to all Pakistani children regardless of their race, colour, creed and religion. In many families, female education is not encouraged so to help attain a 50:50 balance between boys and girls, the teaching staff is entirely female. I am convinced that this charity, by increasing educational attainment in Pakistan, will make the world a better and safer place for us all to live.

The Citizens Foundation web site can be found at:
www.thecitizensfoundation.org

CHAPTER FOUR

-

"In any moment of decision the best thing you can do is the right thing, the next best thing is the wrong thing, and the worst thing you can do is nothing."

Theodore Roosevelt

Insurance Policies for Big Fires

Thomas Thygesen

"One of the fascinating traits of financial markets is their ability to change. Major investment climate changes regularly render time-tested rules of investment useless or even dangerous, new guidelines are gradually discovered and then the process repeats itself."

THE GATHERING STORM

About the Author

Thomas Thygesen has worked for more than 20 years as an economist and investment strategist in the financial sector. Burdened by an Msc in Economics from the University of Copenhagen, his focus has always been on the intersection between economic history, macroeconomic analysis and applied financial theory with a particular emphasis on deep, structural linkages between economics and markets. He is currently in charge of cross-asset research at SEB, the leading Nordic investment bank, advising institutional investors on asset allocation strategies and providing the foundation for the bank's new multi-asset strategy fund.

Insurance Policies for Big Fires
Investment Strategy for a Structural Bear Market

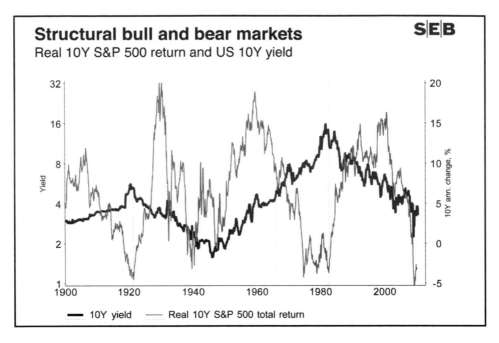

Structural bull and bear markets **S|E|B**
Real 10Y S&P 500 return and US 10Y yield

Source: GFD

One of the fascinating traits of financial markets is their ability to change. Major investment climate changes regularly render time-tested rules of investment useless or even dangerous, new guidelines are gradually discovered and then the process repeats itself.

It is easy to sympathise with the plight of investors entering the past decade with the experience of a two decade bull market to guide them, only to find that the rules had changed. But it must also have been difficult for investors to identify that bull market in the early 1980s after 15 years of negative real returns for both stocks and bonds, and in the late 1960s, when the breakdown of the post-war bull market took everyone by surprise...

Why Static Allocation Doesn't Work: Structural Bull and Bear Markets

In fact, these surprises appear with such regularity that they shouldn't really surprise. Major climate changes have occurred with a frequency of 15-20 years for more than a century. Structural bull and bear markets - long periods where real returns, volatility and asset class correlations systematically deviate from the mean - are the norm, not the exception.

These climate changes affect all the key variables that shape an optimal investment strategy, not just returns. Structural bull markets have above-average equity returns and risk premiums, but also below-average volatility and a low frequency of extreme losses. Structural bear markets have flat equity returns, but also above-average volatility and a high frequency of extreme losses.

This means asset allocation can't be a static exercise. The *"strategic asset allocation"* concept whose demise is so often lamented these days is based on stable long-term risk premiums and correlations. The main reason why it is not working is that the key variables aren't just exposed to the cyclical noise we have learned to expect and to some extent can afford to ignore, but also to persistent changes that last longer than even patient investors can wait.

The problem is compounded by the short data samples used by most practitioners. But even if you were, in some miraculous way, to know the true long-term risk premium for the coming 100 years, a portfolio based on those numbers would systematically provide *"too much"* or *"too little"* protection against the risk of extreme losses for some 10-20 years at a time. A portfolio that dealt adequately with the past 10 years' volatility and extreme losses would have diluted returns unnecessarily in the 1990s and vice versa.

Persistent changes in the key allocation parameters are not necessarily evident in any given year because normal cyclical behaviour continues to dominate short-term market developments. The stock market had bad years in the '90s and good years in the '70s - there were just more good years in the '90s and more bad years in the '70s. Such a frequency change will look a lot like statistical noise at first, and by the time it dominates the data, it's time to move on again. Static allocation is thus unlikely to provide better results in the future, but we can still salvage something from the wreckage by adding an intermediate structural level to the allocation analysis, designed to capture the background radiation from deep, persistent variation in the key parameters.

In order to do this, we need to understand why the deep changes occur and why they seem to be repeating the same patterns over and over again.

The Economics of Structural Bulls and Bears: Deep Cycles

The recurring patterns in key market relationships do not fit well with the generally held perception that history moves along a straight line of continuous improvement. Why would the '70s or the '30s be relevant to a new generation? The world has, like, moved on since then... But, in practice, economic development is not smooth and linear. It makes more sense to see it as a series of overlapping technological revolutions, leading to recurring patterns of growth and upheaval.

Starting with canals and steam power in the late 1700s, economies have been transformed by a series of new techno-economic paradigms. Railroads/telegraph, steel/heavy industry, mass production/electric power and, most recently, IT/mass customisation all triggered major changes in the dominant production model. The scale and complexity rose as each new revolution expanded the industrialised world, but the diffusion of each new technology cluster followed the S-shaped curve known from nature.

Long-term cycles in markets are not universally accepted, perhaps understandably so: Google *"Kondratieff Cycles"* and you'll find some quite fanatical followers of rather half-baked theories. But the economic link between technologic change and economic development has been the subject of intensive empirical studies over the past decades and there seems to be a recurring pattern behind the diffusion, much like a human life-cycle. *

A stylised (i.e. grossly oversimplified) model of this technology diffusion cycle would look like this:

1. As the potential of existing technologies is exhausted, supply starts to fall short of demand, driving inflation up and profits down. New technologies are developed *"below the radar"* but have no macro effect yet.
2. A *"New Era"* investment boom follows the inflation peak as a new business model is rolled out, with high profits in new industries, economic optimism and financial innovation fuelling the mobilisation of capital.
3. The boom ends with over-investment, over-capacity and deflation risks. Financial systems struggle with the debt left behind by the boom, and political systems change in response to social distress.
4. A *"Golden Age"* consumption-driven boom follows as regulation of new industries and redistribution of income reduces over-capacity and allows the new technology to reach its full-scale potential.

Seen through this prism, the structural bear markets mark the extreme of long pendulum swings from over-consumption to over-investment. Real returns are low at both extremes, but from an economic perspective, they could hardly be more different. The high-inflation crisis in phase 1 is a creative destruction of capital to pave the way for a new investment, while the low-inflation crisis in phase 3 is a destruction of debt to pave the way for new consumption.

The most recent technology cycle started in the last half of the 1960s, when the mass production model that drove the post-war boom began to disappoint. Productivity growth entered a 20-year decline, the Bretton Woods fixed exchange rate system collapsed and inflation soared. The result was 15 years of real losses for both stock and bond markets: a high-inflation structural bear market.

By the early 1980s, information technology was starting to transform business practices when central banks finally confronted excess demand and deregulation paved the way for structural change in the corporate and financial sectors. Corporate restructuring, new profits in the ICT

---

* See, for example, *"As Time Goes By"* by Chris Freeman and Francesco Louca or *"Technological Revolutions and Financial Capital"* by Carlota Perez.

sector and financial innovation mobilised capital for an investment boom. Accelerating productivity growth reduced inflation and increased trend growth at the same time, fuelling a *"New Era"* structural bull market lasting almost 20 years.

As the 1990s drew to an end, the climate changed again as supply caught up with demand. The emerging market debt crisis in 1997-1998 triggered a lasting increase in savings in the developing world. After the collapse in the IT bubble, Western policymakers used all available means to stimulate demand, only to find an even worse crisis at the end of a sub-par expansion. Although bond yields continued the decline from the '80s and '90s, the 2000s were a decade of low returns and high volatility for stocks - the first low-inflation structural bear market since WWII. "... caught up with demand. The IT boom had led to rising inequality and stagnant real incomes for the majority of consumers in the US, and the emerging market debt crisis..."

The Situation Today: More Vulnerable Than Ever

Unfortunately, after 10 years of low returns, the core problem of structural over-investment is no closer to a solution. On the contrary, widening global imbalances suggest we have become even more dependent on unsustainable demand sources. Huge capital transfers uphold the balance in what is clearly an unstable global equilibrium, and the instability is starting to show. China's (and by implication Asia's) export-dependent growth strategy is at the core of this problem.

The strategy has been a tremendous success: aided by an undervalued currency and a high saving rate, China has sustained a higher investment ratio and a faster industrialisation process than any country in history. However, over the past decade, as China's national saving rate on average went up by 2 percentage points of GDP per year, it also tilted the global supply-demand balance.

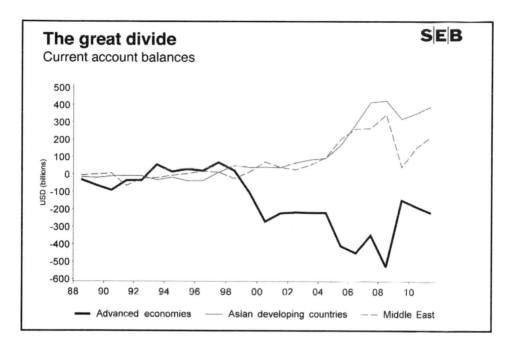

Source: IMF, Reuters EcoWin

A change in Asia's growth strategy has the potential to tilt the balance back. The bulk of the world's low-paid industrial workers are in Asia, and increasing their spending power is the only lasting way to reduce global over-capacity. But this is, at best, a process that could last 5-10 years: Consumers have no direct political representation and trade unions are not very powerful in China, and reforms aimed at stimulating consumer demand are still moving at a very gradual pace.

On the other side of the imbalance, the past 10 years have seen massive consumption of a necessarily temporary nature in the West. A wide range of Western economies have seen private sector debt ratios rise by 50-100% of GDP in less than a decade. With a few exceptions, most notably Germany and Japan, non-financial private debt ratios are close to or even above 200% of GDP, extreme by any historical comparison.

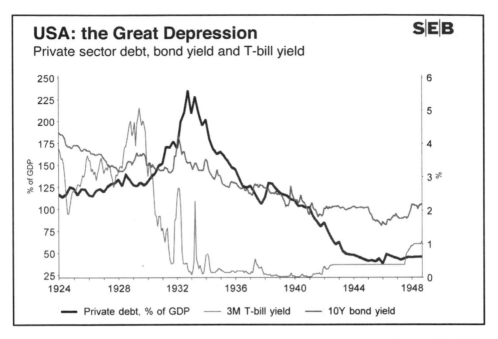

Source: EcoWin

Private sector debt ratios started falling after the financial sector crash of 2008 and policy-makers scrambled (again) to restore demand. While interest rates were cut to zero, governments started borrowing heavily and have so far replaced every Dollar of falling private debt with new public debt. The hope is that if they do it for long enough, private sector debt will start rising. But public debt is on an unsustainable path in most Western economies, so this is no long-term solution either.

At the time of writing (June 2010), aggressive monetary and fiscal stimulus has stabilised house prices and employment in most of the Western world. As in 2003, a temporary demand upswing is possible if the stimulus is maintained, but the risks are asymmetrical. There is no room for any additional monetary or fiscal stimulus if anything happens - and private debt is likely to start falling again in any event if interest rates even start to normalise or fiscal stimulus is withdrawn. Once the private sector embarks on a debt reduction, the two main episodes of sustained debt deflation in the past 100 years - the US depression in the 1930s and Japan since 1990 - suggest that even a zero interest rate may be too high to reverse it. In both cases, private debt ratios peaked close to where many Western debt ratios are today and then declined for more than 15 years, even though interest rates were kept at zero and the public debt and the monetary base expanded significantly.

Global Re-balancing with Major Risks Ahead

The long-term outcome of this struggle is predetermined in the same way as an earthquake is. The global economy's tectonic plates will eventually adjust and the global capital flows will reverse course. We don't know how fast or how violent the adjustment process will be, but it is likely to be marked by continuing political, social, economic and financial volatility and there is a risk that it may result in a devastating quake if a sudden shock unleashes the pent-up tension. The key issue is whether the Western debt consolidation will be slow and controlled so the rest of the world can compensate. The situation in many Western countries is similar to that of Japan in the early 1990s. Japan's economy stagnated as private sector debt declined, even though interest rates were cut to zero and the government added more debt than the private sector repaid. But it never suffered any real collapse in confidence that could upset the global economy.

The big difference between Japan then and the West today is that Japan had a current account surplus. On the one hand, the Japanese surplus meant that FX depreciation was politically unacceptable to the US, cutting Japan off from the most efficient way to inflate the debt away. On the other hand, the current account deficit in the West increases the risk of a disruptive adjustment because it means foreign investors can cut governments off from funding if they lose confidence. Compared with Japan's 20-year slog, this debt adjustment is likely to be faster, but more risky. At first, governments and central banks will try to delay the inevitable, but each new attempt to restore demand with more debt will prove less successful than the last one. With interest rates already at zero and government deficits at unsustainable levels, currency depreciation and money printing will eventually be the only way to avoid a deflationary debt trap.

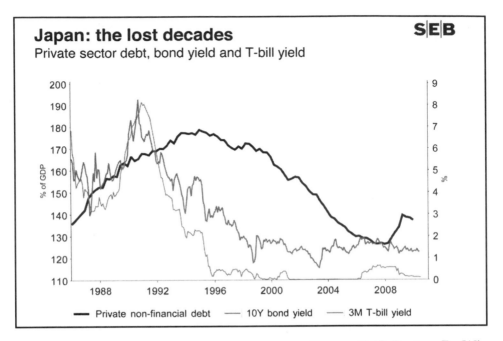

Japan: the lost decades
Private sector debt, bond yield and T-bill yield

S|E|B

Legend: Private non-financial debt — 10Y bond yield — 3M T-bill yield

Source: IMF, Reuters EcoWin

If everything goes right, this could work out as a slightly faster version of Japan's *"controlled consolidation"*, where 5-10 years of Western austerity and domestic stagnation is softened by managed currency depreciation and consumption-boosting reforms in the rest of the world. But this requires almost perfect coordination between capital importers and capital exporters. Markets may force a consolidation that is too fast and destructive for such coordination to work, and there is a risk that political stability in the West will be threatened in the process.

Sovereign Debt Crisis Holds the Key

Europe's sovereign debt crisis in 2010 is, therefore, a pivotal event that could speed up or postpone Western debt consolidation. Speculators probably picked Europe first because they could target Euro zone members individually and with no way to monetise debt. This is fertile ground for speculation as it means that markets can force individual governments into default. If they succeed, they are likely to move on to the real elephant in the fiscal room: the USA.

The US fiscal situation looks significantly worse than the Euro zone aggregate on all the main counts: the public sector deficit and debt, private debt and the current account deficit are comparable to those of the weakest Euro countries. The Fed can postpone the crisis by buying bonds, replacing short-term funding risks with longer-term devaluation risks, but this is no real cure. If over-done, it will lead to capital flight and fears of currency debasement. However, the Dollar also has the added advantage of being the world's reserve currency and this means there are many investors, not least central banks that have a direct interest in supporting it. China, in particular, fears the social risks associated with currency appreciation and has invested trillions in US Dollar assets, but similar strategies are followed across Asia and the Middle East.

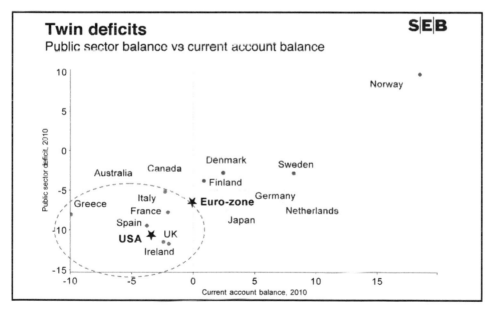

Source: OECD, SEB X-asset

The Euro's 25% decline against both the USD and the CNY as the funding crisis spread has thus delivered an unexpected shock to Chinese exports and increased the US pressure on China to cut the Dollar loose. This is a direct challenge to China's FX strategy, and a further deterioration could force China to reconsider the gradualist approach - or perhaps to extend its *"financial umbrella"* to Europe in order to buy time.

Once again, policymakers are trying to borrow both time and money. The European bail-out plans are an attempt to persuade markets to see it as one relatively healthy borrower rather than as a group of vulnerable and isolated individual borrowers. If they succeed, they may buy some time for global policy coordination. If they fail, the sovereign debt crisis is likely to spread, triggering a faster consolidation across the Western world.

Whether it comes now or later, the next round of serious debt deflation in the West is likely to start with some kind of sovereign debt and currency crisis in the US - the last domino still standing after the Euro slump of 2010. Markets are not likely to have serious doubts about Treasuries as long as US domestic demand is expanding and the budget benefits from cyclical improvement but they will worry when growth falters - and we may not have seen the worst of the structural bear market yet.

Investment Strategy for the 2010s: Insurance Policies

Where does this leave an investor trying to plan for his or her retirement in 2020? The analysis in this chapter suggests that he or she should expect the same investment climate as in the decade that just ended (and in the 1930s): a low-inflation structural bear market, with low or negative risk premiums, high realised volatility, frequent extreme losses and a generally negative correlation between stock and bond returns.

This does not mean that every year will be a bad year for risky assets but it does suggest that there will be just as many bad years as good years - a contrast with the 2:1 or even 3:1 ratio during structural bull markets. In other words, while the '80s and the '90s favoured *"buy-and hold"* strategies, the coming decade is likely to continue favouring *"buy-and-sell"* strategies with more emphasis on active allocation and risk management.

Stock markets are likely to achieve a real return in the low single digits over the coming decade; pretty much in line with what we expect for government bonds. Bond yields are likely to remain on a falling trend and the correlation with equities is likely to be low or negative. Most of the time, a higher allocation to government bonds will thus deliver the traditional hedging effect, limiting losses when equities are under pressure.

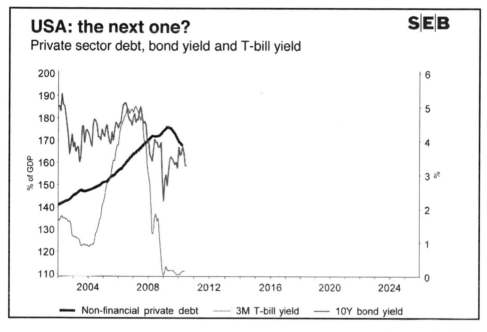

Source: EcoWin

However, there is a significant risk of a pattern-breaking spike in bond yields in connection with a stock market sell-off, even in a deflationary economic climate, if investors start questioning the sustainability of US debt. This happened during the last stage of the US crash in the early 1930s when the Fed bought bonds and markets responded by driving Treasury yields higher and sending capital abroad.

In this extreme case, the traditional allocation response would not do much good. The Treasury position would just add to the losses in the (normally) riskier assets. It may not be the most likely scenario but it is, nonetheless, the key risk that investors should worry about in the coming decade.

And if it happens, the damage is not covered by the normal asset allocation insurance policy. This is a bit like buying a fire insurance that only covers small fires. Of course, it avoids some nuisance but it also leaves you exposed at the time when you really might need insurance. So, a high allocation to Western government bonds alone is not likely to be the smartest way to manage the increased structural risk. What can we use instead?

Gold is the traditional asset of preference when there are doubts about fiscal sustainability and the credibility of paper money, and the past years do not suggest that this role has changed. However, with no direct return from holding physical gold, the price is likely to be volatile and it could fall back significantly if policymakers manage to buy time. Market-neutral hedge funds with low leverage could also provide positive returns if traditional assets go down together but counterparty risk may limit their efficiency as a hedge in a situation with extreme financial stress.

Another idea would be to increase exposure to non-OECD currencies. Normally, hedging currency exposure in developing economies is seen as insurance against risk. From a cyclical perspective this will still be the case but the Western debt problems suggest that the long-term risk is on the other side. Seen from this perspective, exposure to emerging market currencies provides insurance against extreme currency risks in the West. Even in a benign scenario, emerging market currencies are likely to see a trend appreciation over the coming 10 years and, in a worst case scenario, they could see quite an explosive surge. Nonetheless, interest rates are likely to remain higher than in the West, so you actually get paid for taking out the insurance policy - if you can handle the cyclical risk.

Then again, if you are rich and patient enough, you could also fall back on the passive strategies from the textbook. After all, 5-10 years from now when we have all learned the rules for navigating the treacherous waters of a secular bear market, bond yields will be bottoming out and the next great equity bull market will be approaching. And then the process will start all over again..."

Thomas Thygesen:

"I have opted for Amnesty International. I think this links very nicely into the chapter I have submitted as the parallels with the 1930s go well beyond the pure economics. Personal liberties and human rights are likely to come under increasing pressure as economic disappointment, failing institutions and public disenchantment increase political tensions between and within major economies and undermine social and political stability. Amnesty's support for human rights and resistance against political oppression is likely to be more crucial than ever in the coming decade."

The Amnesty International web site can be found at:
www.amnesty.org

CHAPTER FIVE

-

"Truth is tough. It will not break, like a bubble, at a touch.
Nay, you may kick it about all day, and it will be round and full at evening."

Oliver Wendell Holmes, Sr.

Paper Chase
Lee Quaintance & Paul Brodsky

"We think gold is cheap by a factor of almost 7 times."

About the Authors

Lee Quaintance & Paul Brodsky are co-founders and Managing Members of QB Asset Management Company, an investment management firm that oversees discretionary investments using strategic macroeconomic strategies.

Paper Chase

Popular Delusions, The Vampire Squid Industry et al

Discussion Points:

Systemic Distortions: Vast economic and market distortions have emanated from high real inflation and negative real interest rates.

Financialism: Modern currencies and the financial assets denominated in them have no value anchor, which further implies that the Western system of global wealth distribution has no value anchor.

The Sovereignty of the Vampire Squid Industry: Banking systems and bond holders are exercising their sovereignty over global commerce and over the governments that ostensibly oversee them.

Popular Delusions: Jefferson, Lincoln, Lenin & Keynes knew what contemporary man does not seem to: unreserved credit quietly redirects wealth to the few and ultimately leads to social disorder.

Consequences: While few in the private sector may end up defaulting on their obligations in nominal terms, we believe governments and debtors will default in real (inflation-adjusted) terms. Global wealth, regardless of provenance and in whatever form it may take, has begun to lift itself above fiat currencies and financial assets denominated in them. We expect the current US Dollar based global monetary regime to fail and to be replaced by sound (or sounder) money.

The Only Constant: We think gold is cheap by a factor of almost 7 times.

Paper Chase

"Money, when considered as the fruit of many years' industry, as the reward of labor, sweat and toil, as the widow's dowry and children's portion, and as the means of procuring the necessaries and alleviating the afflictions of life, and making old age a scene of rest, has something in it sacred that is not to be sported with, or trusted to the airy bubble of paper currency."

Thomas Paine

Substantial global productive capacity, brought about by the opening of emerging economies over the last twenty years, threatened previous economic equilibriums and trade balances created by established economies in the post-war era. Such globalization meant that global marginal supply and demand growth for goods and services could no longer be controlled by G7 policy-makers because they were vastly out-populated and because their economies had higher domestic social expectations and higher embedded fixed production costs.

Western leaders seemed to encourage their economies to borrow from future output, which stabilized and increased short-term domestic consumption and employment. This politically expedient choice was available to them because, under the global monetary regime as it has been executed since the fall of the Bretton Woods Agreement in 1971, there is no limit on how much currency and credit governments and the private banking system can manufacture. (Prior to 1971, money and credit were claims on a relatively limited amount of gold which, in turn, limited money and credit growth. After 1971, fiat money and credit literally became claims on a country's ability to credibly and predictably print more of it.)

It is impossible to default on such fiat claims in nominal terms as long as treasury ministries and their central bank partners have printing presses (see Weimar Germany, modern Zimbabwe). It is easy, however, for countries to default in real (inflation-adjusted) terms. In fact, we see widespread real credit defaults as having already begun in the US and other developed, deeply-indebted sovereign nations. Regrettably, we see this trend continuing and accelerating.

Systemic Distortions

As credit exploded on public and private sector balance sheets over the last generation, nominal prices of goods, services and financial assets increased and nominal output, employment and tax revenues rose. As time went on, however, the great credit build-up had diminishing marginal economic benefits. Towards the end of this long run, economies grew nominally only, not in real terms, when adjusted for the unprecedented rate of credit inflation. The credit creation and distribution model that was adopted in the West further embedded lasting distortions into economies that would eventually need to be reconciled. Yet there was no reconciliation, such as sufficiently high interest rates that would have restricted new credit growth. *Why?*

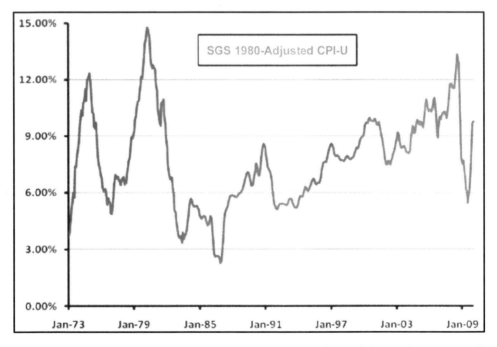

Sources: Shadow Government Statistics (1980 Adjusted CPI-U); QBAMCO

The need for such reconciliation seems to have been hidden through a series of curious policy adjustments, such as substantial alterations of the commonly accepted Consumer Price Index *(CPI)* as a measure of inflation - first in 1980 and again in 1990. *The graph on page 107 "trues-up" the CPI. It* plots Shadow Government Statistics' 1980-Adjusted CPI-U, and it indicates that consumer price inflation has been far higher than the twice-scotched and perpetually scrubbed index currently being released monthly by the Bureau of Labor Statistics.

We suspect consumers would relate more to the far higher ongoing loss of purchasing power implied *in the graph below* than the 1% to 2% annual *"inflation rate"* commonly benchmarked by the BLS and accepted at face value by most economists and investors. From here, we may begin to understand the depth of economic distortions that have been embedded into the global economy. The graph below subtracts Shadow Government Statistics' 1980-adjusted CPI from nominal 20-year and 30-year Treasury yields. We would venture to guess that most people would be startled to learn that real (inflation-adjusted) long-term US interest rates have been functionally negative since 1996.

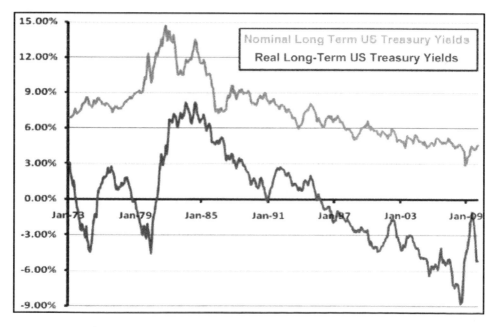

Sources: QBAMCO; St. Louis Fed; Shadow Government Statistics
(1980 Adjusted CPI-U)

108

Accepting that there have been negative real rates begins to explain the nexus of widespread economic distortions that could not otherwise be reconciled. High rates of inflation and negative real interest rates reduced incentive to save, and gave incentive to borrowing homeowners, consumers and businesses to leverage their balance sheets beyond all reasonable and otherwise traditionally-prudent levels.

But what about the other side of the trade? Surely it has been irrational for unleveraged savers to lock in long-term expectations of deteriorating purchasing power. While we would not argue with that rhetorical conclusion, we do think that, despite popular impressions to the contrary, true savers no longer determine long-term interest rate levels. Instead, we think leveraged market players (banks, hedge funds, *"Caribbean banking centres"*) and *"official"* accounts (central banks, foreign finance ministries and SWFs) determine marginal sovereign interest rates.

Positively-sloped yield curves and unlimited access to official short-term borrowing windows make for seemingly juicy carry trade opportunities for the leveraged market community. In terms of the official sector, strongly-accelerating pools of US Dollar reserves have been a great source of the bid for Treasury securities as well. Furthermore, it should be noted that the vast majority of unleveraged investors that invest in Treasury securities are dedicated institutional bond funds, pension funds and insurers. By mandate these investors are generally unconcerned with generating positive real returns. Their first-order fiduciary responsibilities are to match or beat benchmark bond indexes that contain a cross section of whatever prevailing fixed-income product Wall Street index sponsors choose (regardless of credit quality or perceived inflation). Because, by mandate, they are dedicated bond investors, they are not empowered materially to shift capital into other asset classes, even including cash, were they to feel subjectively that prevailing interest rate levels did not reflect price inflation-based fundamentals.

So, we believe that benchmark interest rates that are theoretically supposed to represent the default-free, inflation-adjusted value of money have been, and continue to be, greatly distorted. The Treasury yield curve prices the global reserve currency and is, therefore, the nexus of the pricing function for all global financial assets. Despite continually lower and negative real returns, such distortions allowed banks and shadow banking systems (i.e. non-bank lenders and bond investors) to continually expand their lending activities. This, in turn, produced fundamental economy-wide distortions.

Low or negative real rates incentivised wage earners not to save and, in fact, gave them great incentive to borrow and spend. This activity did not reflect general prosperity and wealth creation but was the rational economic behavior of populations that intuited that their wages and savings were denominated in currencies priced (via interest rates) too cheaply, relative to the rate at which they were losing their purchasing power value.

Meanwhile, the US government continued to borrow in ever-increasing amounts to meet short-term political goals and to satisfy continually rising obligations. It was permitted to do this because there was no outcry from the public that would have to foot the bill, (directly via taxation or indirectly via monetary inflation), and who were also being extended credit in record amounts. Non-US governments and central banks were also forced to inflate their currencies and promote popular credit creation so they could maintain *"competitive"* foreign exchange rates. Corporate borrowers took on more debt too because, if they did not, then they would not be able to compete in the short term with businesses willing to leverage their balance sheets in a price-inflationary world.

Increasing systemic credit synthesized temporary increases in nominal revenues, wages and economic output. Yet these increases were not sustainable because they were tied to debt (claims on currency) that had to be repaid. The nominal values of assets AND liabilities grew and each was used to rationalise growth in the other. Vast borrowing was mostly funded through internal gearing. Consumers, businesses and governments borrowed more to borrow more and businesses, governments and central banks leant more to lend more. *The implicit goal was to generate financial returns for both borrower and lender on each transaction - not to build capital.*

The efficacy of debt assumption dropped dramatically in the US to the point where almost five Dollars of debt became necessary to produce one Dollar of output, as opposed to less than two Dollars of debt thirty years ago. (Perhaps this implies that that current output prices are only 20% of what they should be, since in our current system debt IS money?) Nevertheless, all appeared healthy for a very long time, even as systemic credit exploded. Household and corporate debt-to-equity ratios remained relatively constant because equity values collateralizing the increasing debt rose in sync with assets. Bank balance sheets appeared healthy for the same reason. Government tax receipts rose also, which seemed to justify consistently increased spending. It looked for a long time as though deficits did not matter.

We suppose such a system of ever higher nominal prices, wages and debt loads could, theoretically, have endured forever, were it not for the fact that it becomes impossible for the debt to be repaid in the same currency without further dilutive currency issuance. Paper would have to replace paper. Eventually, wage earners and investors would choose not to accept a futile paper promise; or aging debtors would need to monetize their highly encumbered assets; or trade partners with currency choices would choose to save and invest in other currencies; or the debt would simply climb so high that it could not be serviced. The monetary system would have to fail and the economy would have to re-price to reflect real value. There would have to be reconciliation. (That 5:1 debt to output production ratio comes to mind again here).

Financialism

Finance is, theoretically, the legitimate process of providing funding for capital formation; but it has, through a generation of systemic abuse, become a system based on the tacit promotion of widespread bets to generate short-term financial gains. Such a financial system has been popularly accepted because it has democratically included public stock and housing markets, which further provided widespread (albeit fleeting) prosperity.

According to Robert Shiller, the real earnings of the US S&P 500 advanced from about $35 per share in 1973 to about $55 per share today. (This calculation subtracts the *"official"* CPI from nominal earnings). Shiller's data show that real earnings peaked at around $87 in early 2007, at the height of the credit bubble. Accepting for a moment that the CPI is a valid barometer for the loss of purchasing power, the implication here - that capital wealth is driven more by credit growth than growth in sustainable productive capabilities - is difficult to ignore.

The graph below plots the relationship between the growth of the US M3 money stock measurement and the nominal return of the S&P 500 since 1973. M3 is (and, as of today, was) the only monetary aggregate that includes repurchase agreements between the Fed and its primary dealers. (To cut costs, the Fed stopped publishing M3 in March 2006. The more recent data included in the graph below was taken from Shadow Government Statistics). The repo market ultimately funds much of the credit that supports the financial markets. In short, it seems plain that financial markets have been pulled higher over time by overnight bank system lending.

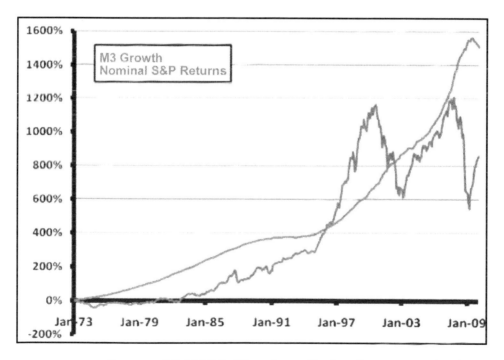

Sources: QBAMCO; Bloomberg; Shadow Government Statistics
(M3 Extension)

This market chimera, along with the obvious short-term economic and political benefits of credit-driven nominal output growth, rising employment and increasing tax receipts, (which allows politicians across the political spectrum to pursue their preferred projects), would make it difficult for even the most well-intentioned monetary policy-maker not to become seduced by maintaining an easy money stance. (As it turned out, there was no need to worry about well-intentioned policy-makers being corrupted, as they seem to have sponsored, endorsed and promoted the scheme.)

The U.S. banking system, including the Fed, has ultimate pricing power over global money because it is able to control the creation and distribution of the world's reserve currency. This control, in turn, gives it (along with other banking systems) ultimate pricing power over global financial assets. Such financial rentiers are attached at the hip to their government policy-makers, who themselves reap great benefits from controlling baseless money.

It is becoming more obvious each day that the G7, in aggregate, is no longer practicing capitalism in the true sense because far less capital is being created and distributed within its societies. Capital is material wealth used or available for use in the production of more wealth. The West is not converting its past and current wealth into sustainable human, natural or productive resources (though this is being done by emerging economies). Instead, developed economies are practicing some form of credit and debit accounting system, based on issuing, leveraging and pursuing money and credit for its own sake, in the curious collective belief, it seems, that all economic participants will be left with positive balances. It is a preposterous scheme. Printing money and extending credit do not create wealth. If they did, all the world's problems could be solved with a few computer keystrokes. At best, expanding money and credit merely redistributes wealth. At worst, they may temper its creation.

In a baseless (conceptually infinite supply) monetary regime, money and financial assets have no value anchor, which means they are not quantifiable stores of value with enduring terms of exchange. In very elementary terms, for a medium of exchange to have *"real money"* properties, its collective value at any discrete point in time must equal all things real and theoretically purchasable. If this equation does not hold, then the nominal exchange value of what is deemed money must change (higher or lower) in order to re-establish that equilibrium. If that change is somehow suppressed, then what was formerly considered money can no longer be deemed as such.

Thus, if money and financial assets denominated in said money have no value anchor (i.e. the equation breaks down), then the entire system of global "paper wealth" distribution must have no value anchor. Today, it is safe to say that wealth is not necessarily where it seems to be based upon where "money" is.

Managing incentives for the accounting system that shifts credits and debits (commonly referred to as *"monetary policy"*) effectively redistributes claims on a contemporaneously static pool of true wealth back and forth between creditors and debtors.

Over time, wealth may be accumulated by an ever-narrower group of beneficiaries:

- Those able to shift from creditor to debtor and back again at the right times.
- Those that take advantage of mispriced leverage that then allows them to generate current income far in excess of unlevered capital producers.
- In the case of the current global economy, foreign capital producers that undercut Western earners and do not have to save or spend their wages in the highly diluting US Dollar-based monetary system.

The cost of succumbing to such financialism has been slowly to diminish the G7's global economic power, which has been migrating to economies capable of producing and distributing (domestically or through exportation) goods, services and resources with sustainable margins. Credit deflation and rising unemployment were inevitable in the West - they were the necessary costs of having maintained a policy of politically-engineered short-term nominal growth through the expansion of unreserved credit.

The credit crisis that began to manifest itself publicly a few years ago was really a currency crisis that continues today. Currency manufacturers seem perfectly willing to continue producing sufficient money and credit to allow West-ern debtors to nominally pay off or refinance their short-term obligations. It can't succeed. It is a Ponzi scheme.

The Sovereignty of the Vampire Squid Industry

Driving through a rural working class area of the US recently, we saw many things for sale (cars parked on the edge of country roads, garage sales, boats, etc.). It was difficult to ignore the reality that most people do not effectively own much outright. They simply lease assets with lifestyle utility from the banking system.

When a new car rolls off the GM assembly line and is sold, most often the title transfers to a borrower. This is not a functional title because, on day one, the bank holds claim to that car despite it having made no effort to build it and having made no commitment to acquire the various factors of production. Following the money, those who bore the burden of production (assembly-line workers) are compensated with bank notes, which the bank-ing system created at no physical cost. Then, the purchaser must borrow those same bank notes that the banking system created at no physical cost. If the purchaser services its loan, the banker merely ends up with more notes at the end than he created. He wins. If the loan fails, the banker ends up with title to a car that it neither worked for in exchange nor produced. He wins again. The same would hold true for housing and all other assets purchased with credit.

In the end, it seems that the banking system spurs real economic activity via its provision of a medium of exchange. In doing so, it demands that a large portion of production be controlled (or ultimately owned) by the banking system itself. In practical terms, the average Joe simply leases his assets from the banking system while the producers of real capital assets work for nothing real in exchange. We suspect the following is true (with further thought necessary):

• Banks are given *"exorbitant privilege"* that is blatantly unfair within the context of a broader economy.

- Producers of real assets and goods work for something more than they accept in terms of exchange.
- Workers work for something more than they accept in terms of exchange.
- Acquirers of the utility of the assets (that they think they *"own"*) are merely leasing these assets and the cost of the lease accrues as a transfer of wealth to the banks.

Good work if you can get it. But wait, there's more. Banking systems have gained economic sovereignty over their governments. The causality should be easy for all to internalise. Banks may create credit from thin air in amounts way above their underlying reserves. This unreserved credit must be denominated in a currency and must eventually be repaid. Doing so permits banking systems to effectively commit their governments to issue actual currency reserves that do not yet exist. In effect, the fractionally-reserved banking system necessitates monetary inflation (monetary growth leading to higher nominal prices) in order to survive.

Thirty-nine years after the forced (but incomplete) monetary reserve discipline on governments and banks ended, systemic claims on currencies are at least 30 times the amount of necessary currency needed to exhaust those claims. (It is estimated that in the US alone there are $60 trillion in public and private debt obligations and about $2 trillion in actual currency plus bank reserves - a.k.a. monetary base.) And so, in the current monetary regime, the vast majority of what we call *"money"* is actually credit - credit that must be repaid by the government with currency that does not yet exist.

So let us place current events in context. If a bank (that helps perpetuate governments' preferred monetary system) is too big to fail, then, theoretically, it must also be too big to indict on criminal charges because doing so would elicit an immediate run on its balance sheet. At the centre of the current global economy then are entities with balance sheets 15 to 20 times larger than their equity values that, as primary dealers, see all coincident public sector market transactions; that as investment banks compete to see all large private transactions; as merchant banks take proprietary positions in opportunities they may find particularly appealing; and finally, and most inequitably to all other market participants, that cannot face criminal charges for unfairly exploiting others in the marketplace.

Nevertheless, we do not expect legislators to address the obvious conflict of interest of entities allowed to toggle as they see fit between agent and principal in various assets across markets that respond to similar economic or market inputs. We think regulatory scrutiny will be limited to discrete transactions and personnel lapses, and will not dare recognize the 800-pound gorilla sitting in the middle of parliamentary discussions - that the source of the issues arising today is systemic, and that policy-makers themselves are also very much to blame.

It is annoyingly easy to make the case that large banks are generally behaving rationally and in concert with public policy. Inequities that periodically capture public notice stem from the banking system's ability (and currently accepted function) to produce and distribute seemingly infinite, unreserved credit - a state of affairs that has been unambiguously endorsed by policy-makers, politicians, financial regulators and respected economists. The largest monetary benefits of this system naturally accrue asymmetrically to the financial mechanics that do the manufacturing and distributing - Wall Street.

The highly charged current public flogging of Wall Street by Washington is dripping with irony. Congress is expressing popular outrage towards large banking institutions that have dutifully and profitably executed government public policy. Both are ultimately responsible for sponsoring a capital allocation system that distorted natural economic incentives and consistently misallocated capital. By our way of thinking, they have been co-conspirators in a global monetary regime that, by its very nature, manufactures credit that then must find expressions for it (junk bonds, mortgage derivatives, dotcom stocks, sub-prime loans, bridges to nowhere, $100 million beach homes, etc).

For politicians, a funny thing happened on the way to satisfying all constituent wants and needs - governments became beholden to their banking systems. What was once the global banking system administering the balm that soothed near-term political and economic adversity morphed into a banking system able to exert its legislated right to control the terms of indebtedness. We believe without equivocation that banking systems and bond-holders are exercising their sovereignty over commerce and the governments that ostensibly oversee them. Together, banks may control the private sector in times of stress because they can lay claim to debtor collateral. They may also act as agent or principal for government bond issuance, which ties government hands. (Sovereign governments, via their mandated partners - the central banks - are the only debtors that may print currency with which to pay their debts, but to sustain those debts without bond investors and primary dealers would clearly be extremely difficult.)

For governments to regain power over creditors, they would have to either abrogate debt contracts or make the burden of the contracts insignificant. The act of printing money - inflation - satisfies the latter, which is why we see substantial inflation as highly likely. Inflation would hurt unleveraged creditors (and Dollar reserve holders). Frankly, we think that this would be a pain with which politicians will learn to live. They will see it as an *"Us vs. Them"* (creditors) decision and the least painful socially, economically and politically. (It is thought that the US went off the gold standard in 1971 after his advisers presented President Nixon with three bad choices, of which he felt abandoning the gold standard was the least bad. Upon signing the order he proclaimed, *"We are all Keynesians now."*)

Most lawmakers, regulators, economists, market participants and media seem focused on finding and fixing second-order causes of the consequences currently capturing public attention. We doubt the Wall Street derivative inquisition will go much deeper, for if it did then politicians would have to indict themselves. We discuss these issues not to purge anger at the inequity of having to compete with entities that seem to have embedded edges (they do in some ways and they do not in others), but to show the long odds of the death of this corrupted system by *"suicide"*. The incentives of powerful people are too great to expect them to change the system. But that does not mean the system will not change - and soon.

Popular Delusions

Why does our take on things seem a hysterical rant to those seeking serenity through conventional wisdom? Admittedly, the overwhelming majority of prominent men and women on the public stage able to influence public opinion might find our conclusions hard to swallow. Ask them why, if you would. If your experience is the same as ours, the discussion will end with a shrug, a smile and the thought: *"all it takes is a little confidence."*

We could be wrong about this (and everything else) but we have the feeling that most established economists, market strategists and policy-makers ascended to their positions through a negative selection process that rewards adherence to political economics rather than pure economic theory. So, we think the public policy class is desperately trying to navigate the current situation by extrapolating cause and effect from a time when nominal output growth better reflected real output growth. It seems that Keynesianism is prohibiting them from understanding that there is no political solution to the current problem - money growth is inflation and we are now trapped in a closed-ended vicious cycle.

It is understandable that *political economists* focus on the importance of nominal aggregate output growth, which benefits governments and banking interests. However, it must be noted that this objective conflicts quite often with the best interests of individuals within that society (and with investors seeking real rates of return in financial assets).

Consider first that if a person is content working eight hours a day, five days a week, then that person is implicitly indifferent to generating any further marginal aggregate economic *"growth"*. At that point, he values leisure time more than the marginal fruits of his labor. Second, consider that real - not nominal - unit growth should be all that matters to living standards. In fact, we would argue that only productivity growth (via economies of scale and innovation) leads to an improvement in living standards over the longer term.

Next, consider that banks do not care directly about real unit-based growth or even productivity growth (unless the latter leads to enhanced asset values). They care only about nominal growth. Banks are leveraged entities concerned only with *"the spread"* and increasing nominal asset (collateral) values, which are generated through monetary and credit inflation. Finally, consider that governments also acquire most of their wealth through the process of inflation. They are the private sector's partner in rising nominal asset values via capital-gains taxes (regardless of whether real exchange values stay constant or even decline). Further, they receive a bigger portion of income through the graduated income tax system. (Governments may further curtail their outflows via the ability to contro or even mechanically suppress?) the perception of inflation by greatly influencing and emphasizing wayward barometers.)

So, we should all agree that productivity growth is unambiguously good for an economy (irrespective of nominal growth). We would add that unit growth is not necessarily beneficial (depending upon whether it is the result of productivity growth or merely more, and perhaps inefficient, labor and resource deployment). Thus, the pursuit of nominal aggregate output growth per se seems to benefit banks and governments while it penalises most discrete economic participants. Recognising the unsustainability of this social arrangement should allow one to anticipate its necessary demise when taken to extremes, as it is today.

We have been asserting from the start that this bank-centric, fiat money-based economic model promotes only notional growth at the expense of real growth. To perpetuate this system there has to be broad deception. Is this possible? We think so, and so did Thomas Jefferson when he warned, *"I deny the power of the government to make paper money or anything else as legal tender"*. And so did Abraham Lincoln: *"The money power preys upon the nation in time of peace and conspires against it in times of adversity. It is more despotic than monarchy, more insolent than autocracy, more selfish than bureaucracy. I see in the near future a crisis approaching that unnerves me, and causes me to tremble for the safety of our country. Corporations have been enthroned, an era of corruption will follow and the money power of the country will endeavour to prolong its reign by working upon the prejudice of the people, until wealth is aggregated in a few hands, and the republic is destroyed."*

A dramatic pronouncement, to be sure, but what about more contemporary social economists? Consider John Maynard Keynes, quoting and commenting on Lenin:

"Lenin is said to have declared that the best way to destroy the capitalist system was to debauch the currency. By a continuing process of inflation, governments can confiscate, secretly and unobserved, an important part of the wealth of their citizens. By this method they not only confiscate, but they confiscate arbitrarily; and, while the process impoverishes many, it actually enriches some. The sight of this arbitrary rearrangement of riches strikes not only at security, but at confidence in the equity of the existing distribution of wealth. Those to whom the system brings windfalls, beyond their deserts and even beyond their expectations or desires, become "profiteers," who are the object of the hatred of the bourgeoisie, whom the inflationism has impoverished, not less than of the proletariat. As the inflation proceeds and the real value of the currency fluctuates wildly from month to month, all permanent relations between debtors and creditors, which form the ultimate foundation of capitalism, become so utterly disordered as to be almost meaningless; and the process of wealth-getting degenerates into a gamble and a lottery."

Lenin was certainly right. There is no subtler, no surer means of overturning the existing basis of society than to debauch the currency. The process engages all the hidden forces of economic law on the side of destruction.

No-one would accuse us of sharing economic sympathies with Lenin and Keynes - just the opposite. But, these men knew what we all should know and don't seem to - that money dilution decreases and reallocates wealth and virtually no-one notices until it is too late. Keynes' logic should not seem quaint or old-fashioned, especially when we can use it to make sense of the current environment that he, ironically, so profoundly influenced. The point here is that the masses can be seduced and fooled by the lure and then tyranny of the short term. Politicians and policy salesmen play the odds and are sadly in the business of providing daily comfort only to the majority of their constituents.

We recently toured the New York Fed. Nothing about the tour was exceptional. We went through airport-like security and came upon a plaque that read: *"Money makes the world go round. Money makes the man and money answers all things. Even time is money. [..] It remains hard to define what it is and how it works."* With 17 other pre-approved guests, we stored our cameras, phones and bags, viewed the coin display in the lobby, and watched a short film on the Fed's cash system. Then we descended five floors below Liberty Street, where we watched another short movie on the Fed's gold vault, which plainly mentioned how the US Dollar is no longer backed by gold, but rather depends on *"faith in the United States"*.

We proceeded along the painted bedrock through an impressive rotating vault door, where we found ourselves in a small barred anteroom from which we could see a few piles of gold bricks. The tour guide told us that most of the US's gold is held in Fort Knox, and that 98% of the 7,000 tons of gold kept there belonged to 60 foreign governments, central banks and official international organizations. (It is funny that the Federal Reserve System is not a federal agency, keeps very little on reserve and hardly pursues its policies systematically.) We were informed that most of the gold stored at the Fed was deposited prior to 1971.

There was no mention why all the security was necessary (given the US Dollar is only backed by "faith in the United States"), or from whom they were protecting the gold (or even why they gave tours in the first place). Then we remembered what we read - *it remains hard to define what (money) is and how it works.* It was a show, like Broadway.

This late stage of our Money Culture may be characterized by an environment of boundless digital fiat money and credit where ledger entries are confused for wealth and where mis-incentivised banks, shamelessly opportunistic politicians and lax regulatory overseers race the real economy off a cliff (as they argue over who did what to whom). Western policy-makers have surrounded G7 economies in a sort of a circular firing squad and have begun to fire.

There is nothing left to do but wait. The necessary collapse of the current regime has become so comically obvious to some that it has been thoroughly war-gamed. Imagine, as the blogger FOFOA recently did, the silliness behind a modern-day bank run. What used to be a rush to get gold from a bank vault before other depositors is now easily *"remedied"* by a printing press - or, more to the point, by an electronic credit in depositor ledgers. (It makes one wonder why the FDIC still pretends to limit depositor insurance when Treasury and the Fed can replace infinite electronic deposits with a few keystrokes?)

Sometime (soon, we think) people are going to catch on that the foundation of the current global economic order is a shared abstraction. Faith in the people, laws, resolve and soundness of the United States and other peaceful, established democracies is not the same as faith in the current global monetary regime or faith in policy-makers to gain courage. In fact, we think the two are mutually exclusive.

World history repeatedly shows that fiat currencies and the central banks that promote them are temporary, backed fleetingly by a popular addiction to a political abstraction before they succumb to the cold realities of organic economics. (The Fed is the US's fourth central bank.) The US and all democratic societies will survive and eventually prosper again because they are more than their bankers, monetary regimes, politicians and the sum of near-term nominal output growth.

While there may not be a multi-generational secret global banking cabal running a grand conspiracy to take over the world, as gold bugs are wont to assert (who can keep a secret these days anyway?), maybe Western societies, including our appointed wise men and professional extrapolators, are merely toiling rationally under false pretences?

Be that as it may, the old guard is re-arranging deck chairs, in our view, desperately trying to stave off short-term economic contraction in nominal terms while increasing economic un-sustainability in real terms. They are futilely pulling out all the stops to sustain an inutile economic system so obviously destined to fail.

Consequences

We see the very high likelihood of extreme hyper-inflation; given the extraordinary amount of debt that cannot be satisfied because there is nowhere near enough *"money"* with which to do so. Western governments are already running budget deficits in excess of 10% of their nation's annual output (and even more credit must be extended to public and private debtors to produce further output growth). Greece is not a one-off event. It is the canary in the coal mine.

Taxes are rising, but this only shifts burdens - it decreases the government's debt repayment burden and increases the burden of debt repayment for the private sector. There is no end in sight to this trend (and, indeed, it seems to be accelerating via the miracle of compounding). Eventually, funding public claims with taxes on the public will fail because it must. Not only will the public reject the idea but it will stop producing goods and services. This would be the point where society breaks down. So, we don't think any politician anywhere on the political spectrum believes raising taxes higher and higher still is a legitimately sustainable solution.

Does all this debt even have to be repaid? To be sure there will (and should) always be claims outstanding to help manage payments and to fund capital projects that, realistically, can service those debts. So, then, no. All of it need not be repaid. However, the debt does have to be serviced, which means that debtors will have to either continue working and allocating ever larger portions of their wages to repay their own and their governments' debts (through taxes), or they will have to sell assets and use the proceeds to pay down their debts. In either of those cases, standards of living, asset prices, economic output, employment and government tax revenues would fall. The result would be a deflationary depression. We do not see this outcome as remotely likely. Remember, there is no legal limit on monetary inflation and no incumbent government structure can survive such an outcome.

Treasury ministries and/or central banks could simply print the money needed by debtors to repay creditors. *The act of making new money to achieve this goal is the very process of inflation (currency devaluation).* The more money that exists to buy goods, services and assets, the more currency is required by sellers of those items to receive equal value in the transaction. Monetary inflation must lead to price increases. Again, the equation must hold.

So, while few in the private sector may end up defaulting on their obligations in nominal terms (were governments to print money and distribute it to all debtors), it is safe to say that governments and debtors will default in real (inflation-adjusted) terms. Politicians will be able to save the day for their indebted constituents by reducing the burden of their debt repayment. Nominal wages will increase with nominal inflation. Fixed debt amounts will not (at least not in the private sector). Most players in a massively-indebted nation would therefore come out winners. Unleveraged bondholders and other forms of pure savers would bear the burden (foreigners and retirees already dependent upon their governments).

The onset of the 2007 credit crisis was an alarm bell. Either credit will have to be defaulted upon in unprecedented amounts or new money will have to be created to satisfy the crushing burden of outstanding claims. Importantly, any new money created by the banking system can only be created by making new credit. They are one and the same. Ironically then, the only agents that can stop the madness are the ones who initially created it - central banks. They can create the money to satisfy the claims via the monetization (purchase) of outstanding assets. They really have no choice.

Indeed, the Fed has been quite active in this process over the past year. This is a limited strategy, though, because the Fed can print new money but not in an amount that acts as an equating offset of new assets. The nominal exchange value of money is therefore destined to contract.

The obvious un-sustainability of the current monetary regime seems to be gaining broader recognition globally. With or without Western policy makers, we think the global economy has begun experiencing a structural transcendence, from one based on coordinated accounting that requires ubiquitous debt assumption (and a limitless capacity to suspend disbelief) towards one based more on organic productivity and a more equitable distribution of global resources.

The only way of measuring which global economic participants will be able to retain true wealth is to determine which are positioned with sustainable future purchasing power, regardless of future nominal prices. In the current environment, creditors have options that debtors do not. A person or entity with excess monetary reserves may convert those reserves into sustainable capital. For example, China is actively converting its paper reserves into scarcer forms of money and natural resources (as are QB investors). Such a conversion from abundance to scarcity should resonate with wealth holders everywhere.

We expect the current US Dollar-based global monetary regime to fail and to be replaced by sound (or sounder) money. We believe sound money would reassert more natural productive equilibriums globally and benefit workers (at every income level) in non-financial industries. We are confident such a reconciliation of accounts will be peaceful, inclusive of all nations, and will be intelligent. The day after the system collapses, we will all wake up in our beds, our cars will still be in the driveways and no one will come for them.

As the plaque at the New York Fed said, you have got to have faith in the United States. We do, which is why we think we know what's coming. It should be plain to all, that gold is the ultimate rip-chord that people and entities will pull to salvage their wealth. It is money, the timeless medium of exchange that represents sustainable purchasing power.

The Only Constant

Global wealth, regardless of provenance and in whatever form it may take, has begun to lift itself above fiat currencies and financial assets denominated in them. True capital has already begun to flow to where it is being treated best - to capital producing economies and to global stores of wealth, from paper money and financial assets to hard money and hard assets. This conversion is entirely rational because it is the only way to generate positive real returns, in our view. Given the substantial monetary inflation we have already seen and expect, we think only marginally positive real returns will look like exceptional nominal returns.

Judging from current global asset pricing, wealth from all corners of the world is concluding that sustainable real purchasing power is the proper objective - not nominal returns measured in notional money. Eventually (three years, three days?) the pendulum will swing back and swing back swiftly towards organic capital formation. Whether or not there will be some form of political intervention, privately-held wealth - now in the form of baseless financial assets - will fly towards true safety before it is transferred through global economic incentives to other pockets.

The safest place to store current and future purchasing power, conceptually, would be in a cash/currency in relatively scarce supply. (Consumable commodities rely more on output growth for appreciation, though they would surely appreciate in an inflationary environment.) Gold is the holy of holies in terms of maintaining purchasing power across all inflationary scenarios except one (e.g. the massive *credit* inflation experienced from 1982 to 2006 that incentivised wealth to invest in ever more leveraged financial assets). Further, gold was, in our view, massively overvalued at its 1980 peak (see our *"Shadow Gold Price"* observations vis-à-vis the spot market price of gold then).

Gold is purchasing power stored in an incorruptible, un-encumbered money form that repeatedly survives all governments and their political, economic and social regimes. Most contemporary investors do not seem to get this. The fluctuation of the spot gold price on commodity exchanges is an odyssey to modern financial asset investors trained to view it as a volatile commodity with no commercial utility. To foreign exchange traders, the ascendance of gold is the one trend that threatens their livelihoods because it implies weakness and fallibility in all paper currencies. It takes away their toys.

Bankers and monetary policy-makers see a rising gold price as a signal that the value and durability of their paper-currency-denominated loan machine is being diminished, and as a viable threat to their power-sharing with governments. And to governments that manufacture baseless paper currencies and demand taxes to be paid in same, a strong gold price is a threat to its sovereignty and power, more terrifying than any advancing army.

Gold held outside government shifts power away from government. Its sovereignty rises above all banking systems, laws, exchanges, regulatory bodies and margin requirements. Yes, gold IS a barbarous relic, as Lord Keynes implied when it was convenient, but that doesn't mean it is quaint or useless or an anachronism. Gold is the ultimate disciplinarian and whoever has it calls the shots. The country with the most gold has always dictated the terms of trade (which is why the US in the twentieth century, and Britain before that, and Spain before that, were so powerful). Yes, it still works that way, no matter what our modern Keynesian economics professors taught us. And, the Chinese know this all too well.

Within this context, the daily change in the gold price on commodity exchanges is almost meaningless, as it represents a barometer of perceived strength or weakness of a *"commodity"* priced in a baseless currency by mismatched commodity speculators. They don't know or are not paid to care that the value of gold is in its strategic potential.

Gold has binary properties. It is the best of all ways to play the mother of all *fat-tail* events. It is effectively a Deep In-The-Money Put on the continuance of the global US Dollar monetary regime (and it is currently priced as though it is way, way out of the money). It is tantamount to owning a credit default swap on stable or increasing purchasing power relative to those who don't own it, at no cost basis and without counterparty risk. Gold is no-one's obligation (with the possible exception of those short it in fiat currency terms).

Statisticians can prove each and every day that nothing startling should happen tomorrow because they measure the vast amount of days that nothing startling happens, which provides them with a large denominator from which to calculate long odds. The presumption of stasis is good business for financial intermediaries, and basing seemingly reasonable investment themes on this statistical probability allows capital holders to overcome their inherent fear of change.

Most investors allocate to the markets by playing the odds which, by definition, gravitates capital to the middle of a bell curve of possible outcomes. This fools the investor into thinking that the probability of future events is somewhat predictable. Of course, history is rife with startling social, economic and political tail events. Stuff happens - things like earthquakes, the bombing of Pearl Harbour, the 1980 US Olympic Hockey team, the demotion of Pluto, dotcom bubbles, liar loans, and even periodic global economic failures and the re-assertion of gold as money.

All those loud gold bugs, burdened (as are we) by righteous indignation at fiscal profligacy and preposterous public policy, ironically have very little money to invest in the stuff. (We understand even John Paulson had trouble raising money for his gold fund.) But that doesn't make them (or us) wrong. Indeed, the fact that very few in the West seem to own gold, despite a ten-year bull market, supports looking deeply into the merits of the trade.

Sources: QBAMCO; Bloomberg; Shadow Government Statistics
(1980 Adjusted CPI-U)

There are sound fundamental economic reasons why we think sophisticated contemporary financial asset investors will re-allocate to gold. First, it remains cheap historically and is getting cheaper with each passing quarter. The graph on the top of the following page plots the nominal and real monthly gold price in USD terms. (To determine the real price of gold, we subtracted the SGS 1980 Adjusted CPI-U from the nominal gold price.) According to this metric, gold, in real terms, is still 30% cheap to its 1980 highs.

But that 30% discount only begins to tell the story of gold's cheapness. *The graph below* plots the return of gold, adjusted for the growth in the US Monetary Base. This is a historically valuable metric with which to value the intrinsic value of gold in US Dollar terms or, alternatively, the US Dollar in gold terms. Over the course of the great credit build-up of the last 25 years, the gold price has declined substantially when adjusted for the dilutive effects of money growth.

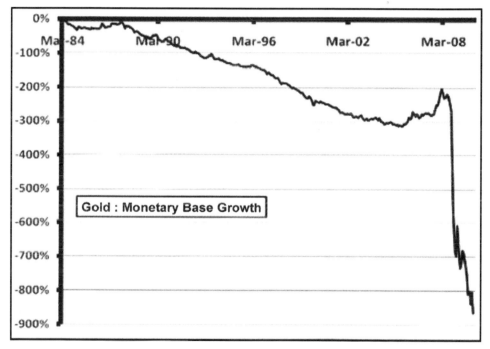

Sources: QBAMCO; World Gold Council; St. Louis Fed

Put another way, the intrinsic monetary reserve value of gold is far higher than current prices. *The graph on the following page* is an updated version of our Shadow Gold Price. The SGP divides Monetary Base by official gold holdings - the Bretton Woods metric for valuing money when the US Dollar, and therefore all other major currencies, was exchangeable into gold.

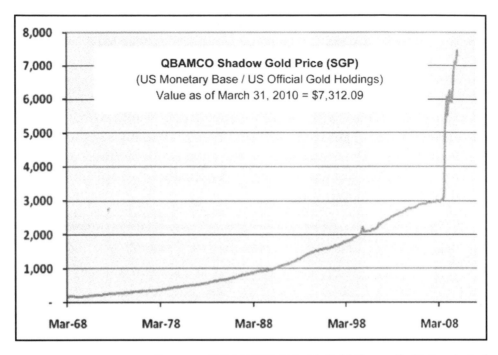

Sources: QBAMCO; World Gold Council; St. Louis Fed

The graph directly above shows visually how much US Dollar purchasing power has been lost. We think gold is cheap by a factor of almost 7 times, which does not necessarily imply a target price for spot gold. The gold price could move higher than that if it experiences a blow off top, like most other bull markets have tended to do historically before exhausting themselves.

Lee Quaintance & Paul Brodsky:

We nominate Juvenile Diabetes Research Foundation and Paul Smith's College as equal recipients for our portion of any charitable donation distributed through Altana Charitable Trust. The JDRF continues to make progress toward a cure for type 1 diabetes and Paul Smith's College provides a diverse private education in the Adirondacks. (Lee Quaintance sits on its board.)

The JDRF web site can be found at:
www.jdrf.org

The Paul Smith College web site can be found at:
www.paulsmiths.edu

CHAPTER SIX

-

"Life is a storm, my young friend.
You will bask in the sunlight one moment,
be shattered on the rocks the next."

Alexandre Dumas

Lessons of the Crisis
Stephen Lewis

"The problem is that, as the 2007-2008 experience teaches, the lag between financial turbulence and economic damage may be fairly long, of the order of a year or more. In the meantime, the economic indicators may remain positive."

About the Author

Stephen Lewis started his career in financial markets with the stockbroking firm, Phillips & Drew, in 1970 after graduating in psychology and philosophy from Balliol College, Oxford. He worked in Phillips & Drew's gilt-edged securities department, becoming a Partner in 1980, a Managing Partner in 1984 and Director of Economic Research in 1985, when the firm incorporated to be subsequently taken over by Union Bank of Switzerland'.

In 1988 Stephen resigned from UBS Phillips & Drew, although continuing for several years as a consultant to that investment bank's Debt Division.

He established his own company, Fifth Horseman Publications, which published newsletters and provided consultancy services on global financial markets to UK and international banks, fund management institutions and to governments.

In 1992 he was a founding partner of The London Bond Broking Co which, in 1996, became a division of Monument Derivatives Ltd (renamed Monument Securities Ltd from June 2001).

Stephen is a member of the Securities Institute and of the Society of Business Economists. He also serves as Treasurer of the Forum for European Philosophy and was, three years ago, elected to the Royal Institute of Philosophy.

Lessons of the Crisis

There was a clear lesson for economic forecasters from the financial crisis that began in 2007 Q3. This was that sharp changes in credit market conditions can have a more profound impact on business activity than standard forecasting models would have led us to anticipate.

Several plausible explanations may be advanced for the failure of the standard models to capture the real economy effects of the financial turmoil. In many instances, forecasts depended on econometric analysis of data-runs that did not cover periods when there had been extreme stress in credit markets. They were based on models that did not adequately allow for credit constraint or, in some cases, admit it as a relevant variable at all. To be sure, it is tempting to dismiss distress in those markets that are far removed from the productive sectors of the economy as having little bearing on the prospects for GDP growth. To a large degree, even I was guilty of assuming that, because the initial institutional casualties of the 2007 crisis operated at several removes from household consumption and business investment, the real economy might not suffer much from the spreading illiquidity in the credit markets.

There are two points to note here, though. The global financial system is nowadays so complex that the linkages between what is happening in one part of that system and another distant part will usually be far from obvious. The second point is that it is sometimes difficult to trace, accurately and comprehensively, the transmission channels between a specific segment of the credit market and the wider economy.

Then again, threats emanating from the credit markets may lie dormant for months, it seems, before their full severity becomes apparent. As they accumulate, business activity beyond the markets may go on much as before until a breaking-point is reached (in the episode that began in 2007 Q3, the Lehman debacle of September 2008), with catastrophic impact on the real economy. This pattern underlies the lags, which may be long and variable, between trouble in the financial sector and a seizure in demand and output. Because the real economy impact of the financial turmoil may take so long to show, forecasters may too readily assume that credit constraint is having, and will have, little or no effect on business activity.

IMF's GDP GROWTH FORECASTS					
		2008	2009	2010	2011
April 2008	world	3.7	3.8	4.8	4.9
	advanced	1.3	1.3	2.7	3.1
October 2008	world	3.9	3.0	4.2	4.8
	advanced	1.5	0.5	2.0	2.9
April 2009	world	3.2	-1.3	1.9	4.3
	advanced	0.8	-3.8	0.0	2.6
October 2009	world	3.0	-1.1	3.1	4.2
	advanced	0.6	-3.4	1.3	2.5
April 2010	world	3.0	-0.6	4.2	4.3
	advanced	0.5	-3.2	2.3	2.4

Source: IMF World Economic Outlook

How the standard forecasting approach failed to pick up on credit-related factors is clear from the recent history of IMF projections of GDP growth for the world and for the advanced economies. We have chosen the IMF forecasts to illustrate our point not, on this occasion, because of any specific shortcomings in the IMF's performance, but because the supranational institution's reports are presented at regular six-monthly intervals. The same case could be made using OECD forecasts or those of national governments.

In October 2007, a few weeks after the credit markets showed their first signs of distress, the IMF shaved its projection for global growth in 2008 by almost 0.5 of a percentage point. But even after this adjustment, it was still forecasting a rise in global GDP of 4.8% and an increase in the aggregate GDP of the advanced economies of 2.2%. Admittedly, the IMF recognised *"risks to the outlook lie firmly on the downside, centring around the concern that financial market strains could continue and trigger a more pronounced global slowdown"*. Nevertheless, the IMF maintained forecasts that were only slightly below the average annual GDP growth in the preceding three years, even though that three-year period had witnessed the strongest burst of expansion in

three decades. By April 2008, there were few signs that illiquidity in financial markets was easing. The IMF cut its forecast for world GDP growth in
2008 to 3.7% and, for the advanced countries, to 1.3%. But it still viewed the
slowdown as temporary, in projecting a pick-up in world GDP growth to
3.8% in 2009 and 4.8% in 2010. By October 2008, the IMF had actually lifted
its 2008 world GDP growth forecast to 3.9% (the actual outcome was 3.0%).
Forecasters would not have had much chance, at that stage, to register the
full impact of the Lehman debacle. By April 2009, they had that chance. A
global growth projection for 2009 that, only a year previously, had been set
at 3.8% was slashed to -1.3%, with a 1.9% recovery envisaged for 2010. That
was the height of despair over the effects of the financial crisis. Since then,
the IMF appears to have adopted an assumption that the financial crisis has
considerably eased. However that may be, it has raised its forecast for global
GDP growth in 2010 to 4.2%, with further growth of 4.3% to follow in 2011.

The challenge now is to estimate what impact the sovereign debt crisis is
likely to have on global economic growth. Standard forecasts are not building in any allowance for this factor. All the same, the IMF, in its latest report,
acknowledged as a key concern, *"sovereign risks in advanced economies could
undermine financial stability gains and extend the crisis"*. This parallels the
IMF's warning of October 2007 about the downside risks from
financial market strains. What appears as a risk may now, as then, be the
early stage in a process that could lead to far more negative growth outcomes than are currently envisaged.

The problem is that, as the 2007-2008 experience teaches, the lag between
financial turbulence and economic damage may be fairly long, of the
order of a year or more. In the meantime, the economic indicators may
remain positive. The US economy did not enter recession until December
2007, five months after the early signs of trouble in the credit markets.
Some other advanced economies did not begin to display negative trends
until well into the second quarter of 2008. That pattern suggests that the
data flow, even if it remains generally positive in the near term, will offer
no guarantee that the upswing in the global economy, from 2009's low point,
will be sustained. If sovereign debt concerns are accompanied by worries over
bank liquidity any more significant than those so far influencing the credit

141

market, another dip in world economic activity would seem a sure thing.

The global economy would face this fresh challenge without any assurance that internationally coordinated action on the scale seen in 2008 Q4 would again be forthcoming. That is not only because much of the scope for fiscal and monetary reflation has already been exhausted. A further lesson of the financial crisis is that global co-operation is nowadays hard to sustain, given longer-term divergent trends and conflicting interests within the G20 group of leading nations.

A shift in power from the advanced economies to the emerging countries is one of the more widely acknowledged consequences of the global financial troubles over the past three years. In recognition of their changed circumstances, G7 leaders formally accepted in September 2009 that the G20, where the more powerful developing nations are represented, should take over as the key decision-making body in global economic and financial governance. The 2007-2008 financial debacle certainly delivered a blow to the moral authority of policy-makers in the advanced countries. They could no longer credibly issue policy-prescriptions to others, either directly or through the IMF, when their pursuit of policies based on the selfsame economic assumptions had brought about such dire conditions at home. However, there is a more concrete way in which the advanced countries have lost out. In less than three years, there has been a change in the relative sizes of globally-important economies on a scale previously unknown over so short a period, outside of wartime.

GDP in advanced and emerging economies

	Peak quarter	Trough	2010Q1		Peak quarter	Trough	2010Q1
Canada	2008Q3	96.7	99.6	Brazil	2008Q3	96.2	102.1*
France	2008Q1	96.0	97.1	China	2008Q1	n/a	118.7
Germany	2008Q1	93.3	94.8	India	2008Q1	n/a	114.9
Italy	2008Q1	94.2	95.0	Indonesia	2008Q1	n/a	110.4
Japan	2008Q1	91.4	95.3	Russia	2008Q1	89.2	91.9
UK	2008Q1	93.7	94.4	Singapore	2008Q3	87,6	101.7
USA	2008Q2	96.2	98.8	South Korea	2008Q2	95.4	103.2
Peak GDP=100							*estimate

Source: Monument Securities

142

In the table, I show how the G7 economies have performed by comparison with a selection of emerging countries since the peak of the last cycle. For those countries that suffered a downswing in economic activity over the past three years, I take the *"peak quarter"* as the one in which they last enjoyed positive GDP growth before turning downwards. For the three Asian economies in the table that did not suffer any downturn, I measure their performance from a notional *"peak quarter"* of 2008 Q1. As a yardstick for each country, I take GDP in the *"peak quarter"* as equivalent to an index level of 100. Then, I present in index terms, for each of the countries where the economy contracted, the level of GDP at the trough and, for all countries, the level of GDP in 2010 Q1.

The G7's experiences have been relatively uniform, compared with those of the emerging countries. Of the G7, Canada has been most resilient throughout, perhaps reflecting the solidity of its banking system. Solid banking has probably had less to do with the recent US recovery than the massive scale of fiscal and monetary support. It may be a surprise to many, given reports of export-driven growth, that Germany has been one of the weakest G7 performers. But we should be careful to note that, even after the past year's rebound, German industrial orders are still running at only 80% of their pre-crisis level. These figures hardly bear out the claim that the Euro has started to fail as a single currency for Europe because the German economy is too strong. The figures in the table also reinforce the impression that the UK economy is dead in the water. When we turn to the emerging economies, the figures further show how misleading it is to think in terms of the BRIC nations as an economically homogeneous class. Russia has been more grievously hurt by the crisis than any G7 member. Brazil has behaved like a supercharged version of Canada. China and India, on the other hand, relying on internal sources of growth, have withstood negative global influences. Plainly, BRIC has become a political concept favoured by Moscow, aimed primarily at shoring up Russia's waning influence as an international power. Because it has no firm economic basis, it seems unlikely to survive long. Indonesia, indeed, has more in common with China and India, in terms of economic performance, than do the other BRIC members. There seems to be a brighter future, therefore, for specifically Asian economic cooperation. We have included Singapore in our table as an example of how a small open economy, partly dependent on trade with the G7, has fared. South Korea has arguably been in a similar position but is more resilient on account of its larger domestic market.

Over the past two years, China has strengthened its economic standing relative to the USA by some 20%, and by 25% or so against Europe and Japan. India's relative gains have been almost as impressive. The political implications of a shift in economic power of this magnitude might be accepted fatalistically by the G7 but are more likely to elicit a defensive response, especially as all these economies are still under water compared with where they were at their previous peaks. China and India, for their part, are likely to feel that they are winning and will see no particular reason to bail out the G7. Consequently, the lesson to be drawn is that the chances of G20 cooperation being effective are remote. Those taking part in the G20 process, noting its very limited progress so far, have been inclined to attribute this to the number of participants involved, but the absence of a common purpose more likely lies at the root of the failure. Weak global governance looks like it will be an enduring feature in international economic relations from now on.

The vital lesson for investors, and bankers, to draw from the crisis has been the importance of liquidity. The behaviour of high-risk asset markets so far in 2010 illustrates the point well. As the year opened, the weight of money was moving into high-risk assets, such as equities, commodities and low-grade corporate bonds, while "safe" assets, such as government bonds and GSE-sponsored MBS, under-performed. These flows persisted through the first quarter and into the second but, then, around the end of April, they abruptly reversed course.

Market observers sought to explain the reversal in high-risk markets in terms of fundamental factors. They pointed to the wide budget deficits of some Euro zone member-states and to China's efforts to tighten monetary conditions as reasons why the markets were taking a less expansive view of prospects for the global economy. Such explanations were never entirely convincing. They did not account for the timing of the sell-off in high-risk assets. After all, Greece's fiscal problems first came to light in October 2009.

By March 2010, it was clear that the Greek Government was failing in its efforts to reassure market participants of its ability and determination to rein back its budget deficit, and that there was a risk of contagion from Greece to other countries in the Euro zone. However, this was widely seen as being no more than a local difficulty. Major equity indices around the world continued to rise, while the prices of crude oil and industrial commodities pushed higher.

Perhaps, it might be said, the markets did not at first fully appreciate the gravity of the situation in Europe. In particular, US investors, harking back to the post-Lehman TARP rescue, might naturally have counted on prompt action from European policy-makers in dealing with sovereign debt problems. They might not have been aware that EU decision-making is fractious and cumbersome, until they witnessed the manoeuvres that eventually gave rise to the proposed EU/IMF safety-net. All the same, there had been plenty of indications prior to this that there might be no practicable solution to the Euro zone's problems.

As for China, it is even less plausible to argue that a shift in the markets' view of Beijing's monetary policy triggered the slide in high-risk asset prices. There had been a sense of shock at Beijing's tough line on bank lending as far back as January 2010. Then, early in that month, China's monetary authorities ordered banks to stop further lending until February and to exercise moderation thereafter. This action was backed by small successive rises in China's Treasury bill rates, a tightening in banks' capital requirements and two rounds of increases in their reserve ratios. All this occurred while high-risk markets were still rising. If we were to believe the standard account of recent events, it was the third hike in the reserve ratio on 10 May that convinced investors the Chinese authorities were in earnest and that more credit-tightening could be expected from them. Why it should have taken the markets so long to reach that conclusion, though, would be a mystery.

In reality, tighter credit in China probably did undermine support for high-risk assets but not, as many market participants supposed, through the negative impact of Beijing's policy announcements on global growth expectations. Though investors had been inclined to interpret the buoyancy of high-risk markets from March 2009 onwards as wholly reflecting and confirming a rebound from the preceding economic downswing, excess liquidity was the essential motive force behind these markets' rallying. Slower credit growth in China was an element in a worldwide shift away from ultra-accommodative liquidity conditions.

Month-to-month changes in Chinese banks' lending in Yuan were erratic and subject to seasonal factors. But data relating to the year-on-year rates of change in this component, which smoothed out such influences, showed clear trends. In January 2009, annual growth in Yuan lending was 21.3% but by March 2009, when high-risk markets staged a turn for the better, it had risen to 29.8%. Lending growth rose further and was sustained around 34% between July and November in 2009. After that, it slackened markedly, to an average of 26.1% in the first quarter 2010 and then to 22.0% in April of this year. Chinese banks' lending in foreign currencies shows a similar, but even more marked, pattern. There were average monthly net repayments of these loans of $2.8bn in 2009 Q1. But then China's banks became net foreign currency lenders at an average monthly rate of $19.9bn in 2009 Q2. By 2010 Q1, the monthly lending rate had fallen to $9.7bn and in April it was $5.2bn.

These loans are small beer, compared with the liquidity infusions stemming from Western central banks' asset purchases. The US Federal Reserve was in the forefront of these operations, with its buying programmes in Treasuries and in mortgage-related securities. In aggregate, these programmes injected some $1.75trn of liquidity between late 2008 and the termination of the Fed's MBS and agencies purchases at end-March 2010. But the Fed was not the only central bank creating liquidity. The Bank of England, through its Asset Purchase Facility, added a further £200bn between March 2009 and the end of January 2010. The rise in high-risk asset prices started shortly after the Fed began its liquidity-easing asset purchases. Indeed, champions of the *"quantitative easing"* (QE) that such purchases represent, argued at the time that part of its beneficial impact on the economy was coming through its effect in lifting asset prices and enabling borrowers to raise funds more cheaply.

It always seemed that less favourable liquidity conditions would follow the cessation of the QE operations, bringing a sharp reversal in those asset prices that had previously benefited from the liquidity-creation. Within four weeks of the Fed's ending its buying programme in MBS and agencies, US equities had topped out. In the four weeks after that, they lost about 10% of their value. Just as the previous market strength was widely attributed to fundamental factors, so the subsequent weakness damaged confidence in the real economy. It was all part of a learning process whereby investors and economists alike have had to pay much greater attention to financial influences.

Stephen Lewis:

My chosen charity is Help for Heroes which supports the recovery of British servicemen and women wounded in the service of their country.

The Help for Heroes web site can be found at:
www.helpforheroes.org.uk

CHAPTER SEVEN

-

"A democracy is nothing more than mob rule,
where the fifty-one percent of the people
may take away the rights of the other forty-nine."

Thomas Jefferson

German Hyperinflation
Dylan Grice

"To call the political climate of the time merely difficult would be a gross understatement."

About the Author

Dylan Grice is a part of Societe Generale's Global Strategy Team where he works with Albert Edwards. Together they were rated the number one team in the 2010 Extel Survey of institutional investors' opinion. Dylan was formerly a director of proprietary trading at Dresdner Kleinwort where he ran thematic macro trading and systematic overlays. Prior to joining Societe Generale he co-founded and ran Vequus, a hedge-fund research firm specialising in systematic macro trading.

Some useful things I've learned about Germany's hyperinflation

For all the ink spilled analysing two of the 20th century's greatest economic tragedies - the Great Depression and Japan's lost decade(s) - little has been spent on arguably the greatest of them all: Germany's hyperinflation. It may be because we're confident we understand it. Everyone knows that unfettered money printing eventually leads to explosive inflation, don't they? The thing is, economists knew that then! So what was going through the mind of the central bank head who presided over history's most pathological currency debasement?

This raises the issue: Is anything more dangerous than a nonsensical idea taken seriously? The esteem of economists has been dented by the financial crisis, though not so severely that the financial community treat economists' views with anything approaching the derision they deserve. The macroeconomic meme is resilient indeed!

Sadly, the situation isn't new. Macroeconomic theory has a long and distinguished history of seducing policy-makers into thinking utopia is just around the corner, a trick brought about by untested hypotheses masquerading as empirical knowledge. Believe it or not, a school of economic thought that was prominent in Weimar Germany during the hyperinflation, and particularly at the Reichsbank as it was aggressively monetising the government deficit, held that the escalating money supply had nothing to do with the exploding rate of inflation!

More on that later. For now, in this new world of policy-making experimentation, it is worth recalling the British Ambassador to Germany's observation on the hyperinflation that *"no-one could anticipate such an ingenious revelation of extreme folly to which ignorance and false theory could lead."*

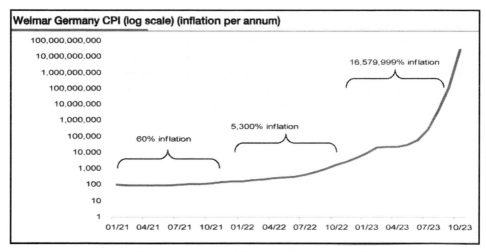

Weimar Germany CPI (log scale) (inflation per annum)

Source: Bresciani-Turroni (1931), SG Cross Asset research

It is often said that the Great Depression so thoroughly destroyed the social fabric of the industrialised world in the 1930s that WW2 became inevitable. But this overlooks the role of Germany's hyperinflation, the horror of which seems under-appreciated in the Anglo-Saxon world. At the height of the crisis in 1923, for example, industrial production fell by the staggering annual rate of 37%. In roughly the same single year, the unionised unemployment rate rose from under 1% in late 1922 to nearly 30%! (And, according to Frank Graham, almost half of the total workforce became unemployed at this time*). **This, remember, is at a time when the rest of the world economy was booming.**

As far as economic pain goes, this probably surpasses the Great Depression yet to come. But it only tells a part of the story: the nation's wealth, held largely in German government bonds was completely wiped out. We can only imagine the nationwide psychological devastation of a proud Germany already feeling victimised and humiliated in the aftermath of WW1. In his *"Ascent of Money"*, Niall Ferguson quotes Elias Canetti's recounting of his hyperinflation experience as a young man in Frankfurt. *"It is a witches"* sabbath of devaluation, where men and the units of their money have the strongest effects on each other. The one stands for the other, men feeling themselves as *"bad"* as their money; and this becomes

* *Please see: Exchange, Prices and Production in Hyper-inflation: Germany 1920-1923. by Frank D. Graham (1930)*

worse and worse. Together they are all at its mercy and all feel equally worthless." Such was the condition of Germany before the Great Depression had even begun.

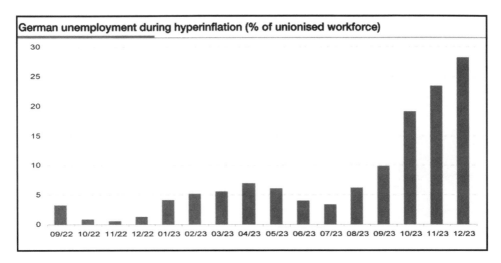

Source: Graham (1930)

Indeed, it is a tantalising counterfactual: would Germany have fallen under the Nazi spell which would ultimately lead the world to a second World War had she not borne the grave burdens of the Great Depression already exhausted, despairing and with ruptured social cohesion? We'll never know, of course, and anyway such events are never so simplistically mono-causal. Nevertheless, it is possible that German hyperinflation played a decisive role in the build-up to WW2 and, therefore, logical to conjecture that the central banker who presided over that hyperinflation is the most influential figure in history you've never heard of.

That central banker was a certain Rudolf von Havenstein. Born in 1857 into an aristocratic Prussian family, he trained as a lawyer and rose to become a county court judge before joining the Prussian Finance Ministry in 1890 and being appointed president of the Reichsbank in 1908. Steeped in the Wilhelmine tradition of devotion to his Kaiser and a passionate believer in the virtue of public duty, he seems to have been liked by all - a true gentleman of the old school - Montagu Norman - then governor of the

BoE - found him to be *"quiet, modest, convincing, and a very attractive man."*

Just how could such a decent, hard-working, intelligent and well-intentioned public servant have given birth to the uncontrollable monster of hyperinflation? How could such a paragon of public integrity preside over the largest currency debasement in financial history, quite possibly sowing the seeds for the most destructive war in the history of civilisation?

He first seems to have developed the habit of monetising government debt during WW1. With a complacency arguably similar to today's policy-makers in justifying their variously creative schemes for monetary and fiscal experimentation, the monetary expansion was justified as merely a stop-gap measure. The war was expected to be short and in any case the losers would be made to foot the bill. No-one really anticipated the long and protracted conflict which occurred, or the financial burden it would impose. So by the end of the War - only 10% of which was financed by taxes - the money supply had ballooned and prices had quadrupled. Nevertheless, Von Havenstein was lauded as a public hero, decorated with honours and even nicknamed der Geld Marschall, which sounds a bit like the 'the Maestro' but in fact translates as the 'Money General.'

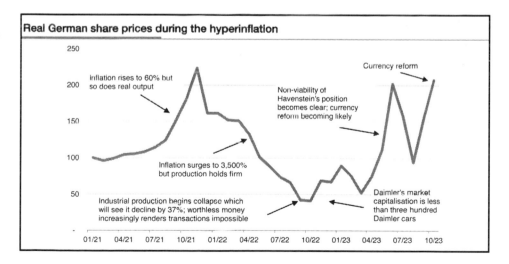

Source: Graham (1930), Bresciani-Turroni (1931), SG Cress Asset Research

Once embarked upon this path though, it became difficult to stop, especially since the early stages of inflation didn't seem too bad. Although inflation rose by 60% in 1921, real industrial production rose by 26% and unemployment stood at only 1% of the unionised workforce. The following chart shows that at one point during this period, real share prices rose by over 100%. But then the inflation intensified. In 1922 it reached 5,300% and on the eve of currency reform in late 1923, the annual rate was 16,579,999%. *How did this happen?*

To call the political climate of the time merely difficult would be a gross understatement. The country was on the brink of civil war: on the far right was the vast and humiliated ex-military which, having been forcibly demobilised by the victorious Allies, had become a seething and vengeful nationalist militia; on the far left were the anti-war workers and communists, the latter inspired by the 1917 Bolshevik Revolution and aiming to achieve the same end in Germany. Meanwhile, with revolution in the air and violent street battles between these polar political opposites playing out nightly, deep-felt resentment towards the foreign powers was fermented by the issue of war-time reparations, whereby Germany was required to hand over 4-7% of GDP each year until full compensation for the war-time devastation had been paid.

It's worth noting that there has been much debate over the extent to which reparations were, in fact, a primary cause of the hyperinflation. Some have argued that the 4-7% budgetary burden was bearable and that the hyperinflation was actually a bluff gone wrong. The German authorities were actually trying to demonstrate just how desperate their situation was as a way to lower their reparation payments. I'm no expert, but I'm not completely convinced by this argument. In passing, it's worth noting that we're about to see how politically feasible such a budgetary burden is, since the 4-7% of GDP range is roughly what Cecchetti et al at the BIS calculate is required to stabilise debt levels at 2007 levels *(see chart on following page)*.

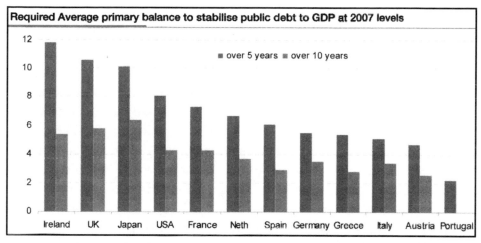

Source: Cecchetti, Monhanty, Zampolli (BIS conference paper, 2010)

I personally think the 4-7% reparations were the last straw for the German authorities facing capital flight in response to the tax measures they'd introduced to shore up the government's budget position (as we're seeing in Greece today), with the monetisation habit now very firmly entrenched and fearful of what might happen should painful deflationist policies be pursued. As Liaquat Ahamed writes in his masterful book on the Great Depression*,

"Were he to refuse to print the money necessary to finance the deficit, he risked causing a sharp rise in interest rates as the government scrambled to borrow from every source. The mass unemployment that would ensue, he believed, would bring on a domestic economic and political crisis, which in Germany's [then] fragile state might precipitate a real political convulsion."

Facing a dilemma orders of magnitude higher but nevertheless familiar to observers of today's situation, faced with the terrifying prospect of even more economic pain should he slam on the brakes, he opted to press his foot further on the accelerator.

Less well-known though is that, as always, economic theory was on hand to furnish Von Havenstein with a *"scientific"* justification for his playing for

* *Please see: Liaquat Ahamed, Lords of Finance. pp 74.*

time. The consensus in Germany was actually that the cause of inflation was external because both the Reichsmark and import prices had moved disproportionately more than the rise in the money supply. Since the external value was caused by the balance of payments, which was largely caused by the reparations, it was foreigners and not budget deficits which caused the inflation. Indeed, Von Havenstein was so enamoured with this theory that he blocked attempts at monetary reform arguing that any measures would be pointless without settlement of the reparations issue. According to Ludvig von Mises, "Herr Havenstein honestly believed that the continued issue of new notes had nothing to do with the rise of commodity prices, wages and foreign exchanges. This rise he attributed to the machinations of speculators... **Speculators always get the blame don't they?***

I don't want to overplay the parallels. In fact, there is one very clear difference between the hand Von Havenstein had to play then and those today's central bankers have to play now, namely the stability of today's political climate. Clearly this can change, but the class warfare, nationalistic xenophobia and revolutionary spirit poisoning the political atmosphere of 1920s Germany is, at the very least, dormant today and certainly not meaningfully visible across the political landscape. But let's not ignore the parallels either: as is the case for today's central bankers, Von Havenstein was faced with horrible fiscal problems; as is the case for today's central bankers, the distinction between fiscal and monetary policy had blurred; as is the case for today's central bankers, the political difficulty of deflating was daunting; and, as is the case for today's QE-enthralled central bankers, apparently respectable economic theory reassured him that he was doing the right thing.

One might think that the big difference is that today we have a greater expertise. Surely we understand what happens when deficits are financed with printed money, and that it is only backward and corrupt states that don't know any better, like Bolivia and Zimbabwe? But just a few years ago didn't we think that it was only backward and corrupt states that suffered banking crises too?

And, anyway, how could Von Havenstein not have known that the con-

* *Please see: The Great German Inflation. Ludwig von Mises*

tinued and escalating printing of money to fund government deficits would cause inflation? The United States' experience of unrestrained money printing during the Civil War had been well documented, as had the hyperinflation of revolutionary France in the late 18th century. Isn't it possible that, like today, he was overconfident in his ability to control his creation and in the economic theory which told him such control was possible? Certainly, in an article in the New York Times on the eve of the First World War, again from Liaquat Ahamed's book, there seems to have been evidence of the general optimism that there would be no *"unlimited issue of paper money and its steady depreciation… since monetary science is better understood at the present time than in those days."*

The fact is we do understand the economics of inflation. Despite what economists everywhere say about being in 'uncharted territory' with QE, we know that if you keep monetising deficits eventually you get inflation, and we know that once you're on that path it can be extremely difficult to get off it. But we knew that then. The real problem is that inflation is an inherently political variable and that concern over debt sustainability and unfunded welfare obligations leaves us more dependent on politicians than we have been in many decades. Frank Graham concluded his 1930 study of the Weimar hyperinflation with the following observation, which I think is as ominous as it is apt today:

"The mills of international finance grind slowly but their capacity is great. It is also flexible. The one condition is that the hoppers be not unduly loaded in the effort to get the whole grist from a single grinding. So much for the economics of the question. What politics has in store is, however, an inscrutable mystery. It can only be said that such financial difficulties as may occur will almost certainly arise from political rather than from economic sources."

THE GATHERING STORM

CHAPTER EIGHT

-

*"The only function of economic forecasting is
to make astrology look respectable."*

John Kenneth Galbraith

A Minskian Roadmap to the Next Gold Mania
Dylan Grice

"The parallel today would be governments winning a mandate to take the difficult decisions ahead on health care and pension entitlement, or even climate change. And who knows what yet-to-be-conceived frauds await?"

A Minskian Roadmap to the Next Gold Mania
(and the signposts to look for before selling)

Despite the strong performance of gold in the past decade there remain many good reasons for continuing to own it today. For one, with the price at which the USD would be fully backed by gold (as it was during the peak of the '70s mania), now standing at $8,000, there is a case for gold being cheap. Also, central banks look as though they're beginning to hoard it. The last time they did that - the late 1960s - proved to be the starting gun for the great gold bull market of the 1970s.

That bull market was propelled by widespread angst concerning tight energy markets, overly accommodative central banks and a nervousness that policy-makers had lost their way. To today's similarly fearful narrative, investors can add developed market government balance sheets which look significantly more stretched than they did then. If problematic inflation is largely a fiscal phenomenon, we could yet see a gold mania to rival that of the 1970s.

Like any other purchase though, it's important to have your eyes wide open to the risks involved. Gold is not the pure safe-haven asset it's often made out to be. Although, historically, it has retained its real purchasing power, it has also swung wildly and for long periods over time. Neither does gold generate any income. By owning it, the holder is forgoing the dividends and interest available from securities.

This forgone income can be thought of as an *"insurance premium"* to be paid to protect against extreme monetary malfeasance. But JP Morgan once said he'd made his fortune by selling too early. It's important to understand that, should such malfeasance come to pass, your *"insurance policy"* will only pay out when you sell. Understanding when to sell gold in the future is as important as knowing why to own it now.

What's a Lump of Shiny Useless Yellow Metal Worth?

"Gold gets dug out of the ground in Africa, or someplace. Then we melt it down, dig another hole, bury it again and pay people to stand around guarding it. It has no utility. Anyone watching from Mars would be scratching their head."

Warren Buffett

In 1965, concerned at the inflationary policies of the US and the attendant threat to their Dollar reserves, the French central bank started converting their Dollars into gold. This set in motion events which saw the central banks of Belgium, the Netherlands, Germany and, eventually, Britain doing the same in 1970. By 1971, the Bretton Woods system, by which all currencies were pegged to the Dollar and the Dollar effectively pegged to gold, had broken. The French had fired the starting gun for the great 1970s bull market in gold and silver.

It's worth pointing this out because central banks aren't known for their investment acumen. Some commentators have mockingly suggested that the Reserve Bank of India's recent decision to buy 200m tons of IMF gold signals the top of the market in the way that heavy selling by the UK signalled the bottom in 1999.

This is cute. I think it's also wrong. Like today, central banks weren't buying gold in the late 1960s to prop it up. They were abandoning attempts to prop up the Dollar. Gold feels frothy today, but the Indian purchase of IMF gold eerily parallels the French purchases of the late 1960s. And ill policy winds are blowing in its favour. With the precious metals consultancy, GFMS, estimating that central banks will be net buyers of gold for the first time since 1988, have the Indians just sounded the same starting gun the French did in 1965?

The last time central banks hoarded gold ....

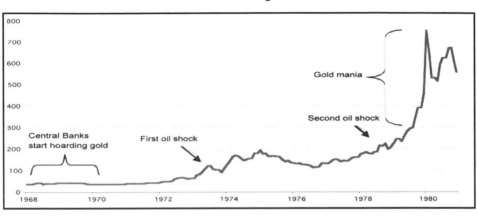

Source: SG Cross Asset Research

The standard reply to Mr. Buffett's views on gold might be that gold acts as a long-term store of value, the most commonly heard rationale for investing in gold. Indeed, the chart below shows the real UK gold price today to be similar to that prevailing in 1265.

But the same chart also shows how unreliable gold has been as a store of wealth. A 15th-century gold bug who'd stored all of his wealth in bullion, bequeathed it to his children and required them to do the same would be more than a little miffed when gazing down from his celestial place of rest to see the real wealth of his lineage decline by nearly 90% over the next 500 years (though he might take comfort from the knowledge that his financial advisor would be burning in hell). More recently, had you bought at the peak of the last bull market in January 1980 for $850, you'd have suffered a nominal decline of 70% by the time it bottomed in 1999. On an annualised basis you'd have lost 6% pa nominal and 9% real.

Seven and a half centuries of real gold prices:

So gold isn't intrinsically safer than any other asset. There is nothing mystical about it either. Like all other assets, it goes up and down according to its fundamental drivers. But what are these fundamental drivers? How can something with no cash flow or earnings power be valued?

The simple answer is that it can't be. Intrinsically, it is pretty much worthless. Indeed, when I tell people I buy gold the most common complaint I hear is that it has no real industrial use. Surely I'd be better at least buying a commodity that industry needs to make stuff with, like silver or platinum? But this *"uselessness"* is exactly what gives gold its value because it makes it the perfect currency. If you own silver, a recession will cause the price (and therefore its purchasing power) to fall because industrial demand has fallen. The same is true for platinum or palladium. But the price of gold will be unaffected by any decline in industrial demand because there is no industrial demand!

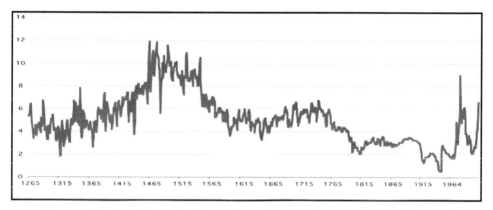

Source: Societe Generale Cross Asset Research, www.measuringworth.org

To value gold it helps to understand that paper money was traditionally based on the stock of gold (and silver). Depositors of bullion would receive a receipt proving their holdings and it soon became easier to use those receipts for commerce than it did the physical gold. So while the use of paper money had become commonplace by the 18th century, that paper was always redeemable into gold or silver. The money supply was always gold-backed.

Full redeemability was increasingly watered down after WW1 so that by the time the Bretton Woods system was imposed following WW2, only central banks had the right to convert paper for gold. But when that broke in 1971 because Dollar holders had become distrustful of US promises to restrain its

170

Dollar printing, the link between paper money and gold was severed completely. Since then, paper money has been backed by nothing more than central banks' promises to maintain the money supply at a stable level.

So, one way to value gold, therefore, is to ask at what gold price the value of outstanding central bank paper would be completely backed by gold. The US owns nearly 263m troy ounces of gold (the world's biggest holder) while the Fed's monetary base is $1.7 trillion. So the price of gold at which the US Dollars would be fully gold-backed is currently around $8,000.

Gold is very cheap - at current prices, the USD is only 14% gold backed

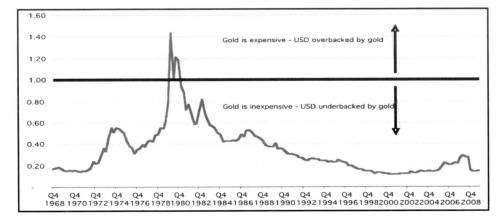

Source: Societe Generale Cross Asset Research

The chart above shows the extent to which the USD has been gold-backed since the late 1960s. It currently stands at 15%, close to the all-time low 12% reached in 2001 but far from the all-time high of 140% reached in early 1980. Interestingly, during that inflation panic, the value of gold rose to such a level that the Dollar became over-backed (the red line is higher than 1). The market value of gold held by the Fed was worth more than the paper money it had issued!

Gold has rallied considerably in recent years, but the monetary base has grown even faster. So a better response to Mr. Buffet might be that you should buy gold because it's cheap…

A Coming Gold Mania?

If my *"valuation"* of gold strikes you as a desperate attempt to value some-thing which can't be valued, it's no different from metrics such as the *"price to clicks"* or *"ARPU"* ratios which were used in the late 1990s during the tech-nology bubble when demand for bullish *"valuation analysis"* mushroomed. They seem crazy now but speculators bought into them during the tech craze. And there may well be a bubbly parallel... Charles Kindleberger, drawing heavily on the work of Minsky, outlined the following *"anatomy of a bubble"*.

Stage 1 sees "displacement". Frequently, this comes about through the introduction of a new disruptive technology (e.g. canals, railways, or the internet) although Kindleberger says it doesn't necessarily have to come from such an innovation. It can arise on the back of greater market liq-uidity, for example, through financial deregulation.

Stage 2 is the "boom". A convincing narrative gains traction (e.g. Asian economies are "miracle" Tiger economies; the Internet will change the world; sub-prime mortgages help financial institutions diversify risk). Price move-ments which seem to confirm the narrative are stoked by credit creation.

Anatomy of a bubble: the Kindleberger-Minsky model

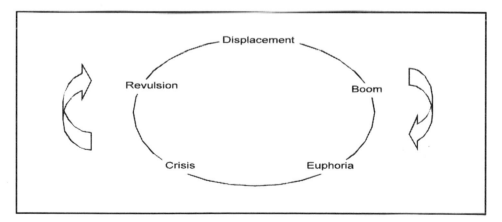

Source: Societe Generale Cross Asset Research

Stage 3 is "euphoria". In the words of Kindleberger, *"there is nothing so disturbing to one's well-being and judgement as to see a friend get rich."* This greed sucks people, who wouldn't normally involve themselves in such practice, into the mania. More and more people seek to become rich without understanding the process involved. Rationality becomes stretched and increasingly fanciful notions excuse what would ordinarily be considered irrational behaviour.

Stage 4 sees the "crisis". The insiders originally involved start to sell. Prices level off and begin to fall. Those who bought at the top find themselves pushed out first and their selling eventually cascades down through the remaining believers. Speculators realise prices can no longer rise and the rush to exit is on. To the extent that leverage was used to finance any purchases at irrationally overvalued prices, savage price declines put banks in trouble too.

Stage 5 sees "revulsion" where prices likely overshoot fundamental values on the downside. Scams and frauds are uncovered. Scapegoats are found for the financial distress caused. The object so richly desired as the bubble inflated becomes an object of ridicule and disgust, along with anyone or anything associated with it.

With this in mind, consider the parallels between the 1st and 2nd phase of the 1970s gold mania with the situation unfolding today. Then, the "displacement" was the collapse of the Bretton Woods system, precipitated by central banks distrustful of inflationary US policies buying of gold. This is very similar to what we are seeing today. Then, the liquidity turning *"displacement"* to *"boom"* came from central bank accommodation of the oil shocks. Today, central banks are monetising government deficits to accommodate the recessionary effect of the credit crisis.

Then the convincing narrative was that with the Middle East controlling our energy from abroad and aggressive trade unions rampant at home, policy-makers were no longer in control. Today, the perception of central bank infallibility has been permanently ruptured by their collective failure to see the 2008 crash coming. Nagging concern at their over-willingness to inflate, at the blurring of monetary and fiscal policy and over long-term government solvency *(see chart below)* gives traction to a similar narrative today.

Our governments are insolvent

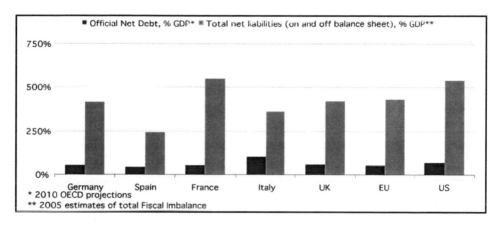

Source: OECD, Jagadeesh Gohale

On the Kindleberg-Minsky map, as I've drawn it, therefore, we've had the *"displacement"* and are only now entering into the *"boom"* phase. The *"mania phase"* lies well ahead. Who knows what unknown unknowns might parallel the two oil shocks of the 1970s?

The top of the gold bubble occurred when politicians won a mandate in the late 1970s / early 1980s to take painful decisions, to take on the trade unions, and to raise interest rates to tackle inflation. Only then, during the *"crisis phase"* did scams such as the Hunt brothers' attempted corner of the silver market come to light. The parallel today would be governments winning a mandate to take the difficult decisions ahead on health care and pension entitlement, or even climate change. And who knows what yet-to-be-conceived frauds await?

When to Sell Gold

I believe these days are a long way off but many believe the time to sell is now. Gold just isn't the misunderstood, widely shunned asset it was a few years ago. Isn't the gold bull market now long in the tooth, with better opportunities to be found elsewhere? I can understand this view. But had you bought stocks at the bottom of the bear market in 1974 and held them for ten years you'd have seen them go from being hated to being loved. And as the number of mutual funds exploded you could have plausibly argued that since stocks were no longer the deeply contrarian plays they'd been, they should be sold. But you'd have missed spectacular gains over the next 15 years (climaxing in the late 1990s mania) because the social contrarian indicators said nothing as to how favourable underlying conditions were for risk assets.

And the underlying conditions today remain favourable for gold. Developed market governments are probably insolvent (*as shown in the chart above*) and while it's not inevitable that this insolvency will precipitate an extreme inflationary event, it might... And though I sometimes wonder if Ben Bernanke is, in fact, the reincarnation of Rudolf von Havenstein - the tragic president of the German Reichsbank who presided over the Weimar Hyperinflation - I don't think he actually is... It's just that he, and other central bankers, might be closer than they think... Gold, like all other commodities, is inherently speculative. Unlike well chosen stocks which you buy to hold to take advantage of their wealth-compounding properties, you only ever buy commodities to sell later. With this in mind, when should you sell gold?

Willem Buiter called gold a 6000-year bubble. The late and great Peter Bernstein subtitled his book about gold *"the History of an Obsession"*. But much as I admire these two great minds, such loaded phraseology implies there to be something irrational about owning gold and I think that's just plain wrong. The fact is that there is a fundamental need for a medium of exchange. Early civilisations used pebbles or shells. Prisoners have used cigarettes.

Having a medium of exchange makes life easier than under barter economy and societies have always organised themselves around the best monetary standard they could find. Until industrialisation of the paper printing process, that happened to be gold, which is small, malleable, portable and with no tendency to tarnish. Crucially, it's also relatively finite and this particular characteristic (in combination with the others) can be very useful in environments characterised by monetary mischief.

I view it primarily as insurance against such environments. It's a lump of metal with no cash flows and no earnings power. In a very real sense it's not intrinsically worth anything. If you buy it, you're forgoing dividend or interest income and the gradual accumulation over time of intrinsic value since a lump of cold, industrially useless metal can offer none of these things. That forgone accumulation of wealth is like the insurance premium paid for a policy which will pay out in the event of an extreme inflation event.

Is there anything else which will do that? Some argue that equities hedge against inflation because they are a claim on real assets, but most of the great bear market troughs of the 20th century occurred during inflation-ary periods. A more obvious inflation hedge is inflation linked bonds, but governments can default on these too. More exotic insurance products like sovereign CDSs, inflation caps, long-dated swaptions or upside yield curve volatility all have their intuitive merits. But they all come with coun-terparty risk. Physical gold doesn't. Indeed, during the *"6000-year gold bubble"* no one has defaulted on gold. It is the one insurance policy which will pay out when you really need it to.

There is nothing mystical about gold and I don't consider myself a gold bug. In fact, I'm not sure I'd even classify gold as an *"investment"* in the strictest sense of the word. Well-chosen equities (not indices) will act as wealth-compounding machines and are likely to make many times the initial outlay in real terms over time. These are *"investments"* because as long as the economics of each business remain firm, you don't want to sell. As they say in the textbooks, you *"buy to hold"*. But gold isn't like that. Like all commodities, it's intrinsically speculative because you only buy it to sell it in the future.

The reason I own gold is because I'm worried about the long-term solvency of developed market governments. I know that Milton Friedman popularised the idea that inflation is *"always and everywhere a monetary phenomenon"* but if you look back through time at inflationary crises from

176

ancient Rome, to Ming China, to revolutionary France and America or to Weimar Germany - you'll find that uncontrolled inflations are caused by overleveraged governments which resorted to printing as the easiest way to avoid explicit default (whereas inflation is merely an implicit default). It's all very well for economists to point out that the cure for runaway inflation is simply a contraction of the money supply. It's just that when you look at inflationary episodes you find that such monetary contractions haven't been politically viable courses of action.

Economists, we find, generally don't understand this because economists look down on disciplines, such as history, which might teach them, because they aren't mathematical enough. True, historians don't use maths (primarily because they don't have physics envy) but what they do use is common sense, and an understanding that while the economic laws might hold in the long run, in the short run the political beast must be fed.

During the Weimar Hyperinflation, Rudolf von Havenstein (then Reichsbank president) was terrified of pursuing the required monetary contraction because he was so fearful of the social consequences that rising unemployment and falling output would elicit. The simple fact is that the agonising dilemma he faced, identical in principle, if not in magnitude, to that faced by policy-makers today, is as old as money itself.

In the 3rd century AD, as the Roman Empire became too large and unwieldy, its borders were consolidated and the great imperial expansion halted. Though necessary, this consolidation posed problems. While the Empire was in growth mode, driven by military conquest which strengthened public finances, the army paid for itself. It was an asset on the national balance sheet. But when that territorial growth was halted, a hole was created in the budget as, while the army was still needed to defend the borders, it was no longer self-funding because there was no territorial expansion.

Roman emperors discovered that contracting expenditure to fit with new lower revenues was a difficult feat to pull off. So, rather than contract military spending, public works or public entertainment - long-term necessities which were painful in the short run - they opted to buy time using successive currency debasements. Ultimately, this culminated in what would become the world's first of many fiscally driven inflation crises *(see charts below)*.

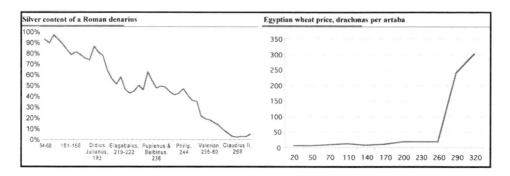

Source: http://www.tulane.edu/~august/handouts/601cprin.htm

Two thousand years ago, the fiscal sobriety so clearly needed in the long-run was subordinated to the short-run requirement to buy time. Hence the age-old short-term temptation to debase the currency and hope no-one notices. Paring overstretched government balance sheets has never been easy. As the Romans should have done in the third century, developed market governments today will have to come clean to their citizens that since keeping the welfare promises they've made over the years will bankrupt them, those promises are going to have to be *"restructured"* and government expenditure substantially tightened.

Fiscal contractions required over 5-year and 10-year periods to stabilise government debt ratios at 2007 levels (% p.a.).

But governments aren't ready to take that step at the moment (the chart above shows just how painful the required measures could be). Indeed, the pressing fear among policy-makers today remains that stimulus might be removed too soon. In the UK, policy-makers refused to *"risk the recovery we've fought so hard for"* to quote PM Gordon Brown (*"fought so hard for"!*). In the US, lawmakers have just expanded the most inefficient health care system on the planet (according to Peter Peterson - ft.com - there are five times as many CT scans per head in the US as there are in Germany, and five times as many coronary bypasses as in France). It has been promised that the increase will be deficit-neutral (which I doubt) but even if it is, current period deficits aren't the correct way to look at health and pension obligations which should be examined on an actuarial basis (and if expanding the program is so difficult, wait until they try contracting it!)

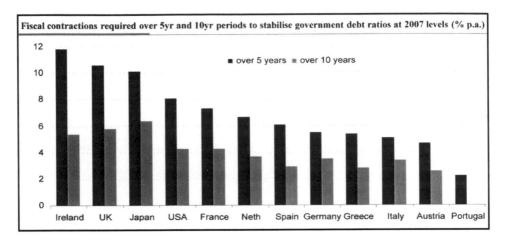

Source: Cecchetti, Mohanty, Zampollo (BIS conference paper, 2010)

But they will face up to these problems one day, because they must. And the good news is that there are precedents for policy-makers adopting the policy of short-term pain for long-term gain. In the UK in the 1970s, for example, the country tired of lurching from one crisis to the next, of militant trade unions and of high inflation. Eventually, they elected Margaret Thatcher who promised to control inflation and smash the unions even if the short-term pain would be severe. She did, and it was. But the rest (despite 364 economists petitioning her that such drastic measures threatened social stability - *"How 364 Economists Got it Totally Wrong"* - Telegraph) is history. The key point to bear in mind is that she was elected with a mandate for short-term pain which hadn't existed five years earlier. The political winds had changed.

Ireland swallowing bitter fiscal medicine today offers a similar example. I've been over there a couple of times in the last few months and it's heartbreaking. Its economy has contracted by nearly 10% since the peak of the credit bubble and my friends in Dublin tell me that, unofficially, house prices are down 60-70% from their peak. Unemployment has spiked to around 15%. The striking thing about being there, though, is that while no one is happy about them, and there have been strikes in protest at the distribution of the pain (which, in passing seems to be a feature of the political climate during such crises) on the whole there seems to be an understanding that such measures are unavoidable. These draconian fiscal policies wouldn't have been possible five years ago. But the political winds have changed.

UK inflation in the 1970s

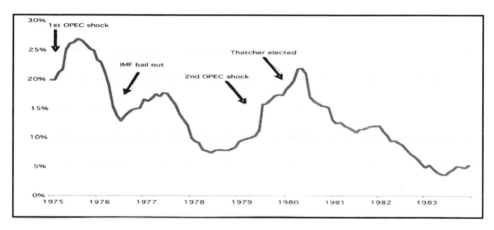

Source: Societe Generale Cross Asset Research

What causes the political winds to change? A government crisis. In 2008, Ireland came very close to going the way of Iceland. They had their crisis. And historians today still refer to the *"inflation fatigue"* in Britain by the end of the 1970s. This was our crisis. So what we learn from these experiences and others like them is that a fiscal crisis is required to force a majority acceptance of the implications of an over-leveraged government.

But the political winds in countries with central banks are a long way from blowing in the direction of fiscal rectitude. And while it's true that more people are at least talking about it, talk is very cheap and no one is yet close to walking the walk. Such steps remain politically unpopular because we haven't had our crisis yet. Given the clear un-sustainability of government finances and the explosive path government leverage is on, a government funding crisis is both inevitable and necessary.

180

Dubai and Greece are merely the first claps of thunder in what is going to be a long emergency.

Eventually, there will be a crisis of such magnitude that the political winds change direction and become blustering gales forcing us onto the course of fiscal sustainability. Until it does, the temptation to inflate will remain, as will economists with spurious mathematical rationalisations as to why such inflation will make everything OK (witness the IMF's recent recommendation that inflation targets be raised to 4%: IMF Tells Bankers to Rethink Inflation - WSJ). Until it does, the outlook will remain favourable for gold. But eventually, majority opinion will accept the painful contractionary medicine because it will have to. That will be the time to sell gold.

Dylan Grice:

I have nominated Kidscape which is a UK charity committed to keeping children safe from bullying and abuse. Kidscape staff equip vulnerable children with practical non-threatening knowledge and skills in how to keep themselves safe and reduce the likelihood of future harm. Kidscape works with children and young people under the age of 16 as well as their parents and carers et al.

The Kidscape web site can be found at:
www.Kidscape.co.uk

CHAPTER NINE

-

*"You have to choose between trusting to the natural stability of gold
and the natural stability and intelligence of the members of government.
And, with due respect to these gentlemen, I advise you, as long as the
capitalistic system lasts, to vote for gold."*

George Bernard Shaw

Warning Flags
Howard Marks

"Investing defensively requires that when everything seems to be going well and investors are feeling positive, we must sense the implicit danger and prepare for negative developments."

About the Author

Since the formation of Oaktree Capital Management in Los Angeles in 1995, Howard Marks has been responsible for ensuring the firm's adherence to its core investment philosophy, communicating closely with clients concerning products and strategies, and managing the firm. From 1985 until 1995, Mr. Marks led the groups at The TCW Group, Inc. that were responsible for investments in distressed debt, high yield bonds, and convertible securities. He was also Chief Investment Officer for Domestic Fixed Income at TCW and President of TCW Asset Management Company, the largest of the TCW companies.

Previously, Mr. Marks was with Citicorp Investment Management for 16 years, where from 1978 to 1985, he was Vice President and senior portfolio manager in charge of convertible and high yield securities. Between 1969 and 1978, he was an equity research analyst and, subsequently, Citicorp's Director of Research.

Mr. Marks holds a B.S.Ec. degree cum laude from the Wharton School of the University of Pennsylvania with a major in Finance and an M.B.A. in Accounting and Marketing from the Graduate School of Business of the University of Chicago, where he received the George Hay Brown Prize. He is a CFA® charterholder and a Chartered Investment Counsellor.

Warning Flags

For about a year, I've been sharing my realization that there are two main risks in the investment world: the risk of losing money and the risk of missing opportunity. You can completely avoid one or the other, or you can compromise between the two, but you can't eliminate both. One of the prominent features of investor psychology is that few people are able to *(a)* always balance the two risks or *(b)* emphasize the right one at the right time. Rather, at the extremes they usually obsess about the wrong one. . . and in so doing make the other the one deserving attention.

During bull markets, when asset prices are elevated, there's great risk of losing money. And in bear markets, when everything's at rock bottom, the real risk consists of missing opportunity. Everyone knows these things. But bull markets develop for the simple reason that most people are buying - ignoring the risk of loss in order to keep from missing opportunity - just when elevated prices imply losses later. Likewise, markets reach their lows because most people are selling, trying to avoid further losses and ignoring the bargains that are everywhere.

The Never-Ending Cycle

Why do people buy when they should sell, and sell when they should buy? The answer is simple: emotion takes over. Price increases excite investors and encourage them to buy, and price declines scare them into selling.

When the economy and markets boom, people tend to assume more of the same is in the offing. They find little to worry about, other than the possibility that others will make more money than they will. Fear of loss recedes, and fear of opportunity costs takes over. Thus risk aversion evaporates and risk tolerance rises.

Risk aversion is absolutely essential in order for markets to function properly. When sufficient risk aversion is present, people shrink from riskier investments and prefer safer ones. Thus riskier investments have to appear to offer higher returns in order to attract capital. That's as it should be. But when people get excited about the prospect of easy money - even if from assets or investment strategies that have become far too popular, turning into overpriced manias - they frequently drop their risk aversion and adopt risk tolerance instead. Thus they swarm into the investment *du jour* without concern for its elevated price and risk. This behavior should constitute an important warning flag for prudent investors.

In the same way that expanded risk tolerance accompanies appreciated asset prices and contributes to the risk of loss, so does risk aversion tend to rise in times of depressed prices, increasing the risk of missed opportunity. When people refuse to buy assets regardless of their low prices, they miss out on the best, lowest-risk returns of the cycle.

Recent History - on the Upside

Just as the recent market cycle was extreme, so was the swing in attitudes regarding the "twin risks." And thus so are the resultant learning opportunities.

Risk aversion was clearly inadequate in the years just before the onset of the crisis in mid-2007. In fact, I consider this the main cause of the crisis. (Last year, *DealBook*, the online business publication of *The New York Times*, asked me to write about what I thought had been behind the crisis. My article, entitled *"Too Much Trust, Too Little Worry,"* was published on October 5, 2009. It offers more on this subject should you want it.) Here's the background regarding the early part of this decade:

Interest rates kept low by the Fed combined with the first three-year decline of stocks since the Depression to reduce interest in traditional investments. As a result, investors shifted their focus to alternative and innovative investments such as buyouts, infrastructure, real estate, hedge funds and structured mortgage vehicles. In the low-return climate of the time, much of the appeal of these asset classes came from the fact that they promised higher returns thanks to their use of leverage, whether through borrowing, tranching or derivatives.

Given the high promised returns, investors forgot about (or chose to ignore) the ability of leverage to magnify losses as well as gains. Contributing to investors' rosy view of leverage's likely impact was their belief that risk had been banished by *(a)* the efficacy of the Fed and its *"Greenspan put,"* *(b)* the combination of securitization, disintermediation, tranching, decoupling and financial engineering, and *(c)* the *"wall of liquidity"* coming toward us from China and the oil producing nations.

For these reasons, few market participants were afraid of losing money. Most just worried about missing opportunity. The unattractive outlook for stocks and bonds meant investors would have to be aggressive and innovative if they were going to earn significant returns in the low-return environment. Thus risk aversion *(a)* was unnecessary and *(b)* would be counter-productive. *"You'd better invest in this new financial product,"* people were told. *"If you don't, you'll miss out. And if you don't and your competitor does - and it works - you'll look out-of-step and fall behind."* When contemplating a virtuous circle without end, investors usually think of only one word: *"buy."*

This describes the process through which fear of missed opportunity can overcome skepticism and prudence. And in this period, that's what happened. No one worried about losing money. Fear of missed opportunity drove most investors, and Citibank's Chuck Prince famously said, ". . . as long as the music is playing, you've got to get up and dance. We're still dancing." Although he worried about a possible decline in liquidity, he worried more about falling behind in the manic race to provide capital.

Recent History - on the Downside

The events from mid-2007 through late 2008 or early 2009 demonstrate the reverse in operation. The upward trend in home prices ground to a halt and subprime mortgages began to default in large numbers. Leveraged vehicles melted down. Credit became unavailable, and financial institutions needed rescuing. Recession caused spending to contract, and corporate profits declined. Bear Stearns, Merrill Lynch, AIG, Fannie Mae, Freddie Mac, Wachovia and Washington Mutual all required rescues. Bank capital, commercial paper and money market funds needed federal guarantees. After the bankruptcy of Lehman Brothers, people began to ponder the collapse of the financial system. As often happens in scary times, *"possible"* morphed into *"probable,"* or at least something very much worth worrying about.

Now a vicious circle replaced the virtuous one of just a few months earlier. And with its arrival, the fear of losing money replaced the fear of missing opportunity. As I've said before, I imagine most investors' cry was, *"I don't care if I ever make a penny in the market again; I just don't want to lose any more. Get me out!"*

For most investors, no assumption was too negative to be true, and no return made the risk of loss worth bearing. High yield bonds at 19% yields. First lien leveraged loans at 18%. Investment grade bonds at 11%. None of these was sufficient to induce risk-taking.

As I wrote in *"The Limits to Negativism"* (October 15, 2008), *"Skepticism calls for pessimism when optimism is excessive. But it also calls for optimism when pessimism is excessive."* By the fourth quarter of 2008, risk aversion ruled and risk tolerance had disappeared. A skeptical view toward excessive pessimism was called for at a time of unprecedented low asset prices, but few people could muster it. The credit markets offered the highest returns in their history, but fear of losing money kept most investors from seizing the opportunity.

In the middle of this decade we saw a manic period in which losses were unimaginable. The resultant shortages of risk aversion and skepticism caused investors to buy at highs and assume unprecedented risks in order to avoid missing opportunity. This was followed - as usual - by a collapse in which no negative event could be ruled out and no return was high enough to induce buying, all because investors wanted nothing other than to avoid losing money.

This cycle produced a treacherous, low-return period in which it was very hard to find investments promising good returns earned with safety, and then a period of collapse in which there were bargains everywhere but few investors possessed the requisite *"dry powder"* and intestinal fortitude with which to buy. That's the background. Where do we stand today?

Signs of the Times

Optimism, adventurousness and unworried behavior characterized the pre-crisis period, and investor behavior reflected those attitudes. In my memo *"It's All Good"* (July 16, 2007), just before the onset of the crisis, I mentioned some of the warning signs in the credit markets:

> Unlike the historic norm, it's routine today to issue CCC-rated bonds. It's easy to borrow money for the express purpose of distributing cash to equity holders, magnifying the company's leverage. It's so easy to issue bonds with little or no creditor protection in the indenture that a label has been coined for them: *"covenant-lite."* And it's possible to issue bonds whose interest payments can be paid in more bonds at the option of the borrower.

> The first requirement for an elevated opportunity in distressed debt is the unwise extension of credit, which I define as the making of loans which borrowers will be unable to service if things get a little worse. This happens when lenders fail to require a sufficient margin of safety. . . The default rate in the high yield bond universe is at a 25-year low on a rolling-twelve-month basis. Under such circumstances, how could the average supplier of capital be expected to maintain a high level of risk a version and prudence, especially when doing so means ceding all the loan making to others? It's not for nothing that they say *"The worst of loans are made in the best of times."*

The inspiration for this article came as my pile of clippings began to swell with indications that pre-crisis behavior is coming back. Here are excerpts from a few, with emphasis added in each case:

On covenant-lite loans

Are debt investors just stupid? That might help explain why they're buying covenant-lite loans again. These deals, which carry few restrictions on borrowers, became a standard bearer for easy money. They may have helped some companies limp through the downturn - but they've left lenders saddled with lots of risk and little return. It's easy to see why companies like covenant-lite loans. . . But for owners of the debt, the attraction is far less clear beyond the familiar short-term reach for yield. . .

Lyondell Chemical is paying (Libor plus 400 basis points) on its recent $500 million covenant-lite deal. And the energy refiner will emerge from bankruptcy with a much slimmer debt load than before it filed for Chapter 11.

Lyondell's terms are better than 2007's crop of covenant-lite loans, to be sure, but lenders still are essentially relinquishing their right to force companies into paying them more money, or exiting the loan entirely, should their creditworthiness tumble.

So why are lenders doing it again? Lyondell Chemical's answer: investor demand for higher yielding assets. This is a familiar mantra while official interest rates remain low. But lenders should be mindful of loosening standards or risk finding themselves once again on the short end of the stick. (*"Don't call it a comeback,"* breakingviews, April 5)

On payment-in-kind loans and flexibility

Clint Eastwood's Dirty Harry character famously held a gun to a suspect and asked: *"Do you feel lucky?"* Investors in credit markets seem to be saying yes, if Cerberus' refinancing of Freedom Group, maker of Remington firearms, is any indication.

A deflating gun bubble backfired on the private equity firm's plans last year for an initial public offering of Freedom. Now trigger-happy credit investors are taking off their safeties and letting Cerberus unload some of its stake.

The $225 million of notes are useful ammo for Cerberus. They allow Freedom to either pay the interest in cash or half in cash and half in additional notes at the company's discretion. The financing allows Cerberus to get cash back on its investment today by buying back preferred stock held by the private equity group ahead of an eventual IPO. . . The buyers of these notes, though, are taking their chances. Freedom doesn't look overleveraged according to its historic cash flow - the company's debt level is about three times *"adjusted EBITDA"* for 2009. But sales of rival gun-makers are continuing to fall. . .

Moreover, these sorts of notes are notoriously difficult to price. The investor has to figure out the risk of the company encountering cash flow problems, whether the firm will actually pull the toggle trigger, and how much the PIK feature may reduce their potential recovery in the event of default. Indeed, many investors took drubbings on similar notes issued at the top of the credit boom. Caution is warranted when investors remove their trigger locks. (*"Do you feel lucky?"* breakingviews, March 31).

On initial public offerings

It is springtime for IPOs. . . KKR and Bain, two of the most aggressive private equity firms during the buyout boom, are now as aggressively looking to cash out. They are leading what is expected to be a season of IPOs as long as the markets continue to stabilize or climb. The IPOs would allow the firms to partially cash out their stakes and return money to investors. They also could use the proceeds to pay down the sizable debt used to finance the takeovers. (*"Bain, KKR to Push New Crop of IPOs,"* The Wall Street Journal, April 9).

On leveraged loans

Even as worries escalate about the ability of highly rated countries to fund themselves, there is a buzz at the other end of the credit spectrum. Leveraged loans, a source of funding for private equity acquisitions, are drawing investor interest again after a long period in the doldrums.

In the U.S., there are signs of life in the collateralized-loan-obligation market, with the year's first deal not only refinancing an existing CLO but bringing in new money, too. In Europe, Harbour Vest Partners is launching a listed fund to invest in mid-market leveraged loans. Leveraged-finance bankers are more bullish, and new loans have started to flow. . .

There are wider implications, too: Cash moving into the loan market represents a greater willingness to hold more illiquid assets, an important development. . . (*"A Pulse Finally Returns to the Leveraged-Loan Market,"* The Wall Street Journal, April 12).

On dividend recaps

Blackstone Group LP and other private equity firms are accelerating sales of junk bonds and leveraged loans to pay themselves dividends in a sign the market for the riskiest debt may be overheating. Apria Healthcare Group Inc., owned by Blackstone, is seeking consent from bondholders to sell notes to issue a dividend, following at least six similar offerings this year, according to data compiled by Bloomberg.

Including loans, companies have raised $10.8 billion in debt to fund payouts this year, compared with $1 billion in all of 2009 and $1.3 billion in the prior 12 months, according to Standard & Poor's LCD.

Private equity firms are taking advantage of record high-yield, high-risk bond sales and a rally in loans to extract cash from companies they own, awaiting a rebound in leveraged buy-outs and initial public offerings. So-called dividend deals, which permeated debt markets in 2006 and 2007 before the credit seizure, may signal investors are becoming too complacent, said William Quinn, chairman of American Beacon Advisors Inc.

"You start to be concerned that you're increasing leverage, which was one of the things that created these problems in 2008," said Quinn, who helps oversee $45 billion for the fund manager in Fort Worth, Texas. *"I understand why private equity firms do it, but I would be concerned."* (*"Dividend Deals Rebound as Black-stone Seeks Cash,"* Bloomberg, April 16).

Companies may increase borrowing to pay shareholder dividends in a record year for junk bonds, Standard & Poor's said. . . *"We are starting to see the proceeds of high-yield issues being channeled to shareholders as dividends, something that is less-welcome from a credit perspective, reminiscent of the leveraged finance market back in 2007,"* analysts led by Taron Wade wrote. . . Companies owned by LBO firms in 2007 issued a record 6.1 billion Euros of loans in the first half to pay dividends to shareholders, data compiled by Fitch Ratings show.

Private equity firms *"essentially decreased the risk of their portfolio equity investments, boosting their near-term equity returns at the expense of the credit quality of the companies themselves,"* according to S&P. (*"Junk Bond Issuers Increase Dividend Deals, S&P,"* Says Bloomberg, April 20).

On collateralized loan obligations

Citigroup is set to launch its second leveraged loan structured products transaction this year, this time for a large private equity client, as debt managers and bankers look to revitalise the markets which drove the buyout boom. . .

If the transaction goes ahead soon, it will be only the second CLO to be sold since the beginning of 2009. Last month Citigroup structured a $525m CLO managed by US fund manager Fraser Sullivan Investment Management. . .

Leveraged finance bankers are hopeful the CLO market can take off again as it would provide greater availability of finance for leveraged loans, the engine of the private equity industry. The market for CLOs ground to a halt after the collapse of Lehman Brothers pushed credit markets into freefall. Even the most actively traded leveraged loans lost as much as a third of their face value in the depths of the crisis. (*"Citigroup markets second CLO,"* Financial News, April 19).

On buyouts

Private equity firms bear some resemblance to children at a fairground: they jump on a ride as dealmaking gathers pace, whizzing faster and faster, before jumping off as the cycle slows down. As the ride starts to gather pace again, buyout firms are back, with some eyeing the biggest rides. (Emphasis in the original).

Mega-deals - transactions over $10 bn that were favored in the boom years of 2006-2008 but have been crimped by the lack of debt - are making a comeback. Last week, Blackstone Group and other investors were in talks to acquire financial data processing company Fidelity National Information Services, according to The Wall Street Journal. The acquisition of Fidelity, which has a market capitalisation approaching $10 bn and about $3 bn in debt, would be the largest leveraged buyout since the credit crisis struck. . .

Bankers and buyout executives said the resurrection of large buyouts was being driven by a booming high-yield bond market. With low interest rates in Europe and the US, investors are more willing to take the risk of weaker credits because it allows them to secure yields unavailable in other forms of lending. (*"Are dealmakers ready for another white-knuckle ride?"* Financial News, May 10).

On investor psychology

Irrational equanimity is back. Not only are developed market stocks back to pre-Lehman levels, but investors' comfort levels are in a zone not seen since the eve of the credit crisis in early 2007. Apart from US stock indices, this shows up in the price investors will pay to insure against volatility, with the CBOE Vix index down to its lowest since the crisis eve of July 2007, and in sharp reductions in cash cushions held by institutions.

Merrill Lynch's widely followed survey of fund managers. . . finds that more now want companies to pay higher dividends or make more capital expenditures than see them pay down debts. . .

Such equanimity is not totally irrational. Macroeconomic data in the past month have run ahead of expectations. When the herd trampling forward is this bullish, it is not a good idea to stand in its way. But it would be easier to feel comfortable with current share price levels if investors showed a little more unease. Complacency on this scale suggests risk of a correction. (*"Investor sentiment,"* Financial Times, April 14).

Just as one returning swallow doesn't make a summer, anecdotal evidence of rising risk tolerance does not mean entire markets have returned to dangerous levels. But it's a fact that issuers and investment bankers can do things today that they couldn't do a year or two ago. The door is open to transactions that wouldn't be possible if risk aversion were running high. The clear inference is that fear of loss has declined and fear of missed opportunity has come back to life. That's an important observation.

Where Did the Unease Go?

Just a short while ago, I believed investors had been sufficiently traumatized that the willingness to bear risk would be absent for years. But it came back in just a matter of months. What explains that?

For one thing, the crisis - as painful as it was - was surprisingly brief. The worst of it began in the third quarter of 2008 with the disclosure of weakness at financial institutions. The onset of the most intense part of the crisis can be dated to Lehman Brothers' September 15 bankruptcy filing. Remarkably, high yield bonds began to recover just three months later, with most of the indices showing gains of roughly 5% for the month of December. So, in the credit markets, the worst pain lasted only about three months and quickly gave way to recovery.

And what kicked off the recovery? Fear of missing opportunity was resurrected by the Fed and other central banks which forced interest rates on short-term government debt to near zero. It might have been the banks' intent, or it might have been an unintended consequence, but those low rates pushed investors to engage in riskier behavior. The returns on T-bills and money market funds went to a fraction of a percent, meaning investors had to crawl out on the limb in pursuit of returns they could live with.

Further, governments flooded the system with liquidity and produced the opposite of crowding out. When governments are big issuers of debt, it can be hard for non-government issuers to raise money. But when governments are big buyers of securities instead, the capital they inject into the markets can make it easy for others to issue securities.

> Investors flooded risky companies with money in March even as the government prepares to shut down a key engine driving one of the greatest corporate-bond rallies in history.
>
> A total $31.5 billion in new high-yield debt, otherwise known as junk bonds, hit the market through Tuesday, exceeding the previous monthly record in November 2006. Partly propelling

the activity: The Federal Reserve's massive mortgage-buying program (which recently came to an end).

By buying $1.25 trillion of mortgage securities, the Fed absorbed a flood of assets that otherwise would have needed buyers. That kept money in the hands of investors, who went searching for something else to buy. The Fed's underpinning encouraged investors to seek riskier, higher-yielding securities. A natural choice: corporate bonds. (*"Bonds Cap Epic Comeback,"* The Wall Street Journal, March 31).

One of the prime tasks investors must perform is to stay alert to extreme behavior and take hints as to what we should do from what we see taking place around us. This is best expressed in Warren Buffett's helpful reminder: *"The less prudence with which others conduct their affairs, the greater the prudence with which we should conduct our own affairs."*

Investor behavior between 2003 and mid-2007 was sending some very worrisome signals. It's obvious, in retrospect, that all one had to do was take heed and lean in the opposite direction. But observations regarding the past are no help for purposes other than education. For observations to be profitable, they must relate to the present and the future.

Investors have made a substantial move back in the direction of pre-crisis behavior. That behavior has to be recognized and monitored. The pendulum has moved away from the depression, panic, skepticism and excessive risk aversion we saw in the fourth quarter of 2008, and with the disappearance of those characteristics have gone the great bargain opportunities.

Uncertainty and fundamental weakness at the depth of the crisis were offset by irrationally low prices and the potential for a rebound in risk tolerance, making most assets a screaming buy. With most of the great bargains gone - along with excess risk aversion - macro uncertainties should no longer be overlooked. Thus, the caution, discipline, patience, selectivity and discernment that were so unnecessary in 2009 are absolutely essential today.

* * *

Investing defensively requires that when everything seems to be going well and investors are feeling positive, we must sense the implicit danger and prepare for negative developments.

In the mid-2000s, I began to warn that with asset prices full, investors optimistic and their behavior aggressive, it was important to worry about things that could come along to derail the markets. When asked what they might be, my list of possibilities would go like this:

- recession
- credit crunch
- $100 oil
- collapse of the Dollar,
- exogenous events such as terrorist attacks, or
- something else

The most dangerous possibility, I pointed out, was the last one. Markets and market participants can adjust to things they see coming. What usually knocks them for a loop are things they don't anticipate. *"We're not expecting any surprises"* is one of my favorite oxymorons. By definition, surprises are things that aren't anticipated, and thus their arrival can be traumatizing.

In January 2010, I published a memo called *"Tell Me I'm Wrong,"* in which I listed a number of things that worried me. These included our reliance on government stimulus and artificially low interest rates; the uncertain outlook for consumer spending, jobs and state and municipal finances; and the risks pertaining to inflation, exchange rates and interest rates. *Here's how I concluded:*

> My goal in this memo isn't to express a forecast. I know that no forecast - and certainly not mine - is likely to be correct. What I do want to do is caution that the considerable risks I see may be less than fully appreciated by those setting asset prices today. The greatest market risks lie in failure of the macro economy to live up to the expectations embodied in today's prices. . .
>
> Most people view the future as likely to repeat past patterns,

which it may or may not do. They tend to think of the future in terms of a single scenario, whereas it really consists of a wide range of possibilities. (Remember Elroy Dimson's trenchant observation that *"risk means more things can happen than will happen."*) And to the extent they do consider a variety of possibilities, few people include ones that haven't been part of recent experience.

The uncertainties discussed above tell me today's distribution of possibilities has a substantial left-hand (i.e. negative) tail, probably greater than at most times in the past. The proper response should be to discount asset prices, allowing a substantial margin for error. Forecasts should be conservative, yield spreads should incorporate ample risk premiums, valuation parameters should be below the long-term norms, and investor behavior should be prudent.

Conspicuously missing from my list of worries was Greece (and all it entails); thus it falls firmly in the category of *"something else."* When the crisis broke it dominated the headlines and depressed markets worldwide. Thus, in this short time, I have proved two things: first, I know little more than others about what the future will bring and, second, when most investors turn optimistic, it becomes important to worry.

The issue of Greece and its debt has been on investors' radar screens for months, but few people seem to have understood its ramifications and the risks it presented to the markets. Then, in recent weeks, things began to be discussed daily in the media - such as Greece's profligacy and the risks involved in admitting it to the European Union; Europe's lack of an established mechanism for dealing with a problem of this nature; and its reliance on Germany to contribute voluntarily to a solution - that, in hindsight, it seems should have been obvious. This tells us a few important things about investing:

- Investors generally overestimate their ability to see the future, and the worst of them act as if they know exactly what lies ahead.

- It's important to worry about what's coming next. The fact that we don't know what it is shouldn't permit us to think there's nothing to worry about.
- Low asset prices allow us to invest aggressively, without much consideration given to worrisome fundamentals and the possibility of negative surprises. But as prices rise, so should our degree of concern over these things.

The bottom line is this: the fact that we don't know where trouble will come from shouldn't allow us to feel comfortable in times when prices are full. The higher prices are relative to intrinsic value, the more we should allow for the unknown.

The recovery of 2009 in the face of significant fundamental uncertainty meant that the markets were reincorporating optimism and were, thus, vulnerable to surprise and disappointment. This, in itself, should be sufficient to induce caution.

Howard's charity of choice is the Marks Family
Writing Center at the University of Pennsylvania.

Penn helped Howard hone his writing skill and enabled him to write things
like *"Warning Flags."* Therefore he funds the writing center out of gratitude.

CHAPTER TEN

-

"Great men, like comets, are eccentric in their courses,
and formed to do extensive good
by modes unintelligible to vulgar minds."

Charles Caleb Colton

Opportunities in the Distressed Debt Market
Marc Lasry

*"Patience, available capital, and careful due diligence
are likely to prove the name of the game."*

About the Author

Marc Lasry is the Chairman, Chief Executive Officer and a Co-Founder of Avenue Capital, a global hedge fund that manages assets valued at approximately $19 billion and specializes in distressed investments. Distressed investing has been the focus of Marc's professional career for over 24 years.

Prior to founding Avenue Capital in 1995, Marc served as the Co-Director of Bankruptcy and Corporate Reorganization Department at Cowen & Company and the Director of Private Debt Department at Smith Vasiliou Management Company.

Marc also clerked for the Honorable Edward Ryan, former Chief Bankruptcy Judge of the Southern District of New York.

Marc received a B.A. in History from Clark University and a J.D. from New York Law School.

Opportunities in the Distressed Debt Market

In the spring of 2009, on the cusp of the worst financial crisis since the great depression and amid widespread fears that the global markets were spiralling toward a full-scale depression, Marc Lasry sat down to record his thoughts on the perilous state of the markets and its unprecedented risks and opportunities.

***

I've spent virtually my entire career in distressed investing. I began my career at Cowen & Company in 1987 and left in 1989 to form Amroc Investments, L.P. In 1995, I co-founded Avenue Capital Group with $7 million in assets with my sister, Sonia Gardner. Avenue currently manages three dedicated distressed debt strategies focused on the U.S., Europe and Asia, as well as several smaller strategies.

Much has already been written about the global market meltdown of 2008, the ongoing massive deleveraging and asset re-pricing, and the long-term effects this may have on economic redevelopment and recovery. Against this backdrop, the question on everyone's mind is: *"When is the bottom?"* Yet amid this carnage, and a recession that will persist through 2009 and likely longer, we are beginning to see the first stages of recovery in certain sectors of the corporate credit markets. For those investors with the ability to effectively apply both fundamental and quantitative analysis in the identification of *"good company/bad balance sheet"* situations, and also have long-term capital, this distressed cycle will present the best opportunity I have seen in over 23 years of investing in this space.

There are three main reasons this distressed cycle is unique and unprecedented. First, largely as a result of the LBO boom, years of excess liquidity, and the explosive growth of derivatives, the size of both the leveraged loan and high yield markets is now over $2.5 trillion. With record amounts of debt outstanding, limited liquidity and risk-adverse markets, there is an increased likelihood of future defaults. Moreover, as opposed to the previous distressed cycle, which was characterized by industry-specific effects (e.g. technology), and by isolated instances of fraud (e.g. Enron, WorldCom), the current cycle spans all industries; from financial institutions to the auto industry, real estate, retail, and the list goes on; further widening the potential opportunity set. Finally, the difficult market of the past year-and-a-half has reshuffled the key players: former investment banks' once-powerful proprietary trading desks have closed down. In addition, there are fewer providers of credit and substantially less competition to buy quality assets at attractive prices. For survivors with capital and distressed expertise, I believe the investment opportunities in this cycle are unprecedented.

There are a few factors that help explain why the opportunities in this distressed cycle are unique. During the leveraged buyout "LBO" fever of the past five years, the loan market displaced the high yield market, as higher valuations of companies were debt-financed in the form of loans (particularly second-lien loans). From 2002-2007, new issue LBO loans grew over nine-fold to $295 billion (falling to just $37 billion at year-end 2008). The total U.S. leveraged loan market grew over 120% between 2002 and 2008, totalling $1.6 trillion at December 31, 2008. This compares to a U.S. leveraged loan market size of $734 billion in 2002, and only $150 billion in 1993. Debt-to-EBITDA ratios for all U.S. LBOs increased substantially from 3.9x in 2002 to 6.0x in 2007 (falling to 4.8x last year). The U.S. high yield market also grew substantially in the past few years, reaching $928 billion by year-end 2008. The sizeable derivatives market has further magnified high yield investment opportunities, with the Depository Trust Clearing Corporation ("DTCC") estimating the size of the credit products market to be $25.5 trillion, while the single-name CDS market to be over $14.8 trillion.

Growth over the past several years in both the high yield and leveraged loan market was driven by a combination of banks providing inexpensive financing and, in large part, by demand from non-traditional investors that are recent entrants to this market, including structured credit vehicles (e.g. collateralized loan obligations ("CLOs") and collateralized debt obligations ("CDOs")), and hedge funds. The increasing demand triggered deterioration in credit quality as increasing amounts of lower-quality debt were issued in both the high yield and leveraged loan markets. This supply-demand imbalance gave borrowers greater negotiating power and increased bank debt issuance with weak or no covenant protection for lenders ("*covenant-lite loans*"). Consequently, unlike previous distressed cycles, borrowers have more lenient terms before they trigger loan defaults. On average, recoveries on both bonds and loans will be lower in this cycle, making solid credit analysis more important. Professor Edward I. Altman of New York University's Salomon Centre estimates an average recovery rate of 24.3% in 2009 for high yield bonds, compared to a weighted-average recovery rate of 42.5% in 2008 and a historic average of 45.1%. Overall recovery rates for leveraged loans fell to 53.9% in 2008, from the 2007 average of 88.7% and the long-term average of 69.56%. Loans are likely to be the fulcrum debt tranche in the capital structure in most restructurings. As a result, fundamental due diligence and the ability to accurately assess relative value will be more important than in previous distressed cycles.

Through the end of 2011, nearly $222 billion of sub-investment grade bonds and loans come due, and over $1.25 trillion through 2014. However, as the financial crisis worsened, risk appetites were significantly reduced, and capital has become substantially more difficult and expensive for companies to obtain. Due to the lack of liquidity in the financial markets, there will be far fewer opportunities for refinancing, which will force many "*good*" companies with strong fundamentals to default or file for bankruptcy. The technical sell-off driven by massive deleveraging has also indiscriminately punished companies, driving prices to record lows. Furthermore, CLO funds, which had been a major source of loan demand over the last five years, are now unwinding at a fairly steady pace, as these vehicles were not designed for a deleveraging environment experiencing a credit crisis. According to S&P LCD, CLOs purchased nearly two-thirds of the debt issued by the $616 billion of LBOs brought to market in the first half of 2007. This spigot has been turned off. In the current market, many CLOs are forced to unload large amounts of loans that have declined significantly in value to avoid breaching covenants, putting further pressure on loan prices. This creates a large supply of attractive opportunities for distressed investors, with the dry powder and acumen to provide financing at very favorable terms, whether in the financial services sector, the auto sector, or more broadly.

The sharp increase expected in default rates also serves as an indicator of the significant expected quantity of the opportunity set in this cycle. Professor Altman forecasts a 13.6% consensus average default rate for year-end 2009, and S&P projects a 13.9% default rate by January 2010, the highest ever in its 28-year series history. While the January default rate of 4.7% (S&P) still trailed these forecasts substantially, bond prices are already reflecting expected defaults for many issuers. This is evidenced by the distress ratio (the percentage of U.S. high yield bonds trading over 1,000 BPS over comparable Treasuries), which climbed to 82% at year-end of 2008, up from 40% in the third quarter and 10% at year-end 2007.

Another way to view the current distressed market opportunity is to look at trends observed by Professor Altman in past cycles. If we take his 13.6% projected default rate for year-end 2009, the implied par value of bonds that will default this year alone would be nearly $150 billion - far higher than the $51 billion that defaulted during the 1989-1992 cycle and approaching the $200 billion total observed in the previous 2001-2003 cycle. Furthermore, taking the ratio of total claims of companies in Chapter 11 to total defaulted bond debt of 3.1x over the last 20 years, and applying that to the $150 billion expected in defaults for 2009, the implied amount of claims in bankruptcies to file this year alone could be over $460 billion, approaching the $475 billion of claims that filed during the past two cycles.

We are beginning to see the first stages of some recovery in the credit markets. TED spreads (defined as the difference between three-month U.S. Treasuries and three-month LIBOR), moved to their widest levels in history on October 10, 2008, reaching 464 BPS following Lehman Brothers' default on September 15th, as banks were reluctant to lend either overnight or for term. As central banks have flooded the market with liquidity, interbank lending liquidity has gradually returned, and TED spreads have fallen to about 104 BPS, similar to levels before Lehman's bankruptcy. The investment grade market has tightened significantly and issuance is on the rise

- $132 billion was already issued in January, the largest single-month issuance ever, and $324 billion has been issued this year through mid-March. High-quality high yield issues are also starting to recover, with BB spreads tightening 13% since the start of the recession, and high yield issuance increasing due to demand from high yield mutual funds. The bank loan market has also started to improve slightly; one widely used measure, the Credit Suisse Leveraged Loan Index posted a record 5.78% return in January, up from its worst return of -13.04% in October of last year. The next stages of a recovery in the credit markets are likely to be the opening of the bank loan market, outperformance of higher quality, lower-rated high yield issuers (B-CCC), outperformance in the distressed index and distressed debt-like investments, and finally, outperformance for equity-like tranches of fulcrum distressed securities as equity valuations improve across the board.

The technical issues that contributed significantly to the indiscriminate selling and massive mark-to-market losses are beginning to abate, and we are beginning to see some re-direction in the markets. Banks have received hundreds of billions of Dollars in bailout capital and have begun to sell their distressed exposure from their prop desks and trading desks. The pipeline of *"hung"* bridge loans has been reduced from over $200 billion in 2007 to under $20 billion, as the loans were either cleared at discounts or deals were cancelled.

One of the most challenging aspects of this distressed cycle is getting the timing right. In past recessions, default rates typically began their upward trend two years (on average) prior to the start of the recession. In this cycle, however, the invention of covenant-lite loans has essentially served to delay defaults. At present, the increase in default rates essentially coincided with the start of the recession, as opposed to preceding it. As a consequence, this cycle will take longer to play out and returns are not likely to pick up until after defaults peak. Investors will need to be diligent in their credit work and prudent in deploying capital to the most attractive opportunities.

In Asia, where Avenue is one of the largest investors in the distressed market (outside of Japan), the challenge is navigating the complex legal systems unique to each country, many of which are neither very creditor-friendly nor predictable. Skilled investment teams with legal expertise and strong local relationships to source attractive opportunities (many of them private deals) dictate the level of success a firm can enjoy at this point in time investing in Asia.

While the ensuing global meltdown has not affected Asia as much as the last Asian crisis of the late '90s, different countries are reacting differently. The more developed countries - Japan, Korea, Hong Kong, Singapore and Taiwan, those with a greater focus on exports - have all been hard hit, while countries such as Indonesia and the Philippines have fared relatively well. In contrast to the U.S., non-performing loans (NPLs) form a large part of the distressed opportunity in Asia, as well as private loans, particularly those tied to hard assets such as real estate, natural resources, and plants and equipment. Currently, we are seeing very attractive opportunities in these non-performing loans (NPLs) and distressed situations, and are still focused on staying senior in the capital structure.

The European markets have been plagued by similar problems as the U.S. - over-levered, aggressive capital structures; banking failures; a large LBO overhang and covenant-lite loans; and forced selling by non-economic sellers - which are creating a unique landscape for distressed investing. Currency issues have played a role in the deteriorating economic conditions across Europe, and Basel II's capital requirements, which began to take effect last year, are forcing banks to offload riskier loans from their balance sheets.

While the size of the high yield and leveraged loan markets is smaller in Europe than in the U.S., the relative lack of competition and the greater relative issuance of bank loans in Europe differentiate the two. Bank loans in Europe account for approximately 80% of the credit market compared to approximately 65% in the U.S., making proprietary sourcing and local networks in Europe paramount to successful investing.

In Europe, we focus on senior secured debt of high-quality single corporate credits at prices ranging from 30 to 70 cents-on-the-Dollar, with the goal of generating equity-like returns with relatively limited downside risk. As high yield bond default rates are also expected to rise sharply in Europe (with Moody's forecasting a 12.5% default rate by the end of 2009 compared to 1.3% in November 2008), it is likely that there will be plenty of promising new opportunities unfolding. In addition, rescue financing should become increasingly attractive over the next 12 to 18 months as capital continues to be scarce and good companies with bad balance sheets need to restructure.

While the current distressed opportunities appear to be significant, today's environment is sobering. The absence of available financing, the deterioration of corporate earnings, and the problems in the banking industry have resulted in massive write-downs on company valuations. For most, the future will be about survival and those who make it through are likely to be rewarded with possibly the best distressed investing opportunities of their lifetimes. Having been through past distressed cycles, we are confident that there will be very promising opportunities to be sourced within this rubble, including those in distressed debt, bankruptcy situations, debt restructurings, merger arbitrage and the like. Patience, available capital, and careful due diligence are likely to prove the name of the game.

This article first appeared in the HedgeFund Intelligence Global Review 2009, and, with minor revisions, is reprinted here with the permission of that publication.

**Marc Lasry is giving his share of the profits
from this book to the Mount Sinai Hospital**

Mount Sinai Hospital was founded in 1852 and remains one of the oldest, largest, and most respected hospitals in the nation. It is located on the eastern border of Central Park and it serves the entire population of New York City and beyond. In 2008 alone, Mount Sinai treated nearly 60,000 inpatients and accommodated approximately 530,000 outpatient visits. In 2009, Mount Sinai Hospital was named one of the best hospitals in the United States by the U.S. News & World Report.

CHAPTER ELEVEN

-

"The free market punishes irresponsibility; Government rewards it."

Harry Browne

Bob Farrell's Market Rules
David Rosenberg

"Pity the poor public. Just as shoe-shine boys were net long ahead of the Wall Street crash, so too the general public are effectively doomed to be part of the herd in financial markets. "

About the Author

David Rosenberg is the Chief Economist & Strategist at Glushkin Sheff with a focus on providing a top-down perspective to the Firm's investment process and Asset Mix Committee.

Mr. Rosenberg received both a Bachelor of Arts and Masters of Arts degree in Economics from the University of Toronto.

Prior to joining Gluskin Sheff in 2009, Mr. Rosenberg was Chief North American Economist at Bank of America- Merrill Lynch in New York and prior thereto, he was a Senior Economist at BMO Nesbitt Burns and Bank of Nova Scotia.

From 2001 to 2008, Mr. Rosenberg was ranked first in economics in the Brendan Wood International Survey for Canada, ranked second overall in the 2008 Institutional Investors Survey for the U.S., and was on the Institutional Investor All American All Star Team from 2005-2008. Mr. Rosenberg also ranked 4th out of 104 economists in the 2009 Thomson-Extel survey of global portfolio managers.

Bob Farrell's Market Rules
David Rosenberg

"Bob Farrell is a Wall Street legend and has a well-deserved reputation as the dean of stock market research."

William Schreyer, (as) Merrill Lynch chairman, 1982

Bob Farrell is one of the few men for whom the epithet *"living legend of technical analysis"* is an appropriate moniker. Joining Merrill Lynch as a junior analyst in 1957, he began deploying multiple facets of fundamental and particularly technical analysis, coupling these with investor sentiment data (at the time a completely new innovation) to endeavour to better understand how markets, collectively, and stocks, individually, would move. He retired after a 25-year career with Merrill Lynch as Chief Stock Market Analyst in 1992, having been in the forefront of market analysis during the *"go-go"* market of the late 1960s, the brutal bear market of 1973-1974 as well as the bull market of 1982 and the crash of 1987, amongst others. Institutional Investor Magazine ranked Farrell the top analyst in "predicting changes in overall stock market direction" an incredible 16 years out of 17 between 1975 and 1992. During his lengthy career Farrell created and refined his 10 *"Market Rules to Remember."*

David Rosenberg subsequently came to repeatedly occupy the Institutional Investors all-stars list during his tenure as a senior analyst at Merill Lynch, deploying the Farrell doctrine to great effect, such as his (initially ridiculed) predictions of a housing price collapse in the US during the mid-1990s.

David outlined the Farrell rules as follows:

1. Markets tend to return to the mean over time

This rule is fairly self-explanatory. Whenever stocks go too far in one direction, they always manage to find a way to return back to their previous levels. Mean reversion is commonplace throughout stock market history whether it is the booms of the railway age and the robber baron era or the dotcom bubble and meltdown in more recent times. I cannot think of a single time when we did not see an extreme in the ratios whether it is Price/Earnings, Price/Book, or the dividend yield becoming over-valued without it then returning back to much more normal levels - usually with a rather sickening thud of bear market activity. No matter how we look at it, expectations on returns can often become extreme and usually are unfulfilled. Ultimately, no matter what the ratio of the stock market to GDP, a form of financial gravity comes to bear on the market and we return to more sensible long-term averages on all key ratios. The most important issue is to keep a clear head and try not to become overly wrapped up in the prevailing euphoria or pessimism of the crowd. Admittedly this is one of the greatest challenges any investor faces as it is very difficult not to become overly optimistic or essentially defeatist when faced with a barrage of media and public statements to those effects as bull and bear markets grind on to their ultimate extremes.

2. Excesses in one direction will lead to an opposite excess in the other direction

In many respects we can consider markets to be a little bit like an elastic band attached to a fixed baseline. Markets rarely (if ever) manage to move neatly from point A to point B. They do so with a lot of relatively volatile zigzag movements. As markets become more extreme, the marketplace will usually not merely revert to the mean, as we mentioned above, but, in fact, overshoot in the opposite direction. Note, too, that the overshoot may be prolonged - markets don't always simply overshoot and revert rapidly to the mean. Take the oil market for instance. In 1979, prices were at 30 Dollars per barrel and then a grinding bear market left prices as low as 12 Dollars in 1998 before the market ticked back up to 20 Dollars in 2002. Therefore, crude prices spent the decade of the 1980s and 1990s significantly below the mean price for oil, in real terms. Finally, the death of production growth caused prices to stir and a new dynamic entered the energy market. Thus we had the remarkable upswing between 2003 and 2008 where prices went all the way to 145 Dollars per barrel. In housing, we had the market boosted between 2000-2006 reaching relatively over-valued levels before the market underwent a severe contraction between 2007 and 2010.

The simple truth of markets holds true for this rule as well as the first: as long as we can keep our sense of perspective on the fundamental valuation of markets then we will be much better placed to avoid being sucked in on the wrong side of the ledger when the market is heading towards extremes and about to reverse direction (often violently).

3. There are no new eras - excesses are never permanent

Ronald Reagan famously posited the most dangerous phrase in politics to be *"I'm from the government and I'm here to help"*. In markets, the phrase *"this time it's different"* is the most frightening remark any investor or investment promoter can ever make. From the South Sea Bubble in England, which peaked in 1720, through countless other markets, the message has always been the same. For some reason, new technology, philosophy or different working practices are championed as having created a whole new methodology which has fundamentally changed the world. While it may be true that crop rotation changed the way the world approached agriculture, the simple truth is that such changes have no long-lasting effects on markets which are cyclical entities that ultimately move be-tween excessive under-valuation and excessive over-valuation. The core reason for this is doubtless plain old human psychology which is largely still operating on a basis of survival instincts liberally coated with greed and fear when it comes to approaching investments.

Therefore, humans have a form of permanent shortage belief when it comes to all major market upswings. However, while a season's orange crop may have been endangered by bad weather, the reality is that there will be a new crop soon, thus ensuring that a permanent high plateau is not achieved for oranges or other foodstuffs. Similarly, when it comes to new technology (from railroads to the internet and many iterations in between, such as the automobile) there may be massive leaps of progress but that does not make the stock markets valuations permanent.

However, it is essential, once again, to emphasise the importance of independent thinking. The permanent shortage belief is a hard-wired fear in the human psyche, it seems. Similarly, when the crowd is going in one direction, the truth is that the crowd has no intention of recognising alternative beliefs. In 2004, I published a report pointing to a housing bubble. While somewhat ahead of the subsequent crash, the report was utterly derided by many observers who felt we were clearly in a new era of housing prosperity.

No matter what sector is the *"new new"* thing attracting a lot of hot investment money in its bullish wake, the truth is that ultimately all innovations ultimately become popularised and commoditised, or simply suffer the same gravitational pull that makes them more *"normal"*. BRIC markets boomed and then fell in half, Japan was going to be the greatest economy power of an era but after the go-go 1990s the stock market collapsed and has never been near its all-time highs, even 20 years later. Ultimately, human nature never changes overall, rendering irrelevant the chorus of *"this time it's different"*.

4. Exponential rapidly rising or falling markets usually go further than you think, but they do not correct by going sideways

In my experience, it has become a standard chant of the broking classes that once we have reached a peak then we can expect a new plateau before the market moves further. Studies of historical price action completely refute this. Remember the elastic band I referred to in relation to rule 2. The truth is that markets tend to move violently from peaks and, similarly, can explode upwards from historical troughs. This is the reality of the asset bubble interconnection. In essence, at the peak of the market every buyer is long and thus markets can only dip quite rapidly (if not collapse fully in the very first instance) as there are simply no more buyers in the marketplace. During the 2002-2007 period, the extra lax credit cycle permitted remarkable moves in housing prices to the upside which ultimately peaked, wobbled and soon collapsed into a deep trough.

Similarly, oil has demonstrated a remarkable volatility in recent years, as I mentioned earlier, going from 20 Dollars to 145 Dollars in relatively rapid succession. This is all tied up in the inherent concept of manias and bubbles which is driven by human psychology. Therefore, it is vital to recall that markets do not correct by levelling off. Rather, the leverage of key players drives markets both up and down by greater extremes as the market cannot accommodate buyers and sellers neatly at peaks or troughs. Therefore, we can reiterate the point that markets go to extremes on both the upside and downside. The key in this rule is to understand that the extremes are usually greater than you can rationalise and, indeed, the after-effects of an extreme are usually themselves fairly severe as markets rarely, if ever, pause for breath just below the peaks or above the excessive troughs.

5. The public buys the most at the top and the least at the bottom

Pity the poor public. Just as shoe-shine boys were net long ahead of the Wall Street crash, so too the general public are effectively doomed to be part of the herd in financial markets. Overall that makes for good sense much of the time as, generally, inflationary market trends tend to push valuations up. However, in more extreme markets, following sentiment indicators and being contrarian can be a very profitable skill set against the market crowd. The general public is essentially linear in its appreciation of market valuations while the market itself is anything but linear. The public may think in terms of substitution effects for their groceries in everyday life (i.e. replacing expensive asparagus with spinach) but in markets they hope for a trend and they tend to ride the trend mercilessly until it peaks and reverses. To this end, Woody Allen's definition of a stockbroker as *"someone who invests your money until it is all gone"* can be deemed somewhat educational.

6. Fear and greed are stronger than long-term resolve

The simple fact is that ordinary investors like being reassured that they are part of a crowd. Therefore, crowd values will always make investors more confident, even if the fundamentals that induced their being a member of that crowd have already dissipated. Seeing an unrealised paper profit has been proven in academic studies to make investors more confident and optimistic. Therefore, investors tend to stick with the long crowd on the way up... In the late 1990s, for instance, the wise *"seek value and preserve capital methodology"* for long-term investing was dislodged as the new paradigm Internet technology bubble exploded. The desire to hold as many (leveraged) technology stocks became the norm amongst the crowd as the longer-term resolve of investors to preserve their capital and minimise their risk profiles dissipated amidst a classic *"this time it's different"* stock market surge. Similarly, we saw at the 2002 lows, a feeling that stocks were to be avoided by the masses and the markets promptly began rising rather strongly all the way to the peaks of 2007... at which stage the crowds greed/fear nexus was centred on property leverage and, hey presto, it transpired that we had all been living in a leveraged bubble and not a new paradigm after all...

If we look at March 2009, we see a clear example of how the market abandoned its resolve for fear. The prevailing view was almost unanimously endorsed that the market could only go down... In fact it started a rather sharp rally which lasted for the rest of the year. In the early stages of upswings and at the birth of bubbles, it is common to have a lingering fear amongst many investors which makes them reluctant to enter the marketplace. Retail investors are always the slowest as a group to buy (or sell) in to a new market phase.

Ultimately, you cannot afford to be drawn in to the crowd without thinking and rethinking your reasons for being a member of that group. You must keep reassessing the fundamentals of the situation. If they fail to add up then you're in a market extreme which has lost sight of core valuations.

7. Markets are strongest when they are broad and weakest when they narrow to a handful of blue-chip names

At major peaks the market often becomes obsessed by a relatively few shares. In the dotcom bubble, for instance, the tech stocks of Intel, Microsoft and Cisco were ultimately the most vital in the marketplace. However, this focus on a narrow range of shares always predicts a weak market position overall. Similarly, at the peak of the housing boom in 2007, only 4 major US metropolitan areas, Boston, Charlotte, New York and Seattle were still actually registering highs.

Equally, look at when the marketplace bottomed in the late 1970s. Here there were broad opportunities throughout the stock market to pick up stock at remarkable value. For instance, the broad market had a price/earning ratio of around 7. In motor companies like Ford this ratio was around 3.5. Even in growth stocks such as Merck and Pfizer, the ratios were still in the range of 12-14. Therefore, in 1982, a great bull market kicked off with broad gains across all shares as they represented great long-term value. However, by 2007, the share market had again ended with a narrow range of *"peaking"* stocks which suggested the market was headed for a decline.

Whenever you see the strength in any index concentrated amongst a relatively narrow number of stocks then we can always be confident that there is trouble lying ahead of that marketplace.

8. Bear markets have three stages - sharp down, reflexive rebound and a drawn-out fundamental downtrend

If we look at the last decade, I think we can see clear evidence of this pattern in action. From 2000-2002 we had a sharp drop followed by the reflexive rebound from 2002 to 2007. (Incidentally, to me, this resembled the bounce in the US stock market between 1932-1936 after the Great Crash and its subsequent volatile price action.) Right now I see the market entering into a long-drawn out decline after the rally of 2009.

9. When all the experts and forecasts agree - something else is going to happen

Quite simply, at the top of the market everybody is bullish (and all contrarian analysts can expect widespread ridicule) while at the bottom of the market the crowd is highly bearish and equally views with degrees of contempt any concept that things may be about to improve. Take, for example, the deep strains of pessimism in many of Jimmy Carter's utterances before he left the White House compared to how Ronald Reagan was able to successfully campaign for re-election as the 1980s bull market was gaining ground with his *"it's morning in America"* advertisements.

The greater the trend, the greater the extent will be to which all opinion becomes polarised to the prevailing trend. Often this can be expressed through the broad media. Take, for instance, the classic Business Week front cover with the banner headline *"The Death of Equities"* which was timed just before the prevailing bear market turned and bull market began.

Ultimately, it takes resolve to disagree with such strong prevailing views but whenever you see a broad consensus amongst the experts then it is absolutely clear that the major event will be contrary to their opinions.

10. Bull markets are more fun than bear markets

This is especially true for those who have *"long only"* mandates. Nevertheless, it applies throughout the retail sector as most private investors really only understand the buy and hold concept while a similar, if more complex, effect perpetuates amongst the professional community. For the sell side, bull markets mean higher trading volumes and thus more brokerage. They also mean more IPOs and takeovers and hence much greater fees for all manner of corporate actions. During bear markets, trading volume tends to dry up while deals are few and far between and while IPOs are often all but non-existent. To that end, the sell side far prefers up markets. Even with the advent of more hedge funds and other money managers who can nominally trade both the up and downside of markets, it is fair to say that their overall returns (with some highly honourable exceptions) tend to be much greater in upwards markets than bearish ones. It is fair to say that the particular skill set for being able to trade long/short portfolios may not yet be as commonplace as some might think.

David Rosenberg was speaking with Patrick L Young

David Rosenberg

Has donated his share of the profits to the Canadian Cancer Society

The Canadian Cancer Society web site can be found at:
www.cancer.ca

CHAPTER TWELVE

-

*"...little is ever really new in the world of finance.
The public has a euphoric desire to forget..."*

John Kenneth Galbraith

How Not To Invest In Emerging Markets

Peter Tasker

"When the bubble is up and running all seems perfectly fine and normal. The stock market may be frothing over like a malfunctioning cappuccino machine, but the excesses are matched and appear justified by excesses in the real economy. The true extent of the economic distortion - the mal-investment and hidden leverage - only becomes obvious after the bubble has burst."

About the Author

Peter Tasker is a founding partner of Arcus Investment, a fund management company specialising in Japanese investments.

A long-term resident of Japan, he has written several books, both fiction and non-fiction, mainly dealing with Japan.

How Not To Invest In Emerging Markets

Imagine you are starring in the financial equivalent of the *"Life On Mars"* TV show. You wake up one morning to find you have time-travelled back to the early nineteen-nineties. The Berlin Wall has just fallen. The triumph of capitalism is unleashing a tsunami of globalisation as billions of people join the market economy as workers and consumers.

Exciting times. Having just arrived from the year 2010, you know this has profound implications for the world of investment. Granted, you didn't pay much attention to how markets actually performed in the decades to come, but you sense an opportunity to become very rich. After all, you have the ultimate form of insider information; a sure knowledge of the economic future.

So, you do the obvious thing - you set up a hedge fund. You rack your brains for the best trades to put on. Keep it simple, you tell yourself. Which economy will make the transformation from emerging to developed in the years ahead? South Korea is the obvious choice. You remember that it becomes a member of the OECD and that its GDP per head soars from $6,100 in 1990 to $28,000 in 2010. Most of all, you remember the astonishing success of Korean brands, which screamed from billboards all over the world in 2010, but are largely unknown in 1990. Why, you even used to own a Samsung mobile phone, a flat-screen TV made by LG, and a Hyundai people carrier!

You decide to leverage up and take a large long position in the South Korean stock market. What short position should you set against it? You know that globalisation creates losers as well as winners. You need to find a clear loser. A good candidate, you decide, is Pakistan. All you remember about the country is bad news; the poverty, the social fragmentation, the rise of Islamic fundamentalism, the political assassinations, the failure to modernise. So you do the logical thing. You balance your Korean long with a short on Pakistan and sit back and watch the profits roll in.

Except, of course, they don't. What happens over the next twenty years is that the Korean Kospi index rises a somewhat underwhelming 40% in US Dollar terms. Meanwhile, Pakistan's Karachi 50 Index rises 350% in US Dollars. Unfortunately the final tally is irrelevant to you since your fund blew up long before.

After a few years of hard scrabble, you decide to have another try in 1995. This time, you'll stake everything on the most obvious trade of all - China. You remember year after year of double digit GDP growth; the Beijing Olympics; the transformation of Shanghai from dowdy backwater to hyper-modern global megalopolis. More to the point, you remember how China emerged apparently unscathed from the global credit crisis of 2008; how its insatiable thirst for raw materials buoyed up the commodities markets; how the shift of economic power from west to east was in the minds of thinking people the world over.

So you go long on China - that's a no-brainer. But what to set against it? This time you decide not to short any Asian markets - they are just too dangerous. But there is one continent that was definitely left behind by globalisation, to the extent that Western charities flocked there and rock stars mounted campaigns for debt forgiveness. You remember reading an article in The Economist which discussed the problems of sub-Saharan Africa in detail. Living standards, it said, had actually gone down over the past forty years. A tragic story, but the investment implications are clear. You take out a large short position on the most liquid market, Nigeria.

This time you know you cannot fail. But somehow you do. Incredibly, this trade turns out to be a bigger disaster than the first one. Between 1995 and 2010, the Chinese market rises 450% in US Dollar terms. An annualised gain of 12% - not bad at all. The real damage, however, comes from the performance of the Nigerian market, which rises an astonishing 1200% in US Dollars over the same period.

Having blown up the fund again, you decide to quit investment and set up a software consultancy to profit from the Y2K bug. But why did your

trades go so wrong? What did you miss? You missed the most fundamental point of all. You were not investing in the statistical construction
known as GDP. You were investing in real-world companies with employees and customers and suppliers. The key determinant of investment
returns is the price paid for the asset - its degree of expensiveness or
cheapness in relation to prospective cash flows. Compared to that, whether
GDP growth is 3% or 8% is a trivial issue.

Trivial? Surely not. Surely it is better to invest in countries with high
growth and rising living standards than those going nowhere. You might
think so, but there is no historical support for that view. Academic studies show little relationship between economic growth and investment
returns. If anything, the correlation is slightly negative. Professor Jay
Ritter of the University of Florida is the author of one such study (1) ranging over a hundred years of data from sixteen different countries. His conclusion is clear: *"Countries with high growth potential do not offer good
investment opportunities unless valuations are low"*.

What lies behind this counter-intuitive finding? One plausible reason is
that shares in fast-growing economies are rarely cheap - in other words,
sentiment is too bullish and growth prospects get priced in at an early
stage. This is a version of the growth paradox in individual shares. Ebay,
for example, has been an extraordinary success as a company. As an
investment, though, it has been an unspectacular performer. As of May
2010, the stock price was no higher than in May 1999. It was a case of too
much too young; the company's explosive growth was fully discounted in
the first year after the IPO.

There is another lesson from the dotcom frenzy that casts light on the
relationship between GDP growth and investment returns. The wild-eyed
dotcom gurus of the late nineteen-nineties turned out to be right about
many things. The internet has indeed spread through the world at warp
speed, becoming indispensable to the lives of billions. It has set off a chain
reaction of creative destruction that has devastated *"bricks and mortar"*
companies and made all kinds of goods and services available at the click
of a mouse.

What the dotcommers failed to predict, however, was the difficulty that even the winners would have in monetising their success. The losers, of which there were many, simply fell by the wayside. While the power of the internet was, if anything, underestimated, the quality of the cash flows it would generate was massively overestimated.

Something similar could be said about emerging economies. By definition, they are in a state of flux. The companies that end up winning the struggle for survival may not even exist yet. That was certainly so in the case of Japan's economic miracle. In the 1950s there were more than one hundred motorbike manufacturers. The market leader, Tohatsu, was driven out of business by the cut-throat pricing of a flaky upstart called Honda.

Even the companies that do survive and prosper - the emerging world's emerging champions - are likely to finance their growth by repeatedly raising large amounts of new capital. This is of no benefit to shareholders without an overall improvement in return on capital; repeated dilution means that while the company itself may experience strong growth, on a per share basis, earnings and dividends will follow a much less impressive trajectory. Emerging economies often have large reserves of under-utilised savings and human resources. Mobilising them is both the key to development and the guarantor of mediocre investment returns. Why waste time attempting to raise returns on your existing capital when you can easily access more?

There's nothing new about emerging market bubbles and investment disasters. In fact, the arrival of a new economic power, like the spread of a transformative new technology, seems almost destined to generate bubbles. The American railway boom of the 1870s, Argentina in the 1880s and 1890s, the US again in the 1920s, Japan in the 1980s, South East Asia in the early 1990s, and BRICs in the 2000s - the bubble-bust cycle seems to repeat endlessly.

Why should this be so? Most investors are mostly rational most of the time. To turn them into bubble jockeys you need what the great American economist Hyman Minsky called a *"displacement"*, meaning a shock to prevailing assumptions. A tectonic shift in the global economy occasioned by the rise of a new power is one such displacement. The internet was a technological example of the same phenomenon. Both convince investors that history has changed course and you need to be on the right side of it. This time, you think, it really does feel different. And yet the iron law of investment never changes. If you pay a lousy price, you get a lousy return.

The other indispensable condition is liquidity; lots of it. For small economies, hot money inflows from hyped-up global investors can be enough to do the trick - as was the case with Thailand, Malaysia and other Asian countries in the lead-up to the mid-nineties Asian crisis. For large countries, you need something more powerful - massive amounts of domestic liquidity sloshing around the financial system. This can only occur if monetary policy is too loose for too long, leading to credit creation well beyond the needs of the real economy.

There are various political and social factors that may encourage the preference for super-easy money. One such is the imperative, especially strong in politically fragile countries, to force rapid industrialisation by capture of export markets. The most powerful weapon in the mercantilist armoury is a cheap currency - maintained by pegs or direct intervention in the Forex market - which generates an invisible subsidy to exporters at the expense of everyone else.

Policy-makers cannot control the external value of the currency and domestic interest rates at the same time. By choosing to target a particular exchange rate, they are giving up on matching interest rates to domestic economic conditions. Instead, they are effectively *"importing"* the monetary policy of the country whose currency they are targeting. If there is not much of a difference in the economic fundamentals of the two countries, that will not matter a great deal. The bigger the difference, though, the bigger the consequences.

The Swedish economist Knut Wicksell defined an economy's natural interest rate as equivalent to the rate of nominal economic growth. Two countries with wildly divergent rates of economic growth will have wildly different natural interest rates too. For a high-growth country to import monetary policy from a low-growth country means importing a much lower than natural interest rate.

What happens if interest rates are much lower than natural for an extended period? You get bubble trouble. In fact it was the Euro zone's *"one-size-fits-all"* monetary policy that set off the vicious boom-bust cycle in Greece, Portugal and Spain. For rapidly growing emerging economies the pathology is slightly different. Rather than consumption binges and trade deficits, you are more likely to see capital investment binges and trade surpluses. That means a classier kind of bubble, but a bubble all the same. And when it bursts the consequences are equally, if not more, devastating. Over-capacity, low returns on investment, excessive reliance on external demand - these are problems that cannot be solved by cost-cutting and belt-tightening.

When the bubble is up and running all seems perfectly fine and normal. The stock market may be frothing over like a malfunctioning cappuccino machine, but the excesses are matched and appear justified by excesses in the real economy. The true extent of the economic distortion - the mal-investment and hidden leverage - only becomes obvious after the bubble has burst. As Chinese premier Jiang Zemin said during the Asian crisis of 1997/8, *"wait for the tide to go down to see who's not wearing any swimming trunks"*.

Behind financial bubbles and real economy bubbles there is always a third, invisible, bubble which spawns the other two. That is the intellectual bubble, the *"this time it's different"* psychology, occasioned by Minsky's *"displacement"*. The concept has to be credible - if it is not, experienced investors would not be persuaded. In the case of a world-class bubble, it has to be a key narrative of the era - the subject of best-selling books, opinion columns, political speeches, dinner party conversations and so on. The rise of China, for example, has such power as a narrative because we can see the evidence before us in our daily lives. As an investor, how can you not want to be part of such an epochal event? Isn't it more risky, not to be involved? After all, a lot of highly knowledgeable and eloquent people are very bullish on its prospects. Needless to say, the investment opportunities in Pakistan and Nigeria could never be packaged in such compelling terms.

What does this tell us about investing in emerging economies? Put simply, that the same rules apply as to investing in anything else:

First, emerging markets, especially those with Dollar-linked currencies, are prone to vicious boom-bust cycles. Buy the busts, not the booms.

Second, as Warren Buffett has said, *"you pay a high price for a bullish consensus"*. Conversely, a bearish consensus may obscure attractive valuations. When there's *"blood on the streets"*, you can still lose 100% of your capital, but you may stand to make considerably more.

Third, GDP growth has little, if anything, to do with investment returns. Shoot your inner economist and concentrate on the fundamentals of the companies.

Fourth, beware of narratives. The more eloquent the narrators, the more cautious you should be. If it looks like a bubble and floats like a bubble, then it probably is a bubble.

Emerging markets have gone mainstream as the principles and infrastructure of financial capitalism have spread across the world. Bold investors have been rewarded with extraordinary profits, and there are still many exciting investment opportunities to be found. They just may not be where you think they are.

(1) "Economic Growth And Equity Returns" - Jay R. Ritter, November 2004.

Peter Tasker has chosen the charity:

"Room To Read", which promotes literacy and gender equality in education in developing areas of the world.

The Room to Read web site can be found at:
http://www.roomtoread.org/

CHAPTER THIRTEEN

-

*"Happiness lies not in the mere possession of money,
it lies in the joy of achievement, in the thrill of creative effort."*

Franklin Roosevelt

Broken Deals
Tom Burnett & Linda Varoli

"Investors buying broken deal stocks need not wait for another bid to benefit from the strategy."

About the Authors

Thomas Burnett, CFA, is Vice Chairman and Director of Research at Wall Street Access. Mr. Burnett provides market information and insights to our trading personnel based on 30 years of experience in domestic and international equity trading, risk arbitrage and equity research.

Prior to Wall Street Access, Mr. Burnett held several positions at Merrill Lynch, including managing director in charge of the international equity department, director of research and manager of the risk arbitrage department.

Mr. Burnett is a graduate of Williams College and the Graduate School of Business of Stanford University.

Mr. Burnett holds the Supervisory Analyst designation and the following licenses: Series 86 and 87, 7, 63, 4, 16, 65, 86 and 87.

Linda Varoli, CFA, is Vice President of Merger Arbitrage Research at Wall Street Access (New York).

Broken Deals:
Opportunities at a Discount

During the autumn of 2008, stock market investors were preoccupied with the crescendo of fears that the global financial system was facing its most serious threat since the 1930s depression. Gigantic financial services companies like Lehman and AIG were toppling and the major governments were preparing record levels of financial aid to keep the system afloat. At the end of August, the S&P 500 Index was trading in the 1,275 to 1,280 range. By the end of October (following the Lehman bankruptcy and the AIG bailout), this index had declined to 968. By the end of 2008, the index had traded below 900 and it closed at 903 on December 31, 2008. In the midst of this financial market turmoil, investors owning shares of SanDisk Corporation (SNDK) were blessed with the good fortune of a hostile bid for their shares (from Samsung Electronics). Ultimately, the hostile bid was withdrawn, as we discuss below, but the trading history of the SNDK shares during and following this event provides an excellent, real-world example of the value that is often found in *"broken deal"* stocks.

Generally, stocks of merger or takeover targets trade at premium prices compared to their pre-announcement levels. Most acquirers are forced to pay a premium for control of their target companies and this premium leads to sharp target share price declines if a merger proposal or a hostile bid is terminated or withdrawn. Often, these target shares are dumped into the marketplace by traders and speculators and merger arbitrageurs who only owned the shares to participate in a completed merger transaction. This selling pressure, after the *"bad news"* has been released, will generally cause the target shares to trade at prices that are below where the shares were trading prior to the announcement of the merger proposal or hostile bid. In many cases, these *"broken deal"* orphans represent a significant opportunity for courageous value investors looking for opportunities at a discount.

The SNDK events began on September 5, 2008, when various press reports suggested that Korean electronics giant Samsung was about to launch a hostile bid for SNDK. The rumours made some sense, since the companies knew each other and Samsung was under contract to pay SNDK millions of dollars in annual royalties. On September 4, 2008, SNDK shares closed at $13.46 on the NASDAQ system. Trading volume that day was a modest 8.0 million shares. When the press reports hit the market the next day, SNDK traded up sharply, closing at $17.64, some 31% above the prior day's closing price. Trading volume increased dramatically to 54.6 million shares, equal to 24% of the 225 million SNDK shares outstanding. For the next ten days, the SNDK shares traded lower as the market anticipated Samsung's next move. Sure enough, on September 16, the Samsung proposal ($26 per SNDK share in cash) was made public. On the same day, SNDK rejected the hostile bid as too low to reflect the SNDK long-term value. On September 27, the SNDK shares rose to $20.92, some 39% above the previous day's close. Trading volume jumped to 32.1 million shares, almost triple the 12.2 million shares traded on September 16. On September 19, rumours that Toshiba was preparing a competing bid for SNDK sent the shares to a closing price of $22.52. Ominously, volume that day was only 12.0 million shares and, in fact, the $22.52 price would turn out to be the highest closing price for the rest of 2008.

On October 2, Toshiba indicated that it would not be making a bid for SNDK, which helped depress the shares on October 3, when they closed at $18.38, down 11% from the October 2 close. The next key event came on October 20, when SNDK reported a loss of $155 million for its September 2008 quarter. The SNDK shares closed down 8.0% on October 20 at $14.42 on 17 million shares. For SNDK investors, the bad news was delivered after the October 21 close when Samsung announced that it had withdrawn its hostile offer to acquire SNDK. On October 22, SNDK shares closed at $10.09, down 31.8% on volume of 42.6 million shares. For the next five trading days, SNDK shares traded between $7.50 and $10 per share, despite the fact that SNDK reported cash and investments of $2.6 billion against debt of $1.22 billion and that the SNDK book value per share on September 30, 2008, was $21.56. Clearly, the SNDK shares' trading level in late October was not only below the pre-deal announcement level, but also below several fundamental value measures that would later be seen as quite attractive. Granted, the stock market was falling sharply and the Philadelphia Semiconductor Index (SOX) was down to 212 in late October from 350 in early September, but the SNDK shares were clearly being tossed into the discount bin by holders disappointed with the failure of the Samsung proposal.

For the next month, the SNDK shares traded in a range of $5 to $10, with a closing low of $5.32 on November 20, 2008. On that date, the SOX index also bottomed, closing at the 171 level. The SNDK shares quickly rallied, however, and they traded above $10 by mid-December before selling off in early 2009, along with the overall market. The $5.32 low price was never touched again and the shares rallied to $15 in late April 2009. Participating in the strong stock market recovery, the SNDK shares rallied throughout 2009, closing at $22.85 on October 22, one year after Samsung dropped its bid. By year-end 2009, SNDK was trading at $28.99. In early 2010, a sharp rally carried the SNDK shares higher, eventually reaching $44.80 in late April. From the November 2008 low to the April 2010 high (an 18-month period), the SNDK shares rose by a multiple of more than eight times.

We summarize these key SNDK events below:

Date	SNDK Closing Price	Event
September 4, 2008	$13.46	Last day before Samsung rumours
September 5, 2008	$17.64	Samsung bid rumours begin
September 17, 2008	$20.92	Samsung bid/SNDK rejects bid
September 19, 2008	$22.52	Toshiba bid rumours begin
October 3, 2008	$18.38	Toshiba announces it will not bid for SNDK
October 20, 2008	$14.42	SNDK reports loss
October 22, 2008	$10.09	Samsung drops bid
November 20, 2008	$5.32	Annual low price
December 31, 2008	$9.60	Rally off bottom
April 30, 2009	$15.72	Recovery off market low
October 22, 2009	$22.85	One year from Samsung dropping bid
December 31, 2009	$28.99	Year-end close
April 26, 2010	$44.61	Subsequent high price

While the SNDK example stands out as a particularly attractive opportunity surfacing during the recent turmoil in the financial markets, there are many other former *"target"* stocks which also rallied sharply off their post-termination prices. Many of these companies were later acquired at prices substantially above the levels where they traded after the first merger proposal was called off. For example, the Bain proposed merger with 3Com (COMS) was terminated on March 20, 2008, due to regulatory issues (the U.S. government could not get comfortable with the participation of a Chinese company in the merger) and the COMS shares traded below $2.00 for several months, eventually bottoming at $1.53 on November 21, 2008. From that low point, the COMS stock price rose steadily until Hewlett-Packard announced a cash merger agreement at $7.90 per COMS share on November 11, 2009. That transaction closed on April 13, 2010, but COMS holders who purchased shares below $2.00 in 2008 could have sold in November 2009, after the $7.90 proposal was announced, at a very large profit. At the time of the COMS merger termination in the March-April 2008 period, the latest Form 10-Q report for the February quarter disclosed that COMS cash and investments exceeded its outstanding debt and the COMS book value equalled $2.80 per share. Despite the negative influence of the merger termination on COMS, the company's balance sheet indicated the presence of a value cushion which proved to be realistic as the stock price recovered and the company became a successful merger target in late 2009.

Investors buying broken deal stocks need not wait for another bid to benefit from the strategy. One further example, similar to the SNDK experience, is provided by Alpha Natural Resources (ANR), whose merger agreement with Cliffs Natural Resources was terminated on November 17, 2008. From a high price above $104 in July 2008, the ANR shares plunged to a low of $14.68 (closing price) on November 20, 2008. By year-end 2008, ANR shares had rallied to the $16.20 level and, six months later, on June 30, 2009, ANR shares closed at $26.27. By year-end 2009, ANR shares were trading above $43 and they closed above $49 on March 31, 2010. To be sure, the rally in ANR shares was greatly assisted by the sharp equity market rally. But the strategy of buying depressed, broken deal stocks can help investors to identify candidates that would be likely to recover on their own or as part of a broad market rally.

This strategy depends on an active merger environment from which *"broken deal"* stocks will emerge. When merger activity slows down, then terminations are less frequent and opportunities to use the strategy are reduced. We present below a table summarizing merger termination announcements for 2007, 2008 and 2009.

Number of Mergers Announced That Were Later Terminated
($500 million minimum size)

2009	2008	2007
14	43	60

Source: Bloomberg

According to this table, there were 60 large merger or acquisition proposals that were announced in 2007 and later called off (the actual termination date may have occurred in a later year). Clearly, there have been ample opportunities to deploy this strategy over the past three years. No investment strategy should be employed in an automatic manner and not all broken deal targets have performed well after the merger termination date. This strategy is best utilized as a screening device that will often turn up attractive investment candidates that merit further investor scrutiny. Only if the investor can get comfortable with the target's management, business outlook and financial structure should he/she go forward with a purchase commitment. This screening/discovery function can be useful, however, in alerting investors to an attractive investment that they otherwise might have missed amid the flurry of negative news that normally surrounds the announcement of a merger agreement termination.

We have also reviewed the strategy of buying the acquirer's stock in a broken deal. This is admittedly a much smaller universe, as many deals involve LBO firms or management of a company, which are not publicly traded. However, our review of a selected universe of terminated mergers (involving the purchase of publicly traded companies with a market capitalisation of over $500 million) between June 1999 and December 2008, indicates that this strategy does not perform nearly as well overall than buying the target companies in broken deals. Again, each situation is unique and the factors surrounding the termination of an individual merger must be analysed to determine whether the acquirer's stock is a good candidate for investment. In addition, the stock of acquiring companies often *"pops"* significantly in the day or two after a merger is terminated (partly due to short-covering by arbitrageurs in the event of a merger that involved stock of the acquirer being issued), so investors should consider waiting a short period after the termination of a merger to invest in the acquirer.

Overall, we find that monitoring announcements of termination of mergers can be an effective screening method for discovering undervalued companies, as we have found that (on average, over the long-term) the returns from this strategy are better than the market returns (using the S&P 500 Index as a gauge of the market). However, investors must keep in mind the varied reasons why mergers are terminated in considering whether to invest in the target or acquirer post-termination. The reasons for termination can vary from resistance to a hostile bid (as in the SNDK-Samsung situation); financial issues at the acquirer (as in the Tyco-CR Bard merger) or target; regulatory disapproval (as in the Sprint-Worldcom and US Air-United mergers); a third-party offer for the acquirer or target; or problems in the overall financial markets (as occurred in several LBO situations in 2007 and 2008), and these reasons must be factored into the investment decision.

Tom Burnett and Linda Varoli have chosen to donate to the:

"Union Settlement Association" in New York City which is closely involved in helping low income immigrants and their families adjust to urban life.

The Union Settlement Association web site can be found at:
www.unionsettlement.org/

CHAPTER FOURTEEN

-

All politicians are Keynesians in times of economic duress.
"For Faust, the lure of Mephistopheles' services is greatly enhanced
by the fact that the price albeit a terrible one is to be paid later.
For politicians, the lure of the support obtained through public
expenditure is similarly enhanced by the fact that the public
debt will be paid (or reneged) by next generations,
often well after the end of one's political career."

Tommaso Padoa-Schioppa

Andrew M Lees
In Search of Energy

"It is the relationship between energy and the economy that is vital to understanding how we should invest. We can measure the cost of energy very easily, but what is more difficult to calculate is the value of energy."

About the Author

Initially on the Buy Side, Andy Lees' early career baptism saw both the 1986 Big Bang and the subsequent '87 crash. In 1993 he decided to move to the Sell side, joining Warburgs with the aim of developing its derivatives exposure to US clients and to index products.

Following the macro story he has his fingers in many pies, but whereas it is common in this industry for people to touch a subject and then move on, Andy has latched on to certain stories and tried to develop themes and understandings as his own. By breaking things down to the lowest common denominator rather than hiding behind the veil of complex terminology and models that a lot of his competition use, he can often see connections that are at first perhaps not obvious. This has often put him in conflict with the more conventional view, but has earned him an extensive client base, to whom Andy is extremely grateful not only for their business but also for the ideas and directions they have pushed him into.

Despite expecting major upheaval over the next 25 years, Andy remains as committed as ever to understanding what is going on, and to hopefully influencing what is going on as per his decision to direct any proceeds from this book to ITER.

In Search of Energy

Economics has long been viewed as the *"dismal science"*, a reputation that the 2007/2008 credit crunch will have reinforced. Debt had been accumulating for many years, with the return on that debt also falling. The western economies had outsourced their jobs to Asia, but had failed to either compensate with productive domestic employment or with reduced consumption. Instead, a house of cards was built, with US domestic consumption increasingly financed by foreign capital, directed by banks.

Capital was allocated inefficiently. The US yield curve, describing the higher return demanded by investors for tying up capital over a longer period of time, inverted in 2005 and remained so until late 2007. This had always indicated a forthcoming recession as it implies that banks, which borrow at the short end and lend at the long end, are losing money and, therefore, have to withdraw credit. Unfortunately the banks thought it was different this time. They thought that they were no longer in the business of lending, instead packaging up loans and selling them to third parties for a fee. What they had foolishly misunderstood was that these third parties would also need a positive yield curve to make money, and that they were actually borrowing from the banks' prime broking divisions to finance the purchases. Even more surprising, the majority of the counterparties buying these securities were special purpose vehicles set up and owned by the banks themselves, but kept off balance sheet. It was clearly a failure of enormous proportions.

The banks thought that they were making money and reported huge profits, but all they were doing was transferring money from their balance sheets into their profit and loss account. They were supporting unproductive investment and consumption on an unprecedented scale, giving the belief of a strong economy. There was plenty of evidence for regulators and central bankers to pick up on such as financial profits becoming a disproportionately large percentage of GDP, and there were plenty of people shouting it from the roof-tops, but unfortunately no-one wanted to listen and so the drunken orgy went on far longer than a lot of us had thought. In the end, it was taken out of the central banks hands and ended by an even bigger force-resource constraint which is where I want to focus my attention.

In 2007 and 2008 food and energy prices started to rise aggressively. Economists dismissed this as irrelevant as these inputs account for a relatively small percentage of GDP. Unfortunately, this goes to the heart of the problem because the related cash flow drain stopped the global growth party in its tracks. It is estimated that there was a nearly five million barrels per day of oil supply shortfall against the market needs. Blackouts started in places like Pakistan and India. Gas shortages in Latin America led to increased use of diesel generators, particularly by the vital mining industries. The US diverted some of its agricultural production to ethanol, adding to a food shortage in various parts of the world. There was simply insufficient food and energy to sustain full economic activity, and so the marginal consumption was squeezed out. Initially it was centred on some of the peripheral countries. Eventually, the weakest link became the heavily indebted US household, which could no longer afford its monthly sub-prime mortgage payments, and so the whole edifice started to collapse.

It is the relationship between energy and the economy that is vital to understanding how we should invest. We can measure the cost of energy very easily, but what is more difficult to calculate is the value of energy. Anecdotal evidence such as the August 2003 blackouts in the United States, where the whole of the Eastern Seaboard ground to a halt, suggests that the value of energy is much higher than its cost. Fossil fuel-based energy is used in every aspect of our production chain, from research and development, through design and manufacture, to operation and, finally, disposal. Things that you wouldn't normally associate with fuel consumption, such as the billions of calculations carried out by computers to analyse weather patterns, for example, can only be done with this enormous energy resource. Cutting through all the complications, economic output is simply the value that we attribute to work done. Measured in calories, about 50 times more work is done by fuels than by labour. Soberingly, most of the calories burned by labour are themselves dependent on fossil fuel-based inputs such as fertilisers and irrigation, without which the estimated carrying capacity of the Earth would be a mere fraction of its present level.

An economy is generally thought to be made up of land, labour and capital, but when you analyse what these actually are, today they are basically derivatives of fossil fuels. The effective size (productivity) of the agricultural land, for example, is about 85% bigger with fuel-based inputs than without and so too, therefore, is the labour force. Capital equipment is also derived from directing energy into the formation of tools rather than end-consumption. Even education is only afforded to us at its present level by fossil fuels lifting us out of the poverty trap, and thereby freeing us from *"survivalism"*. Scientific advancements come from communication, imagination, computer simulation and trial and error, all of which are underpinned by fuel inputs. Ultimately, one hundred percent of economic output is dependent on energy inputs in one form or another, with most of those energy inputs in a modern economy provided by fossil fuels and, to a much lesser degree, other manipulated forms of energy such as hydro, wind and solar.

The cost of energy is the proportion consumed in extracting the fuel from the ground, whilst the value is the economic output derived from the energy. The two are linked by the efficiency of energy extraction. As this efficiency decreases, so the network of capital and technology required to access the fuel will increase. This relationship is crucial to understanding both the present shape of the economy and the energy network. It is also key to understanding how the energy network has evolved and how it will likely develop.

Rather than discuss peak oil where, despite very clear evidence people will argue that black is white, what is not up for debate is that extracting coal, oil and gas from the ground is becoming less efficient. The network of technology and capital required to access the energy is increasing. With oil production, for example, onshore production peaked in 1978 and has gradually declined ever since. Offshore output had to make up the balance, but in recent years we had to rely on lesser forms of oil. By 2008 natural gas liquids - escaping gas from an oil field is put through a centrifuge to collect

273

the tiny droplets of oil - accounted for 11% of world oil or *"liquids"* production, with heavy crude or bitumen comprising 1.8%, tar sands 1.6% and bio-fuels 1.8%. The best way to measure the efficiency of getting the oil out of the ground is to compare the amount of energy that goes into extracting the fuel in terms of capital equipment, etc. with the energy that is returned, i.e. Energy Return on Invested Energy or EROIE.

Overall, the global EROIE mix is thought to be around 20 - for every 1 unit of energy put into the ground, we liberate an additional 20 free units. However, there is a major divergence between different oils and different fuels. Offshore oil production, at around 5 for the North Sea, has a significantly lower EROIE than onshore oil production. The further out to sea and the deeper you go, the more technology and capital is required to extract the oil. The 20% of the tar sands that are surface mined have an EROIE of just 1.7, which would be lower still if we wanted to increase the flow rate as it would need water and other inputs to be transferred from further afield. Moreover, it is debatable whether the 80% of tar sands that are deep underground have a positive EROIE at all as it would need steam injection technology to extract, which explains why there are presently no commercial operations. Corn-based ethanol is also thought to have a very low or possibly negative EROIE. Auditors have recommended that Mexico reduce its stated oil reserves by 7.5 billion barrels because of the very low net recovery rates at its Chicontepec field, which is due to the oil being in very small pockets in the rock structure and at very low pressures. Mexico has so far refused.

The decline rate of production from existing fields is 6.7% per annum, according to the International Energy Agency (IEA), which means that a new Saudi Arabia is required every two years just for production to stand still. Unfortunately the average size of new discoveries is just 20m barrels – average daily consumption is around 85m barrels - compared with nearly 550m barrels in the 1960's and early 1970's, dramatically adding to the cost of production. Even Saudi Arabia's well productivity has fallen 25% between 2005 and 2008 and is down 68% since 1980. With the average new field sufficient to meet just 5.5 hours of world oil demand, the decline rate will accelerate.

The same declining efficiency of extraction is happening in coal and gas. The best seams of coal have been mined already, leaving lower concentrations of coal. High energy anthracite coals have, for all intents and purposes, been exhausted, and bituminious coal is increasingly having to be supplemented with sub-bituminious and lignite coals to meet energy demands. There is a 50% - 60% drop-off in energy per ton between bituminious and lignite coal, which means more effort required to mine, transport, and burn it. As far as gas is concerned, output is being supported by shale gas, whereby the gas is contained in non-porous rocks which require hydraulic fracturing to release the gas. Whilst there are large theoretical reserves, the EROIE is estimated to be around 2.

At a global EROIE of 20, one unit of energy is consumed to liberate 20 free units out of the ground. The cost, therefore, is around 4.8% of the value created from using the fuel, a similar percentage to the *"4% or 5% cost of energy to GDP"* that economists dismiss as insignificant to affecting economic output. The problem is that with the EROIE falling, the size of the energy network is set to rise dramatically as a percentage of the world economy. Even assuming a static production decline rate of 6.7% per annum over the next 10 years, nearly 70% of existing oil output will need to be replaced. Given that we are already turning to very marginal fuels such as the tar sands which have an EROIE of just 1.7, it does not seem too far-fetched to suggest that the global EROIE will fall to around 5 over that time. If that were to happen, the energy network would rise from 4.76% of the global economy to 16.7%. If we were to assume a flat economy, then the energy network would rise by 12.3% pa whilst the rest of the economy would shrink by 1.33% pa.

If we look back to history for evidence of how this would happen, then a very interesting picture arises. The global EROIE has fallen from about 40 in 1990 to about 20 today. That means the energy network has risen from 2.4% to 4.8% of the world economy. The big increase in the energy network did not happen in the North Sea or Alaska, or even the Middle East, but rather in China where its coal production has soared from virtually nothing to almost 50% of world coal production, or in energy equivalent terms, about one-third of world oil production. Not only did the energy network move to China, but it also kept a large proportion of the value added by creating hundreds of millions of new jobs, attracting capital and outsourcing from abroad. Going forward, Brazil has already stated that it will not export any crude oil, only refined product or manufactured goods. Likewise, the Middle East has not increased its oil exports for several years now, instead building up domestic industry so that it can keep more of the value added at home.

At the present relative rate of growth, coal will overtake oil as the world's primary fossil fuel energy source by 2012/2013, a role that it has not enjoyed since the mid 1960s. Oil superseded coal because it has a greater energy density, meaning the concentration of energy is higher and therefore it requires less technology and capital to turn that energy into useful work. For the very same reason, alternative energy has fallen as a percentage of the world fuel mix for the last 200 years, but is now just starting to pick up. The lower energy density has to be compensated for with additional capital and resources, leaving less available for other activities. In the US for, example, it is estimated that based on existing legislation, the country will have to use an additional 206,000 square kilometres of land to meet its 2030 energy requirements, crowding out other industries. This is known as energy sprawl or area inefficiency. On a worldwide basis the maths is simple; to provide the same amount of calories with ethanol as fossil fuels provide would require 50 times as much land and water as we presently use for food production. Even if the US follows through on its ethanol policy, other countries with higher population densities do not have that option open to them. The UK, for example, has already started to offshore its wind farms, but at 2.5 times the cost of onshore wind, it is pricing itself out of the energy market. Beyond 1or 2%, wind and solar power cannot be fed directly into the grid which works in a very tight tolerance zone to safely match demand and supply. Because of the minute by minute variability of wind or solar, the energy will have to be fed into some sort of storage system, and then fed from that back into the grid. The most likely method is using electrolysis to create hydrogen, which would then be combined with carbon dioxide to make natural gas. Unfortunately, there is about a 40% energy loss in the process of turning electricity into hydrogen, a further 25% loss in collecting and combining it with carbon dioxide, and an additional 70% loss in turning that back to electricity.

To compensate for these inefficiencies, greater numbers of wind turbines or solar farms will be required, adding to their demand for land, labour, capital and resources to compensate. If we, once again, look back at recent history for evidence of this, over the last 20 years the growth in the energy network has centred on China. It has been the building of that network which has driven the majority of the global demand for the resources, such as steel, cement and copper, necessary to extract the fuel and to turn it into useful work. Building the network has now started to focus on completely re-plumbing the country to access sufficient water to allow this machine to continue working. China now has the biggest steel industry in the world supporting this network but, despite this, it increasingly has to turn abroad for imports of raw materials, including food. What is more it is exhausting its supply of labour - certainly cheap labour - as it has reached what is known as the Lewis Point. Putting this into perspective, the enormous growth of the Chinese economy has been driven by a relatively small percentage change in the EROIE and a similarly small deterioration in energy density compared with what we now face.

As the EROIE continues to fall, and as the energy density declines, so the energy network will become a larger part of the global economy. This will happen through the relative price of energy rising until it causes demand destruction as per 2007 and 2008. The weakest or marginal demand will be priced out initially, determined by the efficiency of consumption, however, this is likely to be superseded by politics and the geography of the resources. So far the demand that has been priced out has been that financed by debt. Until the West has reduced its reliance on borrowing and has become self-sufficient, it is likely to remain the weak player. As the Greek debacle has shown, investors are far more sensitive to risk now than they were two years ago, withdrawing capital from the markets well before energy starts to act as a constraint. The Greek problem also highlights that whilst Europe as a whole is fairly balanced, that is made up of both big creditor nations and big debtor nations, and making transfer payments from one to another becomes very political when the economies are under stress.

Over the last twenty years China has been a large creditor nation, but this has started to change. It has compensated for reduced demand from the US by simply consuming the goods itself, dramatically reducing its external balance. As China continues to exhaust its own resources and increasingly has to turn abroad for raw materials, its trade position is going to rapidly deteriorate. The scale of numbers involved, however, mean that, despite substantial foreign exchange reserves, the collapse in its finances could be very rapid. Chinese coal production is about 3 billion tons a year, getting on towards 50% of global production. In 2009 it turned a net importer of just over 100m tons, equivalent to around 25% of Australia's (the world's 3rd largest producer and the world's largest exporter) - entire output. It is expected to increase these imports by around 100m tons a year. If we assume that the market can meet these requirements, the adjustment will be relatively smoothly financed out of its foreign exchange reserves, but given the numbers are just so large there may be physical shortages which would lead to a very aggressive forced and potentially uncontrolled restructuring.

The US economy, on the other hand, has the world's largest coal reserves. It is also estimated to have 61bn barrels of oil in the Outer Continental Shelf. It has large shale gas reserves, and it is also the world's largest exporter of grains, accounting around 45% of exports. This puts the US in a very powerful position to buy Middle Eastern oil, where their cost of extraction is also rising. Saudi Arabia, for example, now says that it needs USD71 barrel to balance its budget, but with well productivity declining and water resources depleting, that cost is going only one way. Europe is also in a very powerful position, already getting almost 50% of its power from non-fossil fuels, dramatically better than any other major part of the world. Despite this reliance on a hugely inefficient energy source it is still able to compete head to head with the rest of the world.

Politics and geopolitics will undoubtedly change the dynamics of how the restructuring works. As market forces reallocate resources to the most efficient consumers, governments will do their best to fight this. Massive government transfer payments will be instigated to shift money from the productive workforce to those who have unfortunately lost their job. This is only what you would expect in a modern democracy, but from an economic perspective, it lowers the efficiency of the country as a whole and, therefore, reduces its ability to compete in the wider market for what fuel resources are still available. How one country balances this transfer payment with the need to be competitive, compared to other countries' policies will help to determine their relative economic growth. If a country has its own resources, then it can remove them from the external market and from competing economies. Geopolitical considerations will also come into play in determining resource allocation.

In terms of investment, we have to remember the driving force of this change. Energy is becoming less efficient to extract and turn into useful work, which can only be offset with greater technology, greater capital and more resources. The cost of energy will rise relative to its value. Investments should, therefore, be made in anything that will take advantage of this relative switch, which in recent years has been anything resource, and, therefore, emerging market, focussed. Whilst there will be a common perception that alternative energy will be the area to invest in, the timing is perhaps not as obvious as one might think. I often use the analogy of a Formula 1 car coming in to change its tyres when it starts to rain. If they come in too early they will lose a huge amount of time on slower wet weather tyres, perhaps even destroying the tyres before they start to work; but if they come in too late they risk spinning off the road. Timing the change is critical. Investing in wind or solar too early may end up putting an economy at a huge disadvantage. The energy network could consist of individual countries such as Australia, Canada, Brazil and Russia, but it could equally involve the technology required to extract resources; for example ,the massive floating LNG platforms being built by Samsung Heavy or the companies that specialise in *"safe"* technology for deep sea drilling. The network will also involve massive water transfer programs as well as energy storage, etc. On the short side, I would consider banks and other assets with long duration exposure to the wrong side of this trade, such as to Western office property where the ability to service outstanding debt will deteriorate. If the cost of energy rises relative to the value added, then it won't just be banks that are at risk of rising default rates, but so too pensions and various government commitments. Given the fact that a government's priority must be to look after the health of all its citizens, it will have to make transfer payments through higher taxes, increased budget deficits and the printing of money, all of which I think will end up leading to inflation as the main mechanism of default. Office property, therefore, may not go down in nominal terms, but it will go down in real terms.

If you run this to its conclusion, it is a very depressing story, but it needn't be. We are in the present mess because of a massive misallocation of capital that has been going on for many years. The solution to this energy problem is nuclear fusion. It is an incredibly dense form of energy, and to all intents and purposes, it is unlimited. It is also safe and green, and would drive an industrial revolution on a scale never seen before, opening up other sciences such as nano-technology. The wealth generated would also allow countries to stick to their existing pension commitments, which they otherwise have to default on. The science is there, although we do need to spend heavily on making it a useable energy source. Despite minimal budgets, we have achieved energy breakeven in two different ways. Our ability to contain a heated plasma at a high temperature to enable fusion to occur has doubled every 2 years for the last 50 years or so - known as the Lawson's criterion. The question in my mind is why we haven't already achieved fusion?

This kind of project can only be pursued at the government level as the costs are huge and the benefits and spinoffs will not necessarily be attributed to the original financier, i.e. the science is a public good. US Federal research and development spending has, however, fallen from 2% of GDP in the mid-1960's to about 0.5% today. This has coincided with the end of the Cold War which, whilst praised by politicians and economists as freeing up huge amounts of East European and Asian labour to enter the work force, it also marked the end of a technology race, more commonly referred to as the Arms Race. The so-called benefits that Greenspan used to talk about from the freeing up cheap Eastern labour was nothing of the sort. It did not create a new work force, but rather switched the existing labour force from technological advancement or investing in the future to immediate consumption; the world became a flat horizontal economy rather than a vertical economy. If you analyse war at its most base level, it is about reallocating capital, and particularly in the two world wars about reallocating capital to technological innovation and away from immediate consumption. What the Cold War told us is that we do not need a war to achieve this, but we do need some grown up, responsible thinking by world leaders. Without the innovation and advancement that comes from these big science programmes, a horizontal economy will eventually lead to Malthusianism and the resource constraint that we are seeing.

In terms of cost, world governments have fretted since 1985 about a USD10 billion budget for the International Thermonuclear Experimental Reactor, when the reality is that they should be asking what the cost is of not achieving contained nuclear fusion. It will happen, but the issue is how long and rickety is the bridge before we get there? Private capital can only afford to make relatively small investments in unproven sciences such as this, which inevitably means it would take longer to reach the objective, but again it would eventually happen.

In terms of offsetting the deteriorating efficiency of energy extraction and energy density with efficiency gains elsewhere, this will become increasingly difficult to achieve. As more of the global economy is directed at accessing energy, there will be less available for research and development or even for maintaining existing capital equipment in areas unrelated to the energy network. Rather than increase, productivity will actually slow and decline. It amuses me that economists rave about increased US productivity when GDP is below its peak; the productivity of the employed workforce may have increased but not of the total workforce. It is a step in the right direction and is indicative of a better allocation of capital within the private sector but, unfortunately, that benefit is being diluted by unproductive government transfers. If the overall economy was allocating capital more efficiently, then, by definition, the tax rate and budget deficit would decline as the economic output would be growing sufficiently to dilute it even if that output was coming from the public sector.

Those people denying peak oil are doing the world a major disservice. Embracing it would allow capital to be re-allocated far more efficiently, and with less pain, to the new-look economy. The vociferous nature of the denial infers that oil is the best source of energy we will ever find which, if it were true, would be an extremely depressing state of affairs as it would imply that the world economy has peaked and future generations will never achieve our standard of living again. If, instead, people accepted the hard reality, we could probably achieve a very viable nuclear fusion within 5 to 10 years as a first step to a new exciting economic revolution. In the meantime, there is a huge amount of money to be made and lost from the changing shape of the world economy.

Andrew M Lees:

"Given just how important achieving nuclear fusion is to the world as we know it, and how achieving it would lift the global standard of living to a completely new plane, I would like to donate any profits generated from this project to: ITER, the International Thermonuclear Experimental Reactor. "

The International Thermonuclear Experimental Reactor
web site can be found at:
www.iter.org

CHAPTER FIFTEEN

-

"You would be ill-advised to bet against another ground-shaking financial crisis occurring in the next decade."

Roger Bootle

Kids and Greece

John Mauldin

"In short, times were not all that good, but we got through it. And now, 35 years later, it seems like deja vu all over again."

About the author

John Mauldin, is the author of perhaps the most widely read newsletter in the financial world, *"Thoughts from the Frontline"*, with more than a million regular readers world-wide.

For some years John has been perhaps best known for his rather self-explanatory *'"muddle through economy"* theory while also remaining consistently ahead of the deteriorating economic picture during the middle years of this decade.

His free weekly newsletter is noted for sanguine advice such as the following unbeatable disclaimer:

*"**Warning:** remove sharp objects from the vicinity and pour yourself your favorite adult beverage. This does not make for fun reading."*

All readers of suitably stout disposition are therefore encouraged to read the next two chapters...

Kids and Greece

"To trace something unknown back to something known is alleviating, soothing, gratifying and gives moreover a feeling of power. Danger, disquiet, anxiety attend the unknown - the first instinct is to eliminate these distressing states. First principle: any explanation is better than none... The cause-creating drive is thus conditioned and excited by the feeling of fear..."

Friedrich Nietzsche

"Any explanation is better than none." And the simpler, it seems in the investment game, the better. "The markets went up because oil went down," we are told, except when it went down there was another reason for the movement of the markets. We all intuitively know that things are far more complicated than that. But as Nietzsche noted, dealing with the unknown can be disturbing, so we look for the simple explanation.

"Ah," we tell ourselves, "I know why that happened." With an explanation firmly in hand, we now feel we know something. And the behavioral psychologists note that this state actually releases chemicals in our brains that make us feel good. We become literally addicted to the simple explanation. The fact that what we *"know"* (the explanation for the unknowable) is irrelevant or even wrong is not important to the chemical release. And thus we look for reasons.

How does an event like a problem in Greece (or elsewhere) affect you, gentle reader? And we mean, affect you down where the rubber hits your road. Not some formula or theory about the velocity of money or the effect of taxes on GDP.

This chapter is somewhat of a departure as it is a letter from John to his kids written when they were trying to understand why Greece had him so worked up in his writings.

What Does Greece Mean to Me, Dad?

Tiffani had been talking with her friends. A lot of them read this letter, and they were asking, *"Ok, I get that Greece is a problem. But what does that mean for me here? I want to understand why you think this is so important."* The same day, a friend told me about a conversation she had with her 17-year-old Cal Tech daughter and her daughter's boyfriend, who is also headed to Cal Tech. These are really smart kids, and they were asking her about some of my recent letters. *"We understand what's he saying, but we just don't see what it means."* (For what it's worth, the boyfriend wants to grow up to be Mohammed El-Erian of PIMCO. Go figure; I just wanted to be Mickey Mantle.)

Twice in one day is a sign, I am sure, so I will try and see if I can explain. And since all my kids must be wondering the same thing, this is a kind of letter from Dad to see if I can help them understand why things are not going as well as they would like. (A little background. I have seven kids, five of whom are adopted. A fairly colorful family, so to speak. Ages 16 through 33. Daughter Tiffani runs my business and, except for the youngest boy, they are all out on their own. Four are married or attached. It is not easy to watch them struggle to make ends meet, but Dad is proud. But listening to their stories, and the stories of their friends, help keep me in the real world.)

Dear Kids,

I know what a struggle it has been for most of you, and now three of you have a kid of your own. Expensive little hobbies, aren't they? I know that you read my letter (well, except for Trey) and wonder what it means to you trying to pay your bills. Let me see if I can make a connection from the world of economics to the world of paying your bills. Sadly, what I am going to say is not going to make you feel any better, but reality is what it is. We'll get through it together.

While life looks pretty good for Dad now, when I graduated from seminary in December of 1974 unemployment was at 8%, on its way to 9% a few months later. We lived in a small mobile home, which seemed wonderful at the time. I was proud of it. We scrimped and got by. My first job was a dead end, so I left after a few months. I guess I was lucky that no-one would hire me, because I had to figure out how to make it on my own. All I really knew was the printing business I had grown up in, so I started brokering printing. Pretty soon I was doing just direct mail, and then designing direct mail. But there was never enough money. We were still in that mobile home six years later.

And prices were going up like crazy. We had inflation. I remember going to a bank in the late '70s and borrowing money for my business at 18%, so I could buy paper for a job I had sold. Forget about borrowing for a new home or car. All I knew was that I was struggling to make ends meet (with a new kid!). There were a lot of nights where I would wake up at two in the morning with panic attacks about whether I could make payroll or pay bills until someone paid me. I didn't understand that what the Fed and the government were doing was causing high inflation and unemployment.

I had a bank line I used to buy paper with. One day the bank abruptly cancelled that line and demanded their money, which I didn't have - all I had was a warehouse full of paper and a contract that said I had a year to pay for it. The bank didn't care. I told them they would just have to wait. I swear, they actually called my mother and told her they would ruin me if she didn't pay that $10,000 line. She was scared for me (after all, you had to be able to trust your banker) and paid it without asking me. Turned out the bank finally went bankrupt later in the year. They were just desperate and trying anything they could do to get money, so they wouldn't lose everything. They did anyway.

In short, times were not all that good, but we got through it. And now, 35 years later, it seems like deja vu all over again. Every time we talk it seems like someone we know has lost a job.

And so how do the problems in a small country like Greece make a difference to you? There is a connection, but it's different than the old *"hip bone is connected to the thigh bone to the knee bone"* thing. It is a lot more complicated. Let's go back to a letter I wrote four years ago, talking about fingers of instability. One of the best analogies your Dad has ever written,

293

according to many of his 1 million friends. So read with me a few pages, and then we'll get back to Greece.

Ubiquity, Complexity Theory, and Sand piles

We are going to start our explorations with excerpts from a very important book by Mark Buchanan called Ubiquity, Why Catastrophes Happen. I HIGHLY recommend it to those of you who, like me, are trying to understand the complexity of the markets. Not directly about investing, although he touches on it, it is about chaos theory, complexity theory, and critical states. It is written in a manner any layman can understand. There are no equations, just easy-to-grasp, well-written stories and analogies. www.Amazon.com

We all had the fun as kids of going to the beach and playing in the sand. Remember taking your plastic buckets and making sand piles? Slowly pouring the sand into ever-bigger piles, until one side of the pile started an avalanche? Imagine, Buchanan says, dropping just one grain of sand after another onto a table. A pile soon develops. Eventually, just one grain starts an avalanche. Most of the time it is a small one, but sometimes it gains momentum and it seems like one whole side of the pile slides down to the bottom.

Well, in 1987 three physicists, named Per Bak, Chao Tang and Kurt Weisenfeld, began to play the sand pile game in their lab at Brookhaven National Laboratory in New York. Now, actually piling up one grain of sand at a time is a slow process, so they wrote a computer program to do it. Not as much fun, but a whole lot faster. Not that they really cared about sand piles. They were more interested in what are called non-equilibrium systems.

They learned some interesting things. What is the typical size of an avalanche? After a huge number of tests with millions of grains of sand, they found out that there is no typical number. *"Some involved a single grain; others, ten, a hundred or a thousand. Still others were pile-wide cataclysms involving millions that brought nearly the whole mountain down. At any time, literally anything, it seemed, might be just about to occur."* It was indeed completely chaotic in its unpredictability. Now, let's read these next paragraphs slowly. They are important, as they create a mental image that helps me understand the organization of the financial markets and the world economy.

To find out why (such unpredictability) should show up in their sand pile game, Bak and colleagues next played a trick with their computer. Imagine peering down on the pile from above, and coloring it in according to its steepness. Where it is relatively flat and stable, color it green; where steep and, in avalanche terms, *"ready to go,"* color it red. *"What do you see?"* They found that, at the outset, the pile looked mostly green but that, as the pile grew, the green became infiltrated with ever more red. With more grains, the scattering of red danger spots grew until a dense skeleton of instability ran through the pile. Here, then, was a clue to its peculiar behavior: a grain falling on a red spot can, by domino-like action, cause sliding at other nearby red spots. If the red network was sparse, and all trouble spots were well isolated one from the other, then a single grain could have only limited repercussions. *"But when the red spots come to riddle the pile, the consequences of the next grain become fiendishly unpredictable. It might trigger only a few tumblings or it might, instead, set off a cataclysmic chain reaction involving millions. The sand pile seemed to have configured itself into a hypersensitive and peculiarly unstable condition in which the next falling grain could trigger a response of any size whatsoever."*

Something only a math nerd could love? Scientists refer to this as a critical state. The term critical state can mean the point at which water would go to ice or steam, or the moment that critical mass induces a nuclear reaction, etc. It is the point at which something triggers a change in the basic nature or character of the object or group. Thus, (and very casually for all you physicists) we refer to something being in a critical state (or use the term critical mass) when there is the opportunity for significant change. *"But to physicists, [the critical state] has always been seen as a kind of theoretical freak and sideshow, a devilishly unstable and unusual condition that arises only under the most exceptional circumstances (in highly controlled experiments)... In the sand pile game, however, a critical state seemed to arise naturally through the mindless sprinkling of grains."* Then they asked themselves, could this phenomenon show up elsewhere? In the earth's crust, triggering earthquakes; in wholesale changes in an ecosystem or a stock market crash? *"Could the special organization of the critical state explain why the world at large seems so susceptible to unpredictable upheavals?"* Could it help us understand not just earthquakes, but why cartoons in a third-rate paper in Denmark could cause worldwide riots?

Buchanan concludes in his opening chapter, *"There are many subtleties and twists in the story... but the basic message, roughly speaking, is simple: The peculiar and exceptionally unstable organization of the critical state does indeed seem to be ubiquitous in our world. Researchers in the past few years have found its mathematical fingerprints in the workings of all the upheavals I've mentioned so far [earthquakes, eco-disasters, market crashes], as well as in the spreading of epidemics, the flaring of traffic jams, the patterns by which instructions trickle down from managers to workers in the office, and in many other things.*

"At the heart of our story, then, lies the discovery that networks of things of all kinds - atoms, molecules, species, people, and even ideas - have a marked tendency to organize themselves along similar lines. On the basis of this insight, scientists are finally beginning to fathom what lies behind tumultuous events of all sorts, and to see patterns at work where they have never seen them before."

Now, let's think about this for a moment. Going back to the sand pile game, you find that as you double the number of grains of sand involved in an avalanche, the likelihood of an avalanche is 2.14 times as unlikely. We find something similar in earthquakes. In terms of energy, the data indicate that earthquakes simply become four times less likely each time you double the energy they release. Mathematicians refer to this as a *"power law"* or a special mathematical pattern that stands out in contrast to the overall complexity of the earthquake process.

Fingers of Instability

So what happens in our game? *"... after the pile evolves into a critical state, many grains rest just on the verge of tumbling, and these grains link up into "fingers of instability"* of all possible lengths. While many are short, others slice through the pile from one end to the other. So the chain reaction triggered by a single grain might lead to an avalanche of any size whatsoever, depending on whether that grain fell on a short, intermediate or long finger of instability."

Now, we come to a critical point in our discussion of the critical state. Again, read this with the markets in mind:

"In this simplified setting of the sand pile, the power law also points to something else: the surprising conclusion that even the greatest of events have no special or exceptional causes. After all, every avalanche large or small starts out the same way, when a single grain falls and makes the pile just slightly too steep at one point. What makes one avalanche much larger than another has nothing to do with its original cause, and nothing to do with some special situation in the pile just before it starts. Rather, it has to do with the perpetually unstable organization of the critical state, which makes it always possible for the next grain to trigger an avalanche of any size."

Now let's couple this idea with a few other concepts. First, one of the world's greatest economists (who sadly was never honored with a Nobel), Hyman Minsky, points out that stability leads to instability. The longer a given condition or trend persists (and the more comfortable we get with it), the more dramatic the correction will be when the trend fails. The problem with long-term macroeconomic stability is that it tends to produce highly unstable financial arrangements. If we believe that tomorrow and next year will be the same as last week and last year, we are more willing to add debt or postpone savings for current consumption. Thus, says Minsky, the longer the period of stability, the higher the potential risk for even greater instability when market participants must change their behavior. Relating this to our sand pile, the longer that a critical state builds up in an economy or, in other words, the more fingers of instability that are allowed to develop connections to other fingers of instability, the greater the potential for a serious *"avalanche."*

Another way to think about it is the way Didier Sornette, a French geophysicist has described financial crashes in his wonderful book Why Stock

Markets Crash (the math, though, was far beyond me!) He wrote, "[T]he specific manner by which prices collapsed is not the most important problem: a crash occurs because the market has entered an unstable phase and any small disturbance or process may have triggered the instability. Think of a ruler held up vertically on your finger: this very unstable position will lead eventually to its collapse, as a result of a small (or an absence of adequate) motion of your hand or due to any tiny whiff of air. The collapse is fundamentally due to the unstable position; the instantaneous cause of the collapse is secondary." When things are unstable, it isn't the last grain of sand that causes the pile to collapse or the slight breeze that causes the ruler on your fingertip to fall. Those are the *"proximate"* causes. They're the closest reasons at hand for the collapse. The real reason, though, is the *"remote"* cause, the farthest reason. The farthest reason is the underlying instability of the system itself.

A fundamentally unstable system is exactly what we saw in the recent credit crisis. Consumers all through the world's largest economies borrowed money for all sorts of things, because times were good. Home prices would always go up and the stock market was back to its old trick of making 15% a year. And borrowing money was relatively cheap. You could get 2% short-term loans on homes, which seemingly rose in value 15% a year, so why not buy now and sell a few years down the road? Greed took over. Those risky loans were sold to investors by the tens and hundreds of billions all over the world. And as with all debt sand piles, the fault lines started to show up. Maybe it was that one loan in Las Vegas that was the critical piece of sand; we don't know, but the avalanche was triggered.

You probably don't remember this, but Dad was writing about the problems with subprime debt way back in 2005 and 2006. But as the problem actually emerged, respected people like Ben Bernanke (the chairman of the Fed) said that the problem was not all that big, and that the fallout would be *"contained."* (I bet he wishes he could have that statement back!) But it wasn't contained. It caused banks to realize that what they thought was AAA credit was actually a total loss. And as banks looked at what was on their books, they wondered about their fellow banks. How bad were they? Who knew? Since no one did, they stopped lending to each other. Credit simply froze. They stopped taking each other's letters of credit, and that hurt world trade. Because banks were losing money, they stopped lending to smaller businesses. Commercial paper dried up. All those *"safe"* off-balance-sheet funds that banks created were now folding (what my friend, Paul McCulley, first labelled as the Shadow Banking System). Everyone sold what they could, not what they wanted to, to cover their debts. It was a true panic. Businesses started laying off people who, in turn, stopped spending as much.

As you saw from my earlier story about my bank experience, banks may do what look like unreasonable things when they get into trouble. (Speaking of which, my smallish Texas bank, where I have been for almost 20 years, just cancelled my very modest, unused credit line last month, and told me that letters of credit will not be rewritten without 100% cash against them. Not to worry, Dad is actually in the best shape of his life, business-wise, knock on wood. I hadn't talked personally to a banker in years. When I asked the young clerk on the phone, "What's going on?" he said it was just an order from his director. I switched banks last week, as I can smell a bank in trouble. And I again have a credit line - which I hope not to use. But the fact is, we need banks. They are like the arteries in our bodies; they keep the blood (money) flowing. And when our arteries get hard, we can be in danger of heart attacks. And it's going to get worse, as banks are going to lose more money on their commercial real estate loans. Commercial real estate is already down some 40% around the country.

There are a lot of books that try to pinpoint the cause of our current crisis. And some make for fun reading, like a good mystery novel. You can blame it on the Fed or the bankers or hedge funds or the government or ratings agencies or any number of culprits.

Let me be a little controversial here. The blame game that is now going on is in many ways way too simplistic. The world system survived all sorts of crises over the recent decades and bounced back. Why is now so different? Because we are coming to the end of a 60-year debt supercycle. Not just consumers, but banks borrowed (and not just in the US but all over the developed world) like there was no tomorrow. And because we were so convinced that all this debt was safe, we leveraged up, borrowing at first 3 and then 5 and then 10 and then as much as 30 times the actual money we had. And we convinced the regulators that it was a good thing. The longer things remained stable, the more convinced we became they would remain that way. *The following chart* shows how our sand pile ended up. It's not pretty.

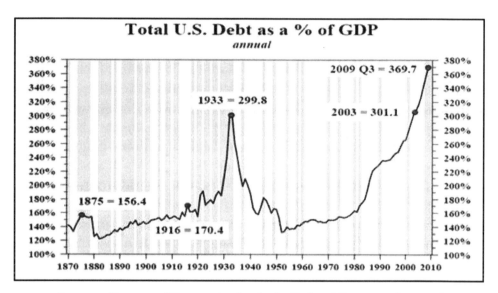

Sources: Bureau of Economic Analysis, Federal Reserve, Census Bureau:
Historical Statistics of the United States Colonial Times to 1970.
Through Q3 2009.

I know Dad always says it is never *"different"* but in a sense this time is really different from all the other crises we have gone through since the Great Depression that your Less-Than-Sainted Papa Joe used to talk about. What the very important book by professors Reinhart and Rogoff shows is that every debt crisis always ends this way, with the debt having to be paid down or written off or defaulted upon. That part is never different. One way or another, we reduce the debt. And that is a painful process. It means that the economy grows much slower, if at all, during the process. And while the government is trying to make up the difference for consumers who are trying to (or being forced to) reduce their

300

debt, even governments have limits, as the Greeks are finding out. If it were not for the fact that we are coming to the closing innings of the debt supercycle, we would already be in a robust recovery. But we are not. And sadly, we have a long way to go with this deleveraging process. It will take years.

You can't borrow your way out of a debt crisis, whether you are a family or a nation. And, as too many families are finding out today, if you lose your job you can lose your home. What were once very creditworthy people are now filing for bankruptcy and walking away from homes, as all those sub-prime loans going bad put homes back onto the market, which caused prices to fall on all homes, which caused an entire home-construction industry to collapse, which hurt all sorts of ancillary businesses, which caused more people to lose their jobs and give up their homes, and on and on. The connections in the housing part of the sand pile were long and deep.

It's all connected. We built a very unstable sand pile and it came crashing down and now we have to dig out from the problem. And the problem was too much debt. It will take years, as banks write off home loans and commercial real estate and more, and we get down to a more reasonable level of debt as a country and as a world. And here's where I have to deliver the bad news. It seems we did not learn the lessons of this crisis very well. First, we have not fixed the problems that made the crisis so severe. The 2,300 page bill that recently passed for financial reform has more unintended consequences that will not help get America back on track. (As an example ,Social Security was 28 pages and the original reg-ulatory reform bill called Glass-Steagall was 35 pages, back in 1934.) And European banks are still highly leveraged.

Why is Greece important? Because so much of their debt is on the books of European banks. Hundreds of billions of dollars worth. And just a few years ago this seemed like a good thing. The rating agencies (yes the same guys who said those subprime bonds were AAA!) made Greek debt AAA, and banks could use massive leverage (almost 40 times in some European banks) and buy these bonds and make good money in the process. (Don't ask Dad why people still trust rating agencies. Some things just can't be explained.) Except, that now that Greek debt is risky. Today, it appears there will be some kind of bailout for Greece. But that is just a band-aid on a very serious wound. The crisis will not go away. It will come back, unless the Greeks willingly go into their own Great Depression by slashing their spending and raising taxes to a level that no one in the US could even contemplate. What is being demanded of them is really bad for them, but they did it to themselves.

But those European banks? When that debt goes bad, and it will, they will react to each other just like they did in 2008. Trust will evaporate. Will taxpayers shoulder the burden? Maybe, maybe not. For a time, it looks like they will. But that won't go on forever. It will be a huge crisis. There are other countries in Europe, like Spain and Portugal, that are almost as bad as Greece. Great Britain is not too far behind.

The European economy is as large as that of the US. We feel it when they go into recessions, for many of our largest companies make a lot of money in Europe. A crisis will also make the Euro go down, which reduces corporate profits and makes it harder for us to sell our products into Europe, not to mention compete with European companies for global trade. And that means we all buy less from China, which means they will buy less of our bonds, and on and on go the connections. And it will all make it much harder to start new companies, which are the source of real growth in jobs.

And then, in January of 2011, we are going to have the largest tax increase in US history. The research shows that tax increases may have as much as a negative 3-times effect on GDP, or the growth of the economy. As we will see later in this book, I think it is likely that the level of tax increases, when combined with the increase in state and local taxes (or the reductions in spending), could be enough to throw us back into recession, even without problems coming from Europe. (And no, Melissa, that is not some Republican research conspiracy. The research was done by Christina Romer, who is Obama's chairperson of the Joint Council of Economic Advisors.)

And sadly, that means even higher unemployment. It means sales at the bar where you work, Melissa, will fall farther as more of your friends lose jobs. And commissions at the electronics store where you work, Chad, will be even lower than the miserable level they're at now. And Henry, it means the hours you work at UPS will be even more difficult to come by. You are smart to be looking for more part-time work. Abbi and Amanda? People may eat out a little less, and your fellow workers will all want more hours. And Trey? Greece has little to do with the fact that you do not do your homework on time. And this next time, we won't be able to fight the recession with even greater debt and lower interest rates, as we did this last time. Rates are as low as they can go and, at some point, if we do not get our government fiscal house in order, the bond market will show that it does not like the massive borrowing the US is engaged in. It is worried about the possibility of *"Greece R Us."*

Bond markets require confidence above all else. If Greece defaults, then how far away is Spain or Japan? What makes the US so different, if we do not control our debt? As Reinhart and Rogoff show, when confidence goes, the end is very near. And it always comes faster than anyone expects. And it always seems to be unexpected.

The good news? We will get through this. We pulled through some rough times as a nation in the '70s. No one, in 2020, is going to want to go back to the good old days of 2010, as the amazing innovations in medicine and other technologies will have made life so much better. You guys are going to live a very long time (and I hope I get a few extra years to enjoy those grandkids as well!) In 1975 we did not know where the new jobs would come from. It was fairly bleak. But the jobs did come, as they will once again.

The even better news? You guys are young, still babies, really. Hell, I didn't have a good year income-wise until I was in my mid-30s, and that was an accident (I literally won a cellular telephone lottery). And it has not always been smooth since then, as you know. But we get through bad stuff. That is what we do as a family and as the larger family of our nation and world.

So, what's the final message? Do what you are doing. Work hard, save, watch your spending, and think about whether your job is the right one if we have another recession. Pay attention to how profitable the company you work for is, and make yourself their most important worker. And know that things will get better. The 2020s are going to be one very cool time, as we shrug off the ending of the debt supercycle and hit the reset button. And remember, Dad is proud of you and loves you very much.

-

This chapter is excerpted from John Mauldin's new book *"The End Game"* which will be published in January 2011.

CHAPTER SIXTEEN

-

"Credit makes war, and war makes peace; raises armies,
fits out navies, fights battles, besieges towns, and, in a word,
it is more justly called the sinews of war than the money itself...
Credit makes the soldier fight without pay, the armies march
without provisions... it is an impregnable fortification...
it makes paper pass for money... and fills the Exchequer
and the banks with as many millions as it pleases, upon demand."

Daniel Defoe

Is This The Endgame?
By John Mauldin

"And yet, and yet... While the Debt Supercycle may not yet have ended, I think we can begin to see a clear case that, like the sandwich-board wearing cartoon prophet warning, "The End is Nigh".

Is This The Endgame?
The Debt Supercycle and the Prospect of Deflation...

The Debt Supercycle

When I mention The End Game, you'll immediately want to know what is ending. What I think is ending for a significant number of countries in the *"developed"* world is the Debt Supercycle. The concept of the Debt Supercycle was originally developed by the Bank Credit Analyst. It was Hamilton Bolton, the BCA founder, who used the word supercycle, and he was referring generally to a lot of things, including money velocity, bank liquidity, and interest rates. Tony Boeckh changed the concept to the more simple *"Debt Supercycle"* back in the early 1970s, as he believed the problem was spiraling private-sector debt. The current editor of the BCA (and Maine fishing buddy) Martin Barnes has greatly expanded on the concept.

Essentially, the Debt Supercycle is the decades-long growth of debt from small and easily-dealt-with levels, to a point where bond markets rebel and the debt has to be restructured or reduced or a program of austerity must be undertaken to bring the debt back to manageable proportions.

As Bank Credit Analyst wrote back in 2007:

The history of the U.S. is characterized by a long-run increase in indebtedness, punctuated by occasional financial crises and subsequent policy reflation. The subprime blow-up is the latest installment in this ongoing Debt Supercycle story. During each crisis, there are always fears that conventional reflation will no longer work, implying the economy and markets face a catastrophic debt unwinding. Such fears have always proved unfounded, and the current episode is no exception.

"A combination of Fed rate cuts, fiscal easing (aimed at relieving subprime distress), and a lower dollar will eventually trigger another up-leg in the Debt Supercycle, and a new round of leverage and financial excesses. The objects of speculation are likely to be global, particularly emerging markets and resource related assets. The Supercycle will end if foreign investors ever turn their back on U.S.

assets, triggering capital flight out of the dollar and robbing U.S. authorities of any room for maneuver. This will not happen any time soon."

I was talking with Martin a few months ago and the topic turned to the ending of the Debt Supercycle. Martin said we are nowhere near the end, as the government is stepping in where private debtors are cutting back. We have just shifted the focus of where the debt is coming from. And he is right, in that the Debt Supercycle in the US, Great Britain, Japan and other developed countries (yes, even Greece!) is still very much in play as governments explode their balance sheets. Total debt continues to grow.

Somewhere Over the Rainbow

And yet, and yet... While the Debt Supercycle may not yet have ended, I think we can begin to see a clear case that, like the sandwich-board-wearing cartoon prophet warning, *"The End is Nigh!"* Greece is the harbinger of fundamental change. Spain and Portugal are pointing to the same outcome, as their cost of debt keeps rising. And Ireland? The Baltics?

There is a limit to how much debt you can pile on. But as the work of Reinhart and Rogoff points out (*"This Time Is Different"*), there is not a fixed limit or some certain percentage of GNP. Rather, the limit is all about confidence, a theme I have written on many times. Everything goes along well, and then *"Boom!"* it doesn't. That *"Boom"* has happened to Greece. Without massive assistance, Greek debt would be unmarketable. Default would be inevitable. (I still think it is!) The limit is different for every nation. For Russia in the 1990s, it was a rather minor total debt-to-GDP ratio of around 12%. Japan will soon have a debt-to-GDP ratio of 230%! The difference? Local savers bought government debt in Japan and did not in Russia.

The end of the Debt Supercycle does not have to mean calamity for each country, depending on how far down the road they are. Yes, if you are Greece your choices are between very, very bad and disastrous. Japan is a bug in search of a windshield. Each country has its own dynamics. Take the US. We are some ways off from the end. We have time to adjust. But let's be under no illusions; we cannot run deficits of 10% of GDP forever. At some point the Fed will either have to monetize the debt or the bond market will simply demand an ever-higher interest rate. Why can't we go the way of Japan? Because we do not have the level of savings they have traditionally had. But their savings levels are rapidly declining which says that if they want to continue their deficit spending at 10% of GDP, they will have to go into the foreign markets to borrow money at a much higher cost, or their central bank will have to print money. Neither choice is good.

The Path to Profligacy

How did we get here? We simply kept borrowing ever greater amounts of money at an increasingly rapid pace. *Look at the chart below.* It is about six months old, but not much has changed.

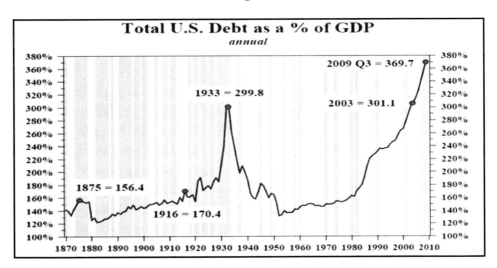

Sources: Bureau of Economic Analysis, Federal Reserve, Census Bureau: Historical Statistics of the United States. Colonial Times to 1970. Through Q3 2009.

In the beginning, each dollar of debt brought about a corresponding dollar of increase in GDP. But that early money was invested in houses and in the means of production, which helped grow the economy. As time went on, and especially after the '80s, more and more of the debt was used for consumption (of which much has come to be from foreign sources) and not for the increase of productive capacity. Toward the end, it took $3 of debt to create a $1 rise in GDP in the US. And now, each $1 rise in debt is government debt, which some research (not neo-Keynesian Paul Krugman's!) says has a slightly negative multiplier - it actually hurts GDP. And it is not just the US. Take a look at the chart of G7 debt (courtesy of GMO, more about which later). That is one ugly and unsustainable chart. In 1950 the G7 countries were recovering from very large war-time debts. Now we don't have that excuse. Nor do we have the option of doing what they did. They cut military spending, inflated a little in nominal terms, and grew their way out of the problem.

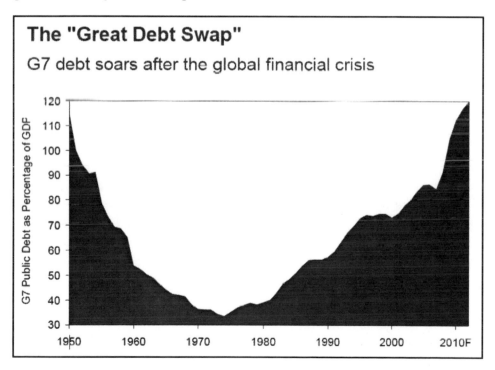

Source: IMF, Independent Strategy.

Things That Cannot Be

Talk about unsustainable. The next chart is one of something that cannot be. The US cannot borrow $15 trillion in the next ten years. It's just not there. Long before that, the bond market will simply rebel, rates will rise, and the aftermath will make the last crisis seem like a cakewalk.

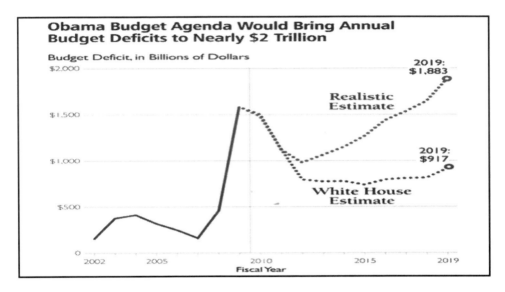

Source: Heritage Foundation calculations based on data from the Congressional Budget Office and U.S. Office of Management and Budget.

For most countries with debt problems, The End Game is a binary-path-dependent future. Countries can elect to get their fiscal houses in order over time, getting the fiscal deficits below the growth of nominal GDP. That is not without consequence, as it will mean slower growth in the short term (less than one year), but cutting deficits year after year, even gradually, will mean a very slow-growth, Muddle Through economy for a sustained period.

Some say the coming election is the most important we have had for a long time. I disagree. It is one thing for the Tea Party movement and independents to elect a Republican Congress. If I am right and the economy is still slow and unemployment lingers around 8% by 2012, it is likely we will see a Republican president at that point. So, some will say 2012 will be the important election.

However, I think the really important election will be in 2014. Let's make the (clearly) optimistic assumption that Republicans get religion and really go to work on the deficits. The economy will not be booming in 2014, as a result of the tightening and move to austerity, whether through cuts or tax increases or both. Cutting more than $1 trillion annually out of spending over 7-8 years is not easy or without pain.

Will voters in 2014 decide there is too much pain? Will they stay the course for fiscal control or will they scream for more stimulus? Will they take the long view and let politicians make hard choices or will they send the message that short-term choices are what they want? Will they give lip service to going on a diet and exercising and then stay on the couch and eat chips and watch TV? Or will they really get fiscal religion and get with the program?

It's all well and good to say that you want fiscal rectitude. It's another thing when it is hitting budgets near and dear to you. And to get back to a remotely sustainable deficit is going to take pain in every corner. It is going to hit near you, gentle reader. Some will get hit harder than others.

And this is the case in every country running large and out-of-control deficits. It is not just a US problem. The Irish are in what can only be called a depression, along with the Baltic states and Hungary. Greece will soon be there, once they have to meet market rates for their debt, or force their labor markets to endure a very serious deflation to make themselves more competitive.

So, can we know how The End Game will turn out? The short answer is no. Each country will have to make its own political choices. Could we see hyperinflation in the US or Britain or Japan? It is possible, with bad policy decisions. I doubt it that it gets to that. But could we see inflation? The answer is yes.

That has been the traditional method of default for many countries over the years. Instead of outright default, they simply inflate away debt. And the logic is compelling. If you have 5% inflation along with 3% real growth, you get a nominal growth rate of 8%. That means in nine years the economy is twice the size in dollar terms, but only about 35% bigger in inflation-adjusted terms. If somewhere along the way you can get your deficits down to "just" 3%, then you can reduce your debt-to-GDP ratio by 5% a year. In less than ten years, you cut your debt-to-GDP ratio in half. Sounds good, right?

Of course, you have destroyed the purchasing power of your currency, given a real hit to the incomes of the middle class, defrauded those who bought your debt, and in all likelihood you did not hold inflation to just 5%. Think the '70s.

And getting the deficit down to 3% is no easy proposition for many countries. Look at the chart below, again from GMO in a paper by Edward Chancellor on sovereign debt. I highly commend it to you. It is all over the net, but the easiest place I found to read it is at

http://www.zerohedge.com/article/must-read-reflections-gmos-edward-chancellor.

We can think of fiscal debt in two ways: structural and cyclical. Structural debt is that caused by government spending programs. Cyclical debt occurs during recessions as revenue drops. One assumes that, at some point, things get back to normal and revenues begin to rise and the cyclical part of the deficit goes away. But that still leaves the structural debt. That can only be dealt with by cutting spending, raising taxes, or holding spending flat while growing your way out of the problem - or some combination of all three.

I find it interesting that Italy has a far less problematic fiscal situation than many of its neighbors. And while politicians in the US always say they will cut out wasteful spending, there just isn't all that much here, percentage-wise. Italy has a lot of places to cut. As an example, there are 629,000 official cars, some of them high-priced Maseratis, that ferry government officials around. That is ten times more than in other European countries and, on a percentage-of-GDP basis, 50 times more than in the US. They could cut out half of them and save about $15 billion, by my back-of-the-napkin calculation, which is more than 0.6% of total GDP. Reduce the number to the European average and you could cut half the structural debt. (I assume about $50,000 per year for maintenance, depreciation, and drivers.) Oh, that we in the US had such easy pickings.

(http://www.economist.com/node/16102798?story_id=16102798)

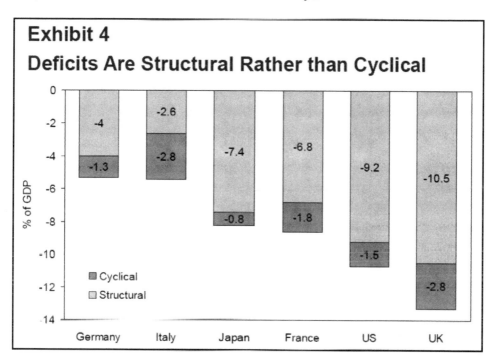

Source: BIS, Independent Strategy.

The Province of Uncertainty

Edward Chancellor closes his paper so eloquently. Let me quote:

As a result of the financial crisis, the world's leading sovereign credit markets have left the world of risk, where probabilities of gains and losses can be measured, and entered the darker province of uncertainty. The future performance of sovereign credits depends on future events and decisions that are unknowable.

"Will the global economic recovery be sustained? Or will economic growth and tax revenues remain weak for a prolonged period? Will policy-makers in leading countries find the political strength to restore their government finances to order? Or will, as some fear, the attempt to cut deficits actually increase them (by hurting the economy and reducing tax revenues)?

"Will central banks engage in further bouts of quantitative easing until they reach the point of no return? Or will they err on the side of caution and tighten too early? Will the current deflationary policies within the Euro zone persist? Or will the ECB turn toward the monetization of excessive debt levels? Will interest rates on long-term government debt remain low? Or will bond vigilantes take fright and demand higher rates as compensation for all this uncertainty and risk?

"These are interesting but intractable questions. Nobody knows their answers. Current yields on government bonds in most advanced economies (PIGS excepted) are at very low levels. Under only one condition - that the world follows Japan's experience of prolonged deflation - do they offer any chance of a reasonable return. But this is not the only possible future. For other outcomes, long-dated government bonds offer a limited upside with a potentially uncapped downside. As investors, such asymmetric pay-off profiles don't appeal to us. Caveat (sovereign) creditor!"

As noted above, The End Game is path-dependent for each country. By that I mean that the end result will stem directly from the course they choose. It is not clear what those choices will be.

For instance, I have often noted that the Euro is not a currency so much as an experiment. However, it is also not an economic currency, but rather a political currency. Whether the Euro lasts in its present form is a political decision to be made by numerous national actors. It is too soon to tell. All of the developed countries that are in trouble have hard decisions to make. To pretend that we know exactly what that involves requires a fair degree of hubris. But we can see the various paths. In most cases, the number of paths is quite limited, because bad choices were made that have brought us to our current set of choices. As we attempt to sort out those paths, we will find there are signposts along the way telling us which path we are taking. As investors, we can then position ourselves accordingly.

And even for countries that, relatively speaking, have kept their act together, we are talking about a large part of world GDP at risk. It is an interesting world in which we live.

The Prospect of Deflation

Meanwhile, discussing deflationary threats has become a very emotive issue. For one thing, a lot of people start equating my analysis with the Paul Krugman camp. The immediate accusation is that I am advocating kicking the can down the road and not reducing the deficit. Wrong. What I have been trying to point out for several years is that we have no good choices. The dilemma is that we are down to bad, and very bad, choices. The very bad choice (leading to disastrous - think Greece) is to continue to run massive deficits. The merely bad choice is to reduce the deficits gradually over time. As I try to point out, reducing the deficits has consequences in the short term. It WILL affect GDP in the short term. Krugman and the neo-Keynesians are right about that. To deny that is to ignore basic arithmetic.

I am not for kicking the can down the road. Not to begin to deal with the deficits, and soon, risks an even worse problem. But - and this is a big but - I don't want to stomp on the can, either.

Nevertheless, the debate over whether we are in for inflation or deflation is likely to remain alive and well for some time to come. It seems that not everyone is ready to join the deflation-first, then-inflation camp I am currently resident in. So, permit me to address some of the causes of deflation - the elements of deflation, if you will, and see if they are in ascendancy. For equity investors, this is an important question because, historically, periods of deflation have not been kind to stock markets. Beginning from that angle, let's see if we can sneak up on some answers. Even on the road (and maybe especially on the road, as I get more free time on airplanes) I keep up with my rather large reading habit. As I prepared

318

this article during mid-summer 2009, the theme in various publications was the lack of available credit for small businesses, with plenty of anecdotal evidence. This was in line with the surveys by the National Federation of Independent Businesses, which continued to show a difficult credit market.

Businesses are being forced to scramble for needed investments, generally having to make do with cash flow and working out of profits. This is an interesting quandary for government policy makers, as 75% of the "rich" that will see the Bush tax cuts go away are small businesses.

Recent research by the Kauffman Foundation has shown that all new start-ups of the past two decades have come from small businesses and start-ups. And yet, as of now, when structural employment is over 10% (if you count those who were considered to be in the work force just a few months ago), we want to reduce the availability of revenues to the very people we want to be hiring new workers, and who are cash-starved as it is.

It is not just that taxes will go from 35% to just under 40%. It is the increase in Medicare taxes coming down the pike, too. We are taking money from private hands, where it has the potential to increase productivity, and putting it into government hands, where it will do nothing for growth of the economy. There is no multiplier for government spending. And tax increases reduce potential GDP by a multiplier of at least 1 and maybe 3, depending on which study you want to cite.

I understand that taxes have to go up. I get it. But we would be better off having a discussion of where we want the tax dollars to come from before we risk hurting an economy that will barely be growing at 2% in the 4th quarter, and may be well below that. It is the increase in taxes that has me concerned about a double-dip recession.

That being said, the announcement by several prominent Democratic senators that they think we should extend the Bush tax cuts is significant. That being said, absent policy mistakes.we may experience A slow-growth world. But an actual double dip is rare.

If Congress were to extend the Bush tax cuts for at least a year, until the presidential commission on taxes is done with its work and THEN have the debate, it would make me far more optimistic. And it would be quite bullish for stocks, I think. Businesses would know how to plan, at least, for a year, and the economy would be given more time to actually recover. I am not ready to channel my inner Larry Kudlow, but from what we see this summer it would make me more optimistic and reduce the chances of a double-dip recession significantly.

Some Thoughts on Deflation

Inflation in the US is now just below 1%, whether you look at the CPI, the Cleveland Fed's measure, or the Dallas Trimmed Mean CPI. The Fed's favorite, the PCE, is also approaching 1%. The Dallas numbers are a little behind, but they are at all-time lows. The classic definition of deflation is an economic environment that is characterized by inadequate or deficient aggregate demand. Prices in general fall, and normal economic relationships start to fall apart.

The Super-Trend Puzzle

I am a big fan of puzzles of all kinds, especially picture puzzles. I love to figure out how the pieces fit together and watch the picture emerge, and have spent many an enjoyable hour at the table struggling to find the missing piece that helps make sense of the pattern. Perhaps that explains my fascination with economics and investing, as there are no greater puzzles (except possibly the great theological conundrums, or the mind of a woman, about which I have only a few clues).

The great problem with the economic puzzles is that the shapes of the pieces can and will change as they rub against one another. One often finds that fitting two pieces together changes the way they meld with the other pieces you thought were already nailed down which may, of course, change the pieces with which they are adjoined; and suddenly your neat economic picture no longer looks anything like the real world.

(Which is why all of the mathematical models make assumptions about variables that allow the models to work, except that what they end up showing is not related to the real world, which is not composed of static variables.)

There are two types of major economic puzzle pieces. The first are those pieces that represent trends that are inexorable: they will not themselves change, or if they do it will be slowly; but they will force every puzzle piece that touches them to shift, due to the force of their power. Demographic shifts or technology improvements over the long run are examples of this type of puzzle piece.

The second type is what I think of as *"balancing trends,"* or trends that are not inevitable but which, if they come about, will have significant implications. If you place that piece into the puzzle it, too, changes the shape of all the pieces of the puzzle around it. And in the economic super-trend puzzle, it can change the shape of other pieces in ways that are not clear.

Deflation is in the latter category. I have often said that when you become a Federal Reserve Bank governor, you are taken into a back room and are given a DNA transplant that makes you viscerally and, at all times, opposed to deflation. Deflation is a major economic game changer. You can argue, as Gary Shilling does, that there is a good kind of deflation, where rising productivity and other such good things produces a general fall in prices, such as we had in the late 19th century. And we have experienced that in the world of technology, where we view it as normal that the price of a computer will fall, even as its quality rises over time.

But that is not the kind of deflation we face today. We face the deflation of the Depression era, and central bankers of the world are united in opposition. As Paul McCulley quipped to me this spring, when I asked him if he was concerned about inflation, with all the stimulus and printing of money we were facing, "John," he said, *"you better hope they can cause some inflation."* And he is right. If we don't have a problem with inflation in the future, we are going to have far worse problems to deal with.

Saint Milton Friedman taught us that inflation is always and everywhere a monetary phenomenon. That is, if the central bank prints too much money, inflation will ensue. And that is true, up to a point. A central bank, by printing too much money, can bring about inflation and destroy a currency, all things being equal. But that is the tricky part of that equation, because not all things are equal. The pieces of the puzzle can change shape. When the elements of deflation combine in the right order, the central bank can print a boatload of money without bringing about inflation. And we may now be watching that combination come about.

The Elements of Deflation

Let's recap. Unemployment is high and is in reality going higher if you count those who would take a job if they could get one. Incomes are weak. Plans to purchase discretionary items are falling. Housing is likely in for a further drop in prices. The stock market is not exactly booming. Treasury yields are falling, not from a credit crisis or a flight to quality, but because of economic conditions (deflation). Money supply is flat or falling. Prices are under pressure. The list goes on, and all factors are indicative of deflation.

Just as every school child knows that water is formed by the two elements of hydrogen and oxygen in a very simple combination we all know as H2O, so deflation has its own elements of composition. Let's look at some of them (in no particular order).

First, there is excess production capacity. It is hard to have pricing power when your competition also has more capacity than he wants, so he prices his product as low as he can to make a profit, but also to get the sale. The world is awash in excess capacity now. Eventually we either grow the economy to utilize that capacity or it will be taken offline through bankruptcy, a reduction in capacity (as when businesses lay off employees), or businesses simply exiting their industries.

I could load the rest of this article with charts showing how low world capacity utilization is, but let's just take one graph, from the US. Notice that capacity utilization is roughly in an area that we associate with the bottom of past recessions (with one exception).

Deflation is also associated with massive wealth destruction. The credit crisis certainly provided that element. Home prices have dropped in many nations all over the world, with some exceptions, like Canada and Australia. Trillions of dollars of *"wealth"* has evaporated, no longer available for use. Likewise, the bear market in equities in the developed world has wiped out trillions of dollars in valuation, resulting in rising savings rates as consumers, especially those close to a wanted retirement, try to repair their leaking balance sheets.

And while increased saving is good for an individual, it calls into play Keynes' Paradox of Thrift. That is, while it is good for one person to save, when everyone does it, it decreases consumer spending. And decreased consumer spending (or decreased final demand, in economic terms) means less pricing power for companies and is yet another element of deflation.

Yet another element of deflation is the massive deleveraging that comes with a major credit crisis. Not only are consumers and businesses reducing their debt, banks are reducing their lending. Bank losses (at the last count I saw) are over $2 trillion and rising.

As an aside, the European bank stress tests were a joke. They assumed no sovereign debt default. Evidently the thought of Greece not paying its debt is just not in the realm of their thinking. There were other deficiencies as well, but that is the most glaring. European banks are still a concern unless the ECB goes ahead and buys all that sovereign debt from the banks, getting it off their balance sheets.

When the money supply is falling in tandem with a slowing velocity of money, that brings up serious deflationary issues. I have dealt with that in recent months, so I won't bring it up again, but it is a significant element of deflation. And it is not just the US. Global real broad money growth is close to zero. Deflationary pressures are the norm in the developed world (except for Britain, where inflation is the issue).

Falling home prices and a weak housing market are one more element of deflation. This is happening not just in the US, but also much of Europe is suffering a real estate crisis. Japan has seen its real estate market fall almost 90% in some cities, and that is part of the reason they have had 20 years with no job growth, and that the nominal GDP is where it was 17 years ago. In the short run, reducing government spending (in the US at local, state, and federal levels) is deflationary. Martin Wolfe, in the Financial Times, wrote (arguing that that the move to *"fiscal austerity"* is ill-advised).

We can see two huge threats in front of us. The first is the failure to recognize the strength of the deflationary pressures... The danger that premature fiscal and monetary tightening will end up tipping the world economy back into recession is not small, even if the largest emerging countries should be well able to protect themselves. The second threat is failure to secure the medium-term structural shifts in fiscal positions, in management of the financial sector and in export-dependency, that are needed if a sustained and healthy global recovery is to occur. Finally, high and chronic unemployment is deflationary. It reduces final demand as people simply don't have the money to buy things.

Deflation that comes from increased productivity is desirable. In the late 1800's the US went through an almost 30-year period of deflation that saw massive improvements in agriculture (the McCormick reaper, etc) and the ability of producers to get their products to markets through railroads. In fact, too many railroads were built and a number of the companies that built them collapsed. Just as we experienced with the fiber-optic cable build-out, there was soon too much railroad capacity, and freight prices fell. That was bad for the shareholders but good for consumers. It was a time of great economic growth.

But deflation that comes from a lack of pricing power and lower final demand is not good. It hurts the incomes of both employer and employee, and discourages entrepreneurs from increasing their production capacity and, thus, employment. That is why it will be important to watch the CPI numbers even more closely in the coming months. The trend, as noted above, is for lower inflation. If that continues, the Fed will act. How would the Fed react? For an answer, we need to go back to Ben Bernanke's famous helicopter speech of November 2002, entitled "Deflation: Making Sure *'It' Doesn't Happen Here."* *

As I discussed in my newsletters frequently, for instance:
http://www.2000wave.com/article.asp?id=mwo070210 and
http://www.2000wave.com/article.asp?id=mwo112802: .

The speech text itself is available at:
http://www.federalreserve.gov/BoardDocs/speeches/2002/20021121/default.htm

(By the way, I have always been convinced that his remark about printing presses and helicopters was an attempt at economist humor, which is why we don't get many offers from comedy clubs.)

Let's sum up the helicopter section: You can create inflation by printing a lot of money. But that is not the interesting part of the speech. Quoting from my letter:

Let's look at what Bernanke really said. First, he begins by telling us that he believes the likelihood of deflation is remote. But, since it did happen in Japan, and seems to be the cause of the current Japanese problems, we cannot dismiss the possibility outright. Therefore, we need to see what policies can be brought to bear upon the problem.

He then goes on to say that the most important thing is to prevent deflation before it happens. He says that a central bank should allow for some 'cushion' and should not target zero inflation, and speculates that this is over 1%. Typically, central banks target inflation of 1-3%, although this means that in normal times inflation is more likely to rise above the acceptable target than fall below zero in poor times.

Central banks can usually influence this by raising and lowering interest rates. But what if the Fed Funds rate falls to zero? Not to worry, there are still policy levers that can be pulled. Quoting Bernanke:

So what then might the Fed do if its target interest rate, the overnight federal funds rate, fell to zero? One relatively straightforward extension of current procedures would be to try to stimulate spending by lowering rates further out along the Treasury term structure - that is, rates on government bonds of longer maturities....

A more direct method, which I personally prefer, would be for the Fed to begin announcing explicit ceilings for yields on longer-maturity Treasury debt (say, bonds maturing within the next two years). The Fed could enforce these interest-rate ceilings by committing to make unlimited purchases of securities up to two years from maturity at prices consistent with the targeted yields. If this program were successful, not only would yields on medium-term Treasury securities fall, but (because of links operating through expectations of future interest rates) yields on longer-term public and private debt (such as mortgages) would likely fall as well.

Lower rates over the maturity spectrum of public and private securities should strengthen aggregate demand in the usual ways and thus help to end deflation. Of course, if operating in relatively short-dated Treasury debt proved insufficient, the Fed could also attempt to cap yields of Treasury securities at still longer maturities, say three to six years.'

"He then proceeds to outline what could be done if the economy falls into outright deflation and uses the examples, and others, cited above. It seems clear to me from the context that he is making an academic list of potential policies the Fed could pursue if outright deflation became a reality. He was not suggesting they be used, nor do I believe he thinks we will ever get to the place where they would be contemplated. He was simply pointing out the Fed can fight deflation if it wants to."

(And now, in 2010, that question might become more than academic.)

With the above as background, we can begin to look at what I believe is the true import of the speech. Read these sentences, noting my bold-faced words: *"... a central bank, either alone or in cooperation with other parts of the government, retains considerable power to expand aggregate demand and economic activity **even when its accustomed policy rate is at zero."***

"The basic prescription for preventing deflation is therefore straightforward, at least in principle: Use monetary and fiscal policy as needed to support aggregate spending...." (As Keynesian as you can get.)

Again: *"... some observers have concluded that when the central bank's policy rate falls to zero - its practical minimum - monetary policy loses its ability to further stimulate aggregate demand and the economy."*

"To stimulate aggregate spending when short-term interest rates have reached zero, the Fed must expand the scale of its asset purchases or, possibly, expand the menu of assets that it buys."

Now let us go to his conclusion:

"Sustained deflation can be highly destructive to a modern economy and should be strongly resisted. Fortunately, for the foreseeable future, the chances of a serious deflation in the United States appear remote indeed, in large part because of our economy's underlying strengths but also because of the determination of the Federal Reserve and other U.S. policy-makers to act pre-emptively against deflationary pressures. Moreover, as I have discussed today, a variety of policy responses are available should deflation appear to be taking hold. Because some of these alternative policy tools are relatively less familiar, they may raise practical problems of implementation and of calibration of their likely economic effects. **For this reason, as I have emphasized, prevention of deflation is preferable to cure.** Nevertheless, I hope to have persuaded you that the Federal Reserve and other economic policy-makers would be far from helpless in the face of deflation, even should the federal funds rate hit its zero bound." And there you have it. All the data pointing to a slowing economy? It puts us closer to deflation. It is not the headline data per se we need to think about. We need to start thinking about what the Fed will do if we have a double-dip recession and start to fall into deflation. Will they move out the yield curve, as he suggested? Buy more and varied assets like mortgages and corporate debt?

What will that do to markets and investments?

Note that last bolded line: *"For this reason, as I have emphasized, pre-vention of deflation is preferable to cure."* If he is true to his words, that means he may act in advance of the next recession if the data continues to come in weak and deflation starts to actually become a threat. That is the thing we don't see in all the economic data - the potential for new Fed action. Let's hope that, like the deflation scare in 2002, it doesn't come about.

However, if the US gets into outright deflation, I expect the Fed to react by increasing their assets and by outright monetization, buying treasuries from insurance and other companies, as putting more money into banks when they are not lending does not seem to be helpful as far as deflation is concerned. More mortgages? Corporate debt? Moving out the yield curve? All are options the Fed will consider. We need to be paying attention.

Never forget. Recessions are, by definition, deflationary. One of the things we learned from This Time is Different by Rogoff and Reinhart is that economies are more fragile and volatile and that recessions are more frequent after a credit crisis. Further, spending cuts are better than tax increases at improving the health of an economy after a credit crisis.

I think we can take it as a given that there is another recession in front of the US. That is the natural order of things. But it would be better to have that inevitable recession as far into the future as possible, and preferably with a little inflationary cushion and some room for active policy responses. A recession next year would be problematic, if not catastrophic. Rates are as low as they can go. Higher deficits are not in the cards. Yet unemployment would shoot up and tax collections go down at all levels of government.

That is why I always worried so much about taking the Bush tax cuts away when the economy is weak. Now, maybe those who argue that tax increases don't matter are right. They have their academic studies. But the preponder-ance of work suggests their studies are flawed and, at worst, are guilty of data mining (looking for data that supports your already-developed conclusions). As Professor Michael Boskin wrote in the Wall Street Journal:

"The president does not say that economists agree that the high future taxes to finance the stimulus will hurt the economy. (The University of Chicago's Harald Uhlig estimates $3.40 of lost output for every dollar of government spending.) Either the president is not being told of serious alternative viewpoints, or serious viewpoints are defined as only those that support his position. In either case, he is being ill-served by his staff."

There's a reason economics is called the dismal science and, therefore, we need to think any tax increase through very thoroughly.

John Mauldin has chosen to donate to:

"My charity is Knightsbridge International, a group of heroes bringing relief to those who are in places where it is dangerous to go. They put themselves into harm's way to help those who are desperate".

The Knightsbridge International web site can be found at:
www.kbi.org

CHAPTER SEVENTEEN

-

"The first panacea for a mismanaged nation is inflation of the currency; the second is war. Both bring a temporary prosperity; both bring a permanent ruin. But both are the refuge of political and economic opportunists."

Ernest Hemingway

US Stock Market Returns - What is in Store?

Prieur du Plessis

"It is one thing to trade the market's rallies and corrections, but this is easier said than done, with not many people actually getting it right with any degree of consistency. Others are of the opinion that the recipe for creating wealth is simply to follow the patient approach, saying that 'it's time in the market, not timing the market' that counts."

About the Author

Dr Prieur du Plessis is chairman of Cape Town-based Plexus Asset Management and is author of the Investment Postcards from Cape Town blog: *http://www.investmentpostcards.com* (to which readers are invited to subscribe free from the home page).

Prieur is also professor extraordinaire at the University of Stellenbosch Business School and serves as Honorary Consul of Slovenia for South Africa.

US Stock Market Returns
What is in Store?

Stock market movements, since the start of the credit crisis, have been characterised by relatively high volatility as uncertainty became paramount. And as new pieces of the economics puzzle are added every day, investors are increasingly struggling to make sense of the most likely direction of stock prices.

It seems to be a case of so many pundits, so many views. Has the market started topping out and is a primary bear market about to resume, or is a new secular bull market merely correcting the strong rally that commenced in March 2009, before moving higher? Or is a *"muddle-through"* trading range in store?

It is one thing to trade the market's rallies and corrections, but this is easier said than done, with not many people actually getting it right with any degree of consistency. Others are of the opinion that the recipe for creating wealth is simply to follow the patient approach, saying that *"it's time in the market, not timing the market"* that counts.

This gives rise to the all-important question: does one's entry level into the market (i.e. the valuation of the market at the time of investing) make a significant difference to subsequent investment returns?

In an attempt to cast light on this issue, my colleagues at Plexus Asset Management have updated a previous multi-year comparison of the price-earnings (PE) ratios of the S&P 500 Index (as a measure of stock valuations) and the forward real returns, as done by Jeremy Grantham's GMO. Our study covered the period from 1871 to June 2010 and used the S&P 500 (and its predecessors prior to 1957). In essence, PEs based on rolling average ten-year earnings were calculated and used together with ten-year forward real returns. In the first analysis the PEs and the corresponding ten-year forward real returns were grouped in five quintiles (i.e. 20% intervals). *See diagram A.1.*

Diagram A.1

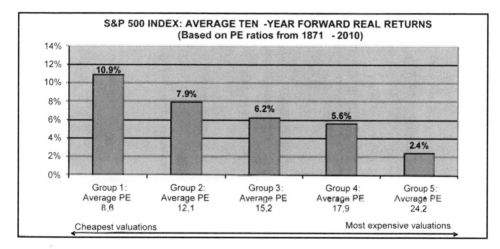

Source: Plexus Asset Management (based on data from Prof Shiller and I-Net Bridge)

The cheapest quintile had an average PE of 8.6 with an average ten-year forward real return of 10.9% per annum, whereas the most expensive quintile had an average PE of 24.2 with an average ten-year forward real return of only 2.4% per annum.

This analysis clearly shows the strong long-term relationship between real returns and the level of valuation at which the investment was made.

The study was then repeated with the PEs divided into smaller groups, i.e. deciles or 10% intervals *(see diagrams A.2 and A.3).*

Diagram A.2

S&P 500 INDEX: TEN-YEAR FORWARD REAL RETURNS					
Group		**Minimum**	**Maximum**	**Average**	**Spread**
Group 1:	PE Ratio < 6	9.5%	20.0%	16.1%	10.5%
Group 2:	PE Ratio 6 & 7	1.8%	20.0%	12.7%	18.1%
Group 3:	PE Ratio 8 & 9	4.0%	18.8%	9.7%	14.8%
Group 4:	PE Ratio 10 & 11	0.4%	17.6%	9.3%	17.1%
Group 5:	PE Ratio 12 & 13	-4.2%	15.2%	6.3%	19.3%
Group 6:	PE Ratio 14 & 15	-4.6%	16.1%	6.3%	20.8%
Group 7:	PE Ratio 16 & 17	-4.0%	15.7%	6.1%	19.7%
Group 8:	PE Ratio 18 & 19	-2.6%	12.2%	5.0%	14.8%
Group 9:	PE Ratio 20 & 21	-3.3%	9.0%	3.4%	12.3%
Group 10:	PE Ratio 21 >	-5.9%	7.5%	1.1%	13.5%

Source: Plexus Asset Management (based on data from Prof Shiller and I-Net Bridge)

Diagram A.3

S&P 500 INDEX: TEN-YEAR FORWARD REAL RETURNS					
Group		**Minimum**	**Maximum**	**Average**	**Spread**
Group 1:	PE Ratio < 6	9.5%	20.0%	16.1%	10.5%
Group 2:	PE Ratio 6 & 7	1.8%	20.0%	12.7%	18.1%
Group 3:	PE Ratio 8 & 9	4.0%	18.8%	9.7%	14.8%
Group 4:	PE Ratio 10 & 11	0.4%	17.6%	9.3%	17.1%
Group 5:	PE Ratio 12 & 13	-4.2%	15.2%	6.3%	19.3%
Group 6:	PE Ratio 14 & 15	-4.6%	16.1%	6.3%	20.8%
Group 7:	PE Ratio 16 & 17	-4.0%	15.7%	6.1%	19.7%
Group 8:	PE Ratio 18 & 19	-2.6%	12.2%	5.0%	14.8%
Group 9:	PE Ratio 20 & 21	-3.3%	9.0%	3.4%	12.3%
Group 10:	PE Ratio 21 >	-5.9%	7.5%	1.1%	13.5%

Source: Plexus Asset Management (based on data from Prof Shiller and I-Net Bridge)

This analysis strongly confirms the downward trend of the average ten-year forward real returns from the cheapest grouping (PEs of less than six) to the most expensive grouping (PEs of more than 21). The second study also shows that any investment at PEs of less than 12 always had positive ten-year real returns, while investments at PE ratios of 12 and higher experienced negative real returns at some stage.

A third observation from this analysis is that the ten-year forward real returns on investments made at PEs between 12 and 17 had the biggest spread between minimum and maximum returns and were, therefore, more volatile and less predictable.

As a further refinement, holding periods of one, three, five and twenty-years were also analysed. The research results (not reported in this article) for the one-year period showed a poor relationship with expected returns, but the findings for all the other periods were consistent with the findings for the ten-year periods.

Although the above analysis represents an update to an extension of an earlier study by GMO, it was also considered appropriate to replicate the study using dividend yields rather than PEs as valuation yardstick. The results *are reported in diagrams B.1, B.2 and B.3* and, as can be expected, are very similar to those based on PEs.

Diagram B.1

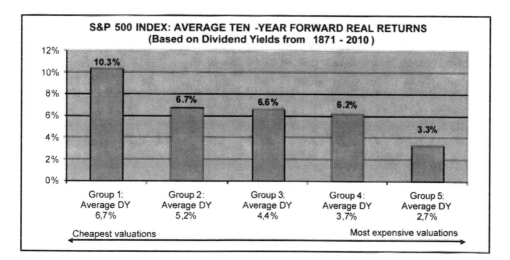

Source: Plexus Asset Management (based on data from Prof Shiller and I-Net Bridge)

Diagram B.2

Group			Minimum	Maximum	Average	Spread
Group 1:	Div Yield	9% >	6.6%	14.1%	9.5%	7.6%
Group 2:	Div Yield	9%	4.3%	15.0%	10.0%	10.7%
Group 3:	Div Yield	8%	4.3%	16.3%	11.6%	12.1%
Group 4:	Div Yield	7%	2.5%	18.8%	10.9%	16.3%
Group 5:	Div Yield	6%	1.1%	20.0%	11.0%	18.8%
Group 6:	Div Yield	5%	-4.2%	18.2%	7.1%	22.4%
Group 7:	Div Yield	4%	-4.6%	15.4%	6.4%	20.1%
Group 8:	Div Yield	3%	-4.0%	16.1%	5.3%	20.1%
Group 9:	Div Yield	2%	-4.0%	10.9%	4.1%	14.9%
Group 10:	Div Yield	<2%	-5.9%	5.2%	-0.6%	11.1%

Source: Plexus Asset Management (based on data from Prof Shiller and I-Net Bridge)

Diagram B.2

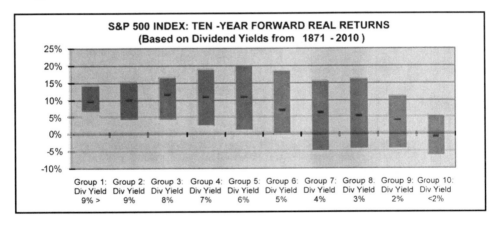

Source: Plexus Asset Management (based on data from Prof Shiller and I-Net Bridge)

Based on the above research findings, with the S&P 500 Index's current ten-year normalised PE of 19.7% and dividend yield of 2.1%, investors should be aware of the fact that the market is, by historical standards, above *"average value"* territory. As far as the market in general is concerned, this argues for unexciting long-term returns, and possibly a *"muddle-through"* trading range for quite a number of years to come.

Although the research results offer no guidance as to calling market tops and bottoms, they do indicate that it would not be consistent with the findings to bank on above-average returns based on the current valuation levels. As a matter of fact, there is a distinct possibility of below-average returns.

Dr Prieur du Plessis has chosen to support:

"My preferred charity is Proud Partners, a South African charitable organisation aimed at uplifting previously disadvantaged communities through the
provision of musical instruments and tuition to a large number of schools".

The Proud Partners web site can be found at:
www.proudpartners.co.za

CHAPTER EIGHTEEN

-

"The fact that an opinion has been widely held is no evidence whatever that it is not utterly absurd; indeed, in view of the silliness of the majority of mankind, a wide-spread belief is more likely to be foolish than sensible"

Bertrand Russell

A World of Opportunity
By Patrick L Young

"For one thing, the east has been a net creditor to the west for several years now. In other words, the west is reliant on the emerging world to prop up its profligacy. I don't feel entirely comfortable that the emerging world is ultimately going to support anything other than a pure business case to keep buying western debt which can only make the storm all the more intense when we reach the real crisis..."

A World of Opportunity

Amidst the Riskiest Markets of a Lifetime

"Cheer up, the worst is yet to come."

Philander Johnson

Without wishing to pile dismal news upon the existing heap of dismal news that has emanated from the, well, dismal, science, things do not look good. In fact, there is clear evidence that not only is the party over but that there is a massive quantity of wreckage accumulating in what could mount to the biggest highway pile-up in history and nobody has yet really felt the slightest twinge of post-party hangover. That experience is to come. Nevertheless, before any reader takes away the concept that the world is uniquely poised for a prolonged gloomy phase there cannot be enough emphasis on the fact that, despite the dreadful economic outlook for governments who have overspent with gusto for decades, the truth is that spring will see new shoots of growth and the seasons will continue much as they always have done. Indeed, there is clear evidence that periods of recession stimulate great creativity as it requires genuinely innovative design to prise money from consumers' wallets. Sports events will continue albeit with perhaps slightly less hubris and razzmatazz than in recent years. In other words, life will go on.

However, financial affairs could get really, really, ugly.

Nevertheless, it is also vitally important to bear in mind that no matter what may happen in many parts of the world there will always be markets which grow and economies which flourish during periods of severe recession elsewhere. A trip to Argentina provides a perfect example of both what can work to the upside as the others are failing while, equally, it is a grim lesson in just how things can deteriorate when governments lose their grip completely. Wandering through the many antiques shops of Buenos Aires, the visitor is always struck by the plethora of exquisite items dating from the 1920s through to the 1950s which are for sale, often at great prices and frequently in excellent condition. During the inter-war years the

Argentine economy driven by its foodstuff exports, amongst other products, was a fast emerging global powerhouse. Neutrality in the second world war helped see Argentina become the 7th largest economy on earth, thanks to prudent economic management and, of course, the collapse of the defeated Axis powers.

Alas, more or less ever since, Argentina has been in decline, driven by a series of governments who feasted on debt and then struggled to repay it. Argentina is a nation with remarkable potential nowadays, thanks to decades of relative decline, but it has dropped (even after a degree of rebound) to the 23rd largest economy in the world, according to the IMF (2009). Nevertheless, it is a shining example of a nation which grew strongly despite the travails of the developed world during the 1920s and 1930s economic contractions.

In the current environment it is fair to suggest that, despite inter-linkage with the established west, there are many *"emerging markets"* with enormous potential to largely ride out the gathering storm in the west. For one thing, the east has been a net creditor to the west for several years now. In other words, the west is reliant on the emerging world to prop up its profligacy. I don't feel entirely comfortable that the emerging world is ultimately going to support anything other than a pure business case to keep buying western debt which can only make the storm all the more intense when we reach the real crisis... Similarly, flexible eastern economies will likely adapt to local opportunities as well as export markets as the western *"end game"* plays out. Am I therefore entirely bearish on the prospects for the west? Well, as a matter of fact, broadly I am. As the Charlemagne column in the Economist appositely noted (July 17th, 2010):

"Viewed from afar, Europeans are a complacent, ungrateful lot. Nannied from cradle to grave by the world's most generous welfare systems, they squeal like spoiled children when asked to give up just a few of their playthings. As governments in the euro zone trim benefits and raise the retirement age in the wake of the sovereign-debt crisis, a wail of indignation has rung out and a wave of protests set in."

Ultimately, I really find it hard to justify living in a high tax western European EU state but, then again, I emigrated from the UK more than 15 years ago precisely because the Blair/Brown manifesto for change was little more than a glorified debt disaster waiting to happen.

At the same time, while investment in the nations of western Europe may be a particularly challenging class to manage in the near future, I would note that, here too, opportunities are available for the canny investor, albeit with a particular risk appetite! Arguably the best place to seek such innovations may be the proven home of rather sclerotic financial governance but the finest entrepreneurial nation ever known to man: the United States of America. The inventiveness of Europeans and Americans alike is a consistent wonder to behold and I believe the next decade will see incredible developments as the nascent *"miracles"* of nanotechnology revolutionise our lives... For those who doubt the coming benefits of nanotechnology, I'll be happy to bet them a bottle of the finest champagne when I celebrate my 150th birthday to prove just how much nanotech has improved our lives. Similarly, the trading of markets will continue to grow, even if established assets such as equities prove to be in a long-term cyclical bear market as other contributors to this book have argued so exquisitely.

Nevertheless, while innovation may help create small pockets of investment in the west, it will be in the east that the opportunities will occur en masse. True, there are some governments who have already worked so diligently to model their economies on the old established debt rich western models that the likes of Hungary look like a total fiscal mess in need of deep and painful surgery. However, while the west and sundry nations who binged on debt convalesce for the next decade or two (if not longer), the world has a massive opportunity ahead of it Make absolutely no mistake, there are a great many opportunities out there but, at the same time, this looks like the end game for the west as a rich power. At best, it is the *"beginning"* of the end game". Europe itself is being rebalanced to the east (as I type this article from Poland). Yes, there have been immature bubbles in smaller nations such as the Baltic states and so forth but they will recover a lot faster than the old-fashioned rigid hegemonies in Britain, France, Greece or wherever. Poland has reached the top table as the 20th largest economy in the world (IMF 2009) and yet it is clearly only in the warm up phase of its development - a development which has so far weathered the storm of economic crisis to the west and north. Moreover, there is tangible value to be achieved in many of these nations - property bubbled in several CEE/SEE nations but at the time of writing property yielding 10% or more is widely available in many areas of the former Warsaw Pact. As we journey east to Belarus/Ukraine/Russia or south-east to the Balkans, yes there are nations with issues concerning governance transparency and the rule of law, but for every nation to be avoided there are at least two providing bounteous op-portunities. There is, of course, also the thorny issue of tax. The western governments, including the USA have made many shrill cries about tax-ation threats from small islands. Actually, it's the onshore nations that they ought to be worried about. Even balancing budgets in the Baltics has only resulted in tiny ratchets of rates to the low or mid-20% range. Many other nations have flat tax rates, with Russia at just 13% - lower than *"low tax"* Jersey (20%)! Ultimately, eastern Europeans value their flat tax as being a key symbol of national growth that encourages investors. In the west, the French and Germans, let alone the Italians and Spaniards, view the system of flat tax with a scorn driven from their fear of impending bank-ruptcy. I suspect, dear reader, you will have no difficulty discerning where my thoughts lie on which system is going to win out once the storm has ravaged the west. Meanwhile, thanks to their profligacy, the west is only making things worse by printing money, borrowing more and more while seeking to further raise the tax burden on their beleaguered workforce.

Prosperity is rising in the east and I don't just mean the rapidly rising powerhouse nations of China and India which are close to repeating their massive economic power from the 16th and 17th century. Rather, even to the east of the European landmass, the future of the continent is now developing in the centre and the south, not the established *"heritage centres"* of London, Paris and Rome. Economic growth does not have to be a zero sum game but the way the west has gone about it, they look like securing a unique economic *"achievement"*.

Perhaps the west can come through this storm rapidly and settle itself into another round of growth. Maybe, just maybe. Then again what rate can western Europe grow at, given the red tape cocooning the states? When it comes to investing, I far prefer having the deck of cards balanced as far as is fairly possible in my favour. To understand how to grow *"developed"* nations, the west could learn from Singapore - scheduled for 15% growth in 2010 as I write - despite a very advanced first world standard of living!

Despite the ugly economics of the west, the possibilities for profit in this world abound. Ladies and gentlemen, this is a world of opportunity. To prepare for the future, ensure that you have not merely secured your wealth against the future economic tsunami, but also make sure that you have looked to enhance your investment returns by embracing economic growth whether it be the nano and bio technology fields or the vast future economic engine of the world. The geography of opportunity begins at the Oder river on the border between Germany and Poland and stretches a long, long, way east...

Even allowing for the fact that nano technology will help me live a great life to 150 years old (and far beyond!) I see little point in wasting a couple of decades of investment in the west - after all the past decade has been a complete write-off. The problem is the losses are likely to really mount up as the power of government proves to be negligible against the mountain of debt it has created. Remember Argentina: a global powerhouse in 1946 and nowadays a beautiful, if somewhat faded, relic of a bygone age. That's the future which awaits the west without a sea change in attitude and gover-nance. Defend your assets pro-actively and at the same time make the world a better place - I urge you to invest in growth: the growth of the east.

Patrick L Young:

Let me tell you a little bit about my friend Wyatt, the son of my good friend *"Kip."* Wyatt has autism and his movement is constrained by dyspraxia. At 11 he is a wonderful, constantly smiling, happy go lucky little boy. Alas Wyatt can speak only a couple of words and will require permanent care for the rest of his life. Wyatt never fails to brighten up my life. Wyatt loves to play and he even shares my passion for motorsport. Yet we really have no clear idea just how much Wyatt understands. Even worse, I often find myself fumbling to understand his actions and signals. Lee presciently created this book to help all members of our society. Thinking of Wyatt inspired me to edit this book for Lee. Fortunately for Wyatt, his family have the means to support him and endeavour to give him the best possible experience of what is often a rather confusing life. Therefore, I am supporting a charity which seeks to support the disabled and provides the best opportunities for a fulfilling life. The *"Fundacja Anny Dymnej 'Mimo Wszystko.'"*

"Against the Odds" was created by a wonderful Polish actress, Anna Dymna. The Foundation aims to help level the playing field in all aspects of life and work between disabled people and non-disabled people. Anna Dymna's work has inspired Poles for many years and I am delighted to support her charity to build the best society for us all.

The Mimo Wszystko web site can be found at:
www.mimowszystko.org

354

"Paper money has had the effect in your state that it will ever have - to ruin commerce, oppress the honest, and open the door to every species of fraud and injustice."

George Washington

Altana Charitable Trust

Altana Charitable Trust is a UK registered charity. The trustees and support staff contribute their efforts for no cost so other than any credit card payment fees 100% of your contribution goes to the charity.

The charity supports a wide range of charities with the current list below which makes it simpler to give to a broad range of charities as you send the money to us and we do all the work.

www.altanacharitabletrust.com

The trustees are:
Sean Laird and Neville Newman (a partner of Harris & Trotter LLP).

Harris & Trotter LLP

Harris & Trotter LLP are a general practice firm of accountants located in central London. The firm was established in 1940 and has 11 partners, 55 staff members with over 2000 clients.

Harris & Trotter developed a scheme whereby a voluntary £7 charge to be added to every invoice raised and when paid is then matched by the firm so that £14 is donated to charity for every invoice raised. Each quarter a charity committee meets and distributes the funds to charities nominated by the firm's clients, staff and partners.

Neville's chosen charity to which his share of the book sale proceeds will be donated is the Harris & Trotter charitable trust.
www.harrisandtrotter.co.uk

Sean Laird

Sean is a Portfolio Manager at Trafalgar Asset Managers. Prior to Trafalgar, Sean worked at Bank of America, Tillinghast Towers-Perrin and MED Ltd. Sean is a qualified Actuary, CFA charter holder and holds a BSC (Hons) in Mathematics from Glasgow University.

Sean's chosen charity is Trees for Life
www.treesforlife.org.uk

Trees for Life is an award-winning charity working to help restore the Caledonian Forest, which formerly covered a large part of the Scottish Highlands. Just 1% of the original forest survives today, as isolated stands of mostly old trees. Since 1989 we've been helping to bring this forest back from the brink, both through natural regeneration and by planting trees. Our long term vision is to restore the forest, and all its constituent species, to a 600 square mile area west of Inverness, including our 10,000 acre Dundreggan Estate.

Rostron Parry Ltd

Rostron Parry Ltd *(www.rostronparry.com)* is a London-based PR and marketing support company specializing in hedge funds and financial markets infrastructure clients. Simon Rostron and John Parry, its founders, were originally financial journalists who established their company in 1991 just as derivatives markets were taking off and as hedge funds began to attract more public interest.

The company's expertise in the field of hedge funds and exchanges/brokers/IT is unparalleled, which is why its principals have frequently taken part in conference programmes, seminars and other public debates on these subjects. As a result it is also often used as an independent resource by journalists seeking fair, intelligible explanations of complex issues. It is that skill which also makes it most effective when representing clients' interests.

Rostron Parry have provided PR services to *"The Gathering Storm"* free of charge and they have also nominated the armed forces veterans charity Help for Heroes as their chosen charity:

www.helpforheroes.org.uk/

The current charities receiving a share of the proceeds are:

- Batten's Disease Family Association - *www.bdfa-uk.org.uk*
- Child's i Foundation - *www.childsifoundation.org/*
- The Citizen's Foundation - *www.thecitizensfoundation.org*
- Amnesty International - *www.amnesty.org*
- Juvenile Diabetes Foundation International - *www.jdrf.org*
- Paul Smith College - *www.paulsmiths.edu*
- Help For Heroes - *www.helpforheroes.org.uk*
- Kidscape - *www.Kidscape.co.uk*
- The Marks Family Writing Center at the University of Pennsylvania
- Mount Sinai Hospital, NY
- Canadian Cancer Society - *www.cancer.ca*
- Room To Read - *www.roomtoread.org/*
- Union Settlement - *www.unionsettlement.org/*
- The International Thermonuclear Experimental Reactor - *www.iter.org*
- Knightsbridge International - *www.kbi.org*
- Proud Partners - *www.proudpartners.co.za*
- Against the Odds Foundation - *www.mimowszystko.org*
- Make a Wish Foundation - *www.make-a-wish.org.uk/*
- Trees for life - *www.treesforlife.org.uk*
- Harris & Trotter charitable trust
- Albert II Foundation *www.fpu2.com*

If you would like to donate via credit card or bank transfer
then please go to the website
www.altanabooks.com
or send a cheque payable to Altana Charitable Trust to

Altana Charitable Trust
c/o Neville Newman
65 New Cavendish Street
London
W1G 7LS

The Gathering Storm supports the Albert II Foundation:

"I decided to set up a Foundation whose purpose is to protect the environment and to encourage sustainable development (...). By definition, this is a common global challenge that requires urgent and concrete action in response to three major environmental issues: climate change, biodiversity and water."

H.S.H. Prince Albert II of Monaco

The Albert II Foundation strives to act as an accelerator of projects and solutions for the environment. It promotes sustainable and equitable management of natural resources and places the individual at the centre of its projects. It encourages the implementation of innovative and ethical solutions in three main areas: climate change, biodiversity and water.

The Albert II Foundation web site can be found at:
www.fpa2.com

About Derivatives Vision Publishing

Derivatives Vision Publishing specialises in books on financial markets. It includes the derivatives.com books imprint and has been producing books since 2001. All our books have been authored and edited by financial professionals.

DV Publishing commissions books under its own auspices and produces under contract for third parties, such as the Swiss Futures & Options Association (*"An Intangible Commodity"*) and the Association of Futures Markets (*"The Exchange Manifesto" first edition*).

"The Gathering Storm" has been produced for charity and, as such Derivatives Vision is making no profit from the publication or sale of the book although our staff are working diligently to ensure it achieves the maximum of revenue for charity!

During 2011 Derivatives Vision Publishing will release several new books concerning the future of financial markets and also some intriguing historical volumes.

For further details about Derivatives Vision Publishing
and our forthcoming releases please contact our
Chairman Patrick L Young:
patrick@derivativesvision

Bibliography

"The Unthinkable, who survives when disaster strikes and why,"
by Amanda Ripley - Arrow Books, London, 2009

"Manias, Panics, and Crashes: A History of Financial Crises"
By Charles P. Kindleberger - John Wiley & Sons inc., New York, 2000

"A Week in December"
By Sebastian Faulks - Hutchinson, London, 2009

"The Drunkard's Walk: How Randomness Rules Our Lives"
By Leonard Mlodinow - Pantheon Books, New York, 2008

"The Little Book of Behavioral Investing: How Not to be Your Own Worst Enemy"
By James Montier - John Wiley & Sons inc, New Jersey, 2010

"Mobs, Messiahs, and Markets: Surviving the Public Spectacle in Finance and Politics"
By William Bonner & Lila Rajiva - John Wiley & Sons inc, New Jersey, 2007

"Gold and Iron: Bismarck, Bleichroeder and the building of the German Empire"
By Fritz Stern - Random House Inc., New York, 1977

"Lords of Finance: The Bankers Who Broke the World"
By Liaquat Ahamed - Penguin Books ltd, London, 2009

"This Time Is Different: Eight Centuries of Financial Folly"
By Carmen M. Reinhart & Kenneth Rogoff - Princeton University Press, United Kingdom, 2009

"Extraordinary Popular Delusions & the Madness of Crowds"
By Charles Mackay - Wilder Publications, Radford, 2008

Index

A

B